NATURE'S WAY

The Great Blue Heron

(Ardea Herodius)

By BUD SIMPSON

NATURE'S WAY

The Great Blue Heron

(Ardea herodius)

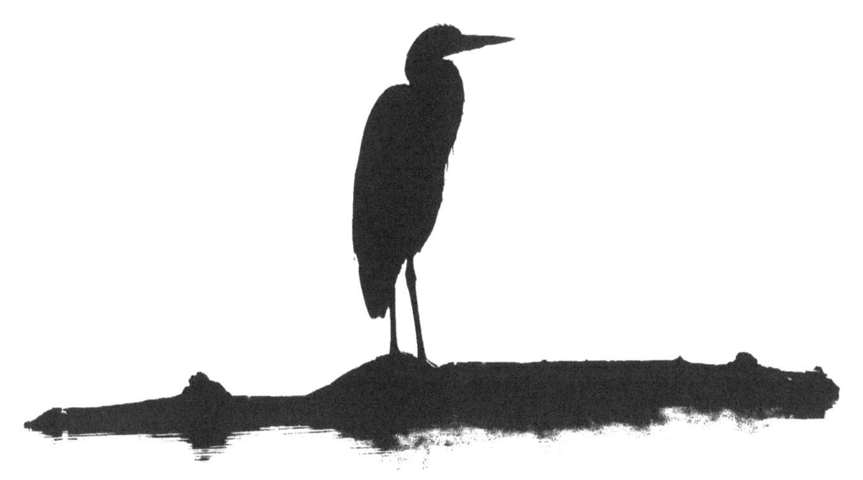

By BUD SIMPSON

All photographs in this book, and on the covers, unless otherwise noted, were taken by the author.

ISBN: 978-1-62249-291-6

Published by
The Educational Publisher, Inc.
Biblio Publishing
BiblioPublishing.com

This small book is dedicated to all who love Mother Nature and all her creatures, but in particular, all its feathered creatures.

He walks the shallow with an antic grace.
The great feet breaks the ridges of the sand,
The long eyes notes the minnow's hiding place.
His beak is quicker than the human hand.

From, *The Heron*, by Theodore Roethke
(1908-1963)

Bud Simpson

INTRODUCTION:

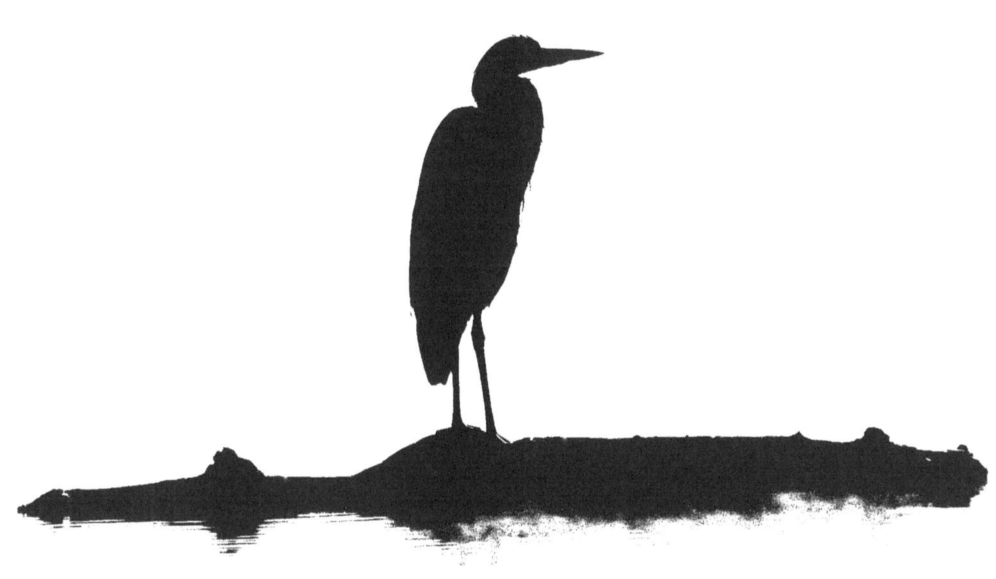

This book is intended as a photographic essay concerning one bird species, the Great Blue Heron. It is not a technical piece by any means. My intent is to let these photographs speak for themselves as much as possible. I might interject my observations into its photographic narration at some points, but only as clarification or to point out an observation of my own pertaining to what these great birds have taught me about themselves. They were the teachers, I was the eager student. They still have much to teach me. I'll never live long enough to know it all. I was amazed to find that I had over 9,000 images of Great Blue Herons in my computer folders. I know I will run across some photographs later on and say to myself: I should have included this one, or that one. I still take more heron photos each time I go to my lake. I can't help myself. Who knows if the next photo will teach me something else about these aptly named birds. I'm almost afraid to check my picture files for all the other species I have photographed. If all goes well with this offering, I may do other books on other species at some point in the future.

Foreword by Paul Knoop

THE GREAT BLUE HERON

Henry David Thoreau, In 1882, made this notation in his notebook: "Scared up three great blue herons in the little pond close by; quite near us. It was a grand site to see them rise, so slow and stately, so long and limber, with an undulating motion from head to foot, undulating also their large wings, and looking warily about them. With this graceful, limber undulating motion they arose, their two legs trailing parallel far behind."

Of all the birds that grace our waterways the great blue heron is perhaps everyone's favorite. While in flight its long legs are stretched out behind and its long neck drawn in - affording a characteristic "S" silhouette against the sky. It is a stately bird, dignified in its bearing, graceful in its movements; an artistic feature of the landscape.

While searching for its prey the great blue heron stands motionless for many minutes at a time knee deep in water. Here it patiently waits with indrawn neck until some luckless fish or frog has ventured near enough. Suddenly, and as quick as lightning, the sharp bill and long neck shoot downward, the wiry body sways forward on reed-like legs and the unfortunate prey, seized in the spear-like bill, soon disappears down the capacious gullet. It is a show not to be missed.

These great birds are social animals and nest in large colonies called rookeries. The nests are placed in the tops of the largest trees, often reaching sixty or eighty feet above the ground. Built of sticks the nests are three or four feet across and a foot deep. To be near a rookery during the nesting season is quite an experience. The adult birds are landing in the treetops on stilt-like legs, wings held high for balance. The young in the nests are emitting loud cackling sounds and the returning adults have gullets full of fish and other prey which they regurgitate into the mouths of the noisy young. In addition there is a musty odor that permeates the air, resulting from large amounts of heron droppings covering the trees below. This so-called "whitewash" is a strong fertilizer and often kills the trees in which the herons nest.

The lives of great blue herons have not always been so tranquil. A bit more than a hundred years ago these birds were being slaughtered to satisfy the millenary trade; their plume-like feathers were placed on women's hats. So many birds were killed that extinction was eminent. Fortunately federal and state protection came just in the nick of time.

All the photographs in this small book were taken by Bud Simpson in Logan, Ohio at wetland areas near his home. To get such intimate photos was an amazing feat considering the time and patience involved. Obviously this was a labor of love and the entire book speaks to the wild beauty that surrounds us.

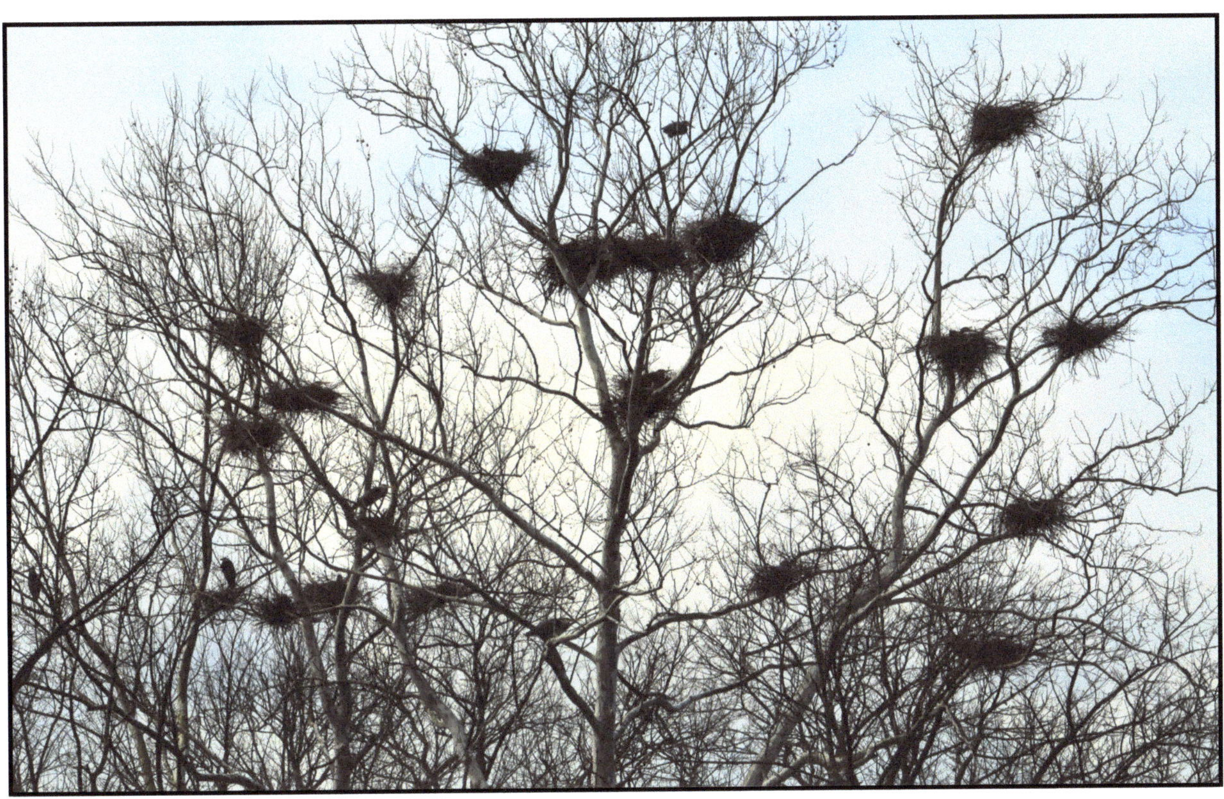

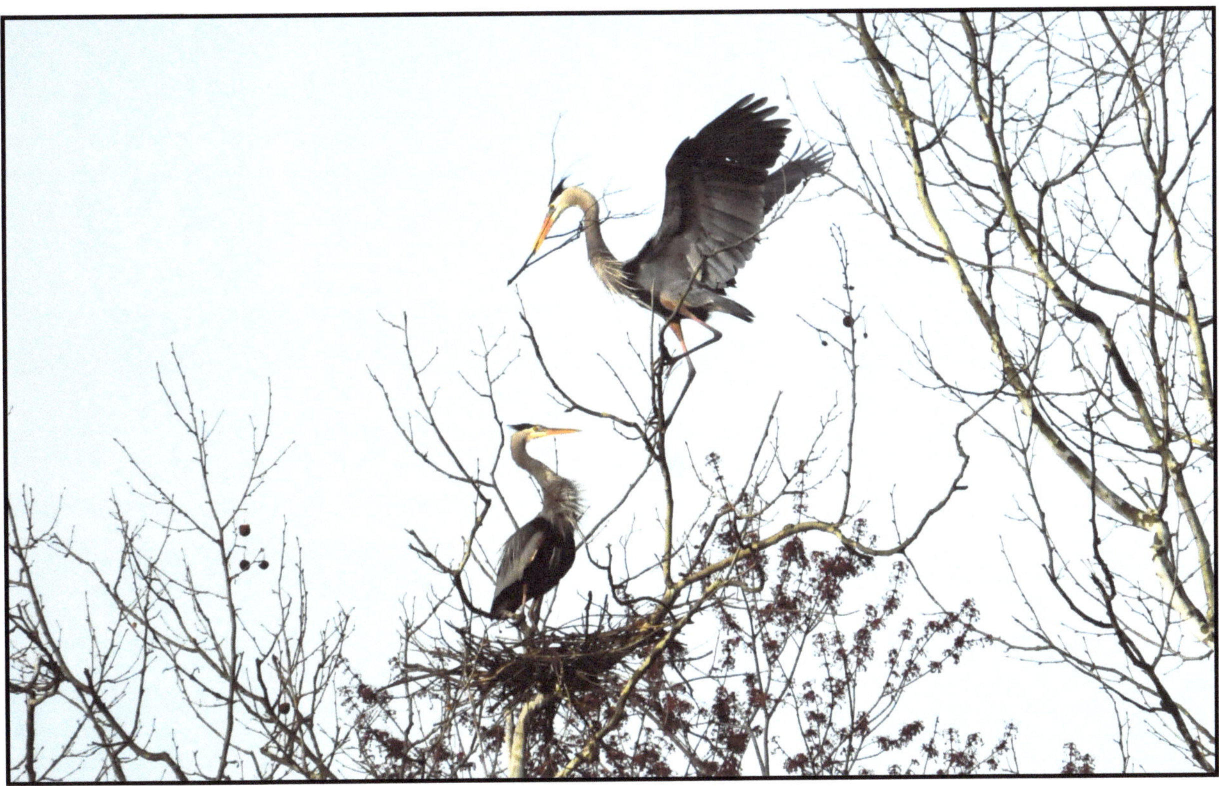

It all starts here; in the Heron rookery. Many Great Blue Herons gather communally, sometimes filling many trees with what appears to be, loosely built nests of sticks and twigs. The males bring the material to the nest and the female inserts the twigs into just the right spot for a strong structure.

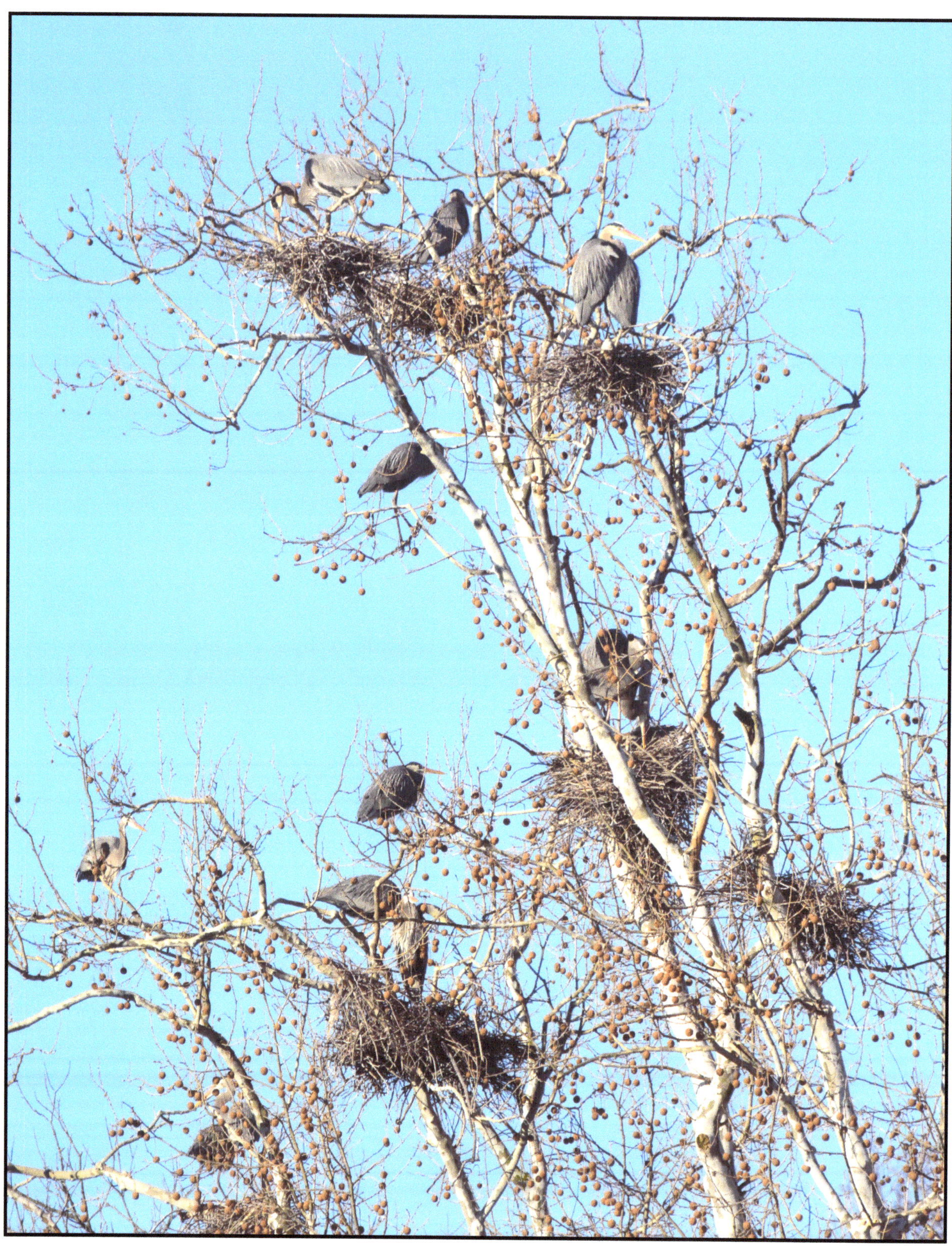

This photograph shows but part of a rookery. Other nearby sycamore trees are not shown here, but still have about the same density of nests as these. These nests are near completion of their yearly refurbishing.

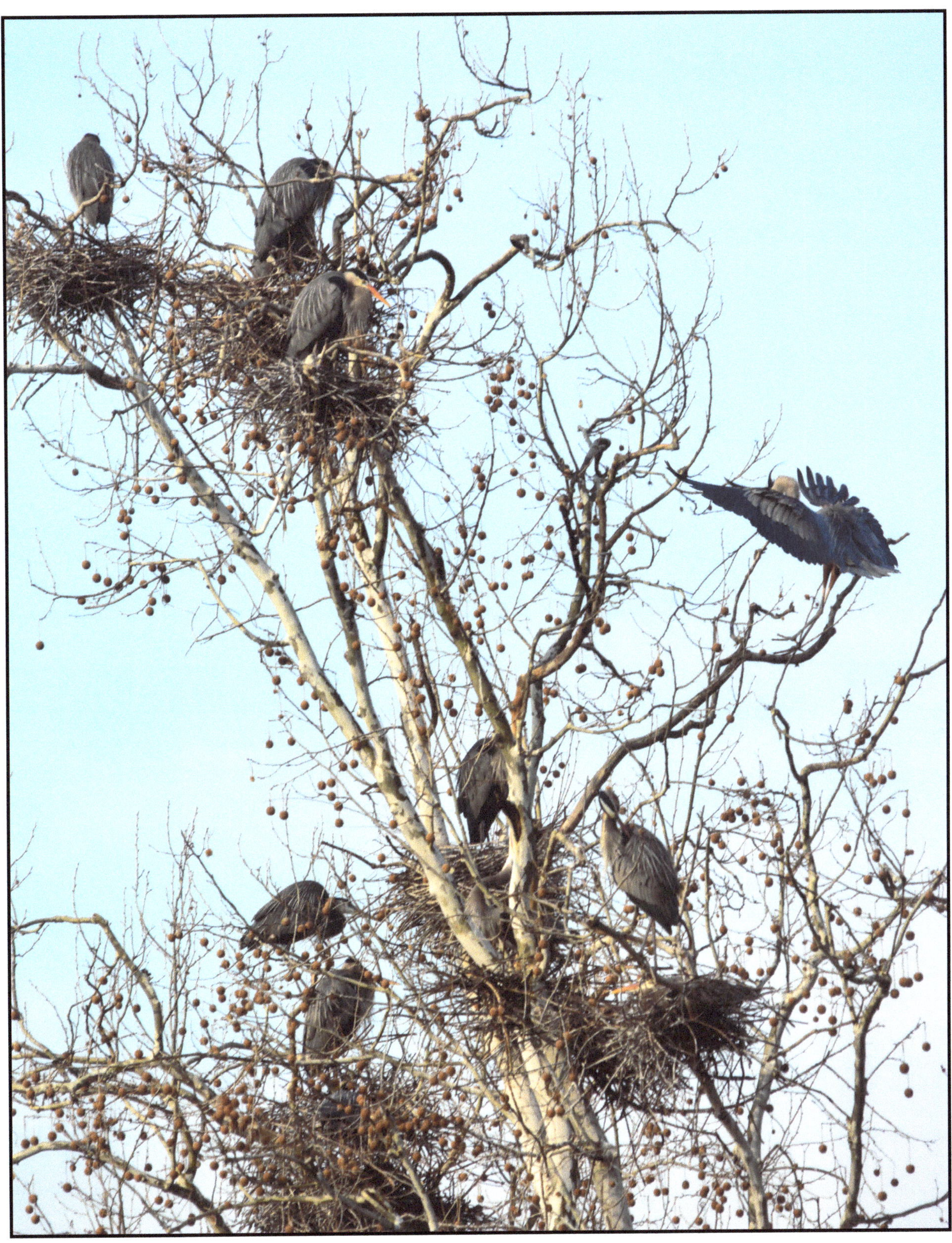

Soon, the building and rebuilding ends and the Herons get down to the real purpose of these nests; raising healthy families. Usually, they produce two or three new Great Blue Heron chicks.

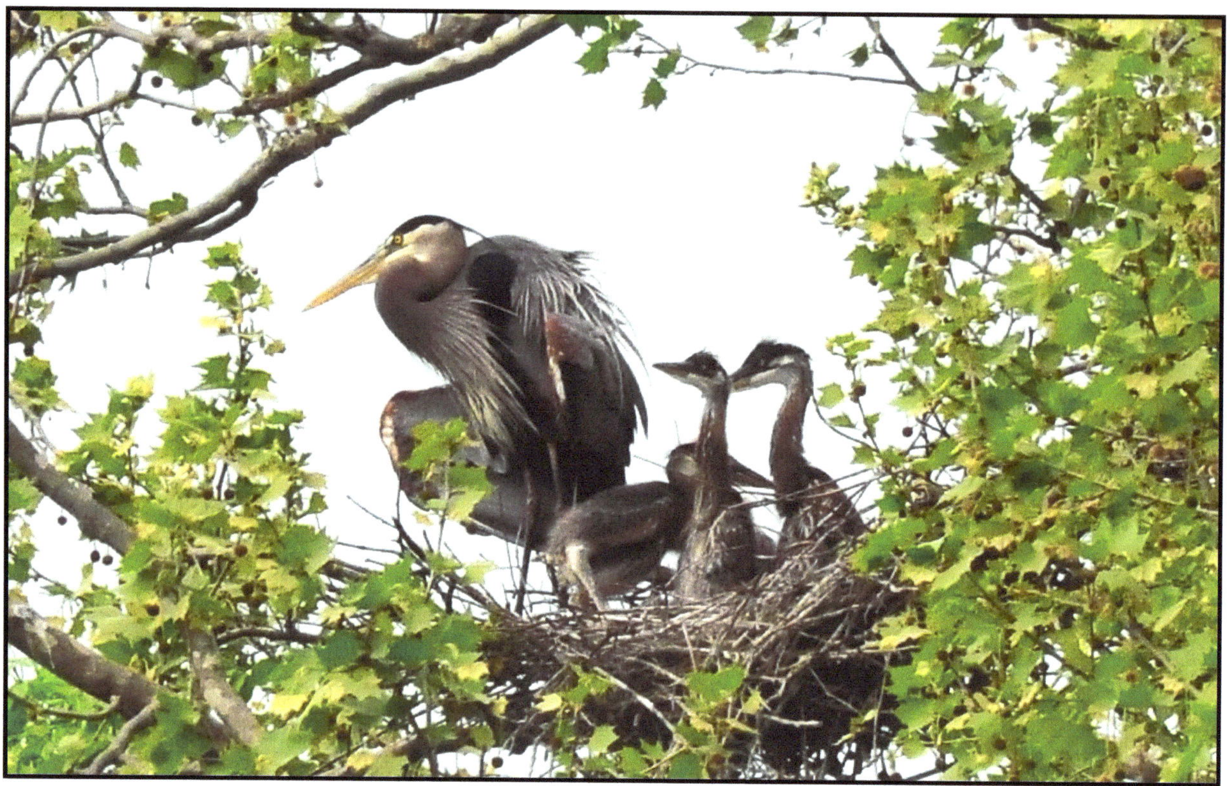

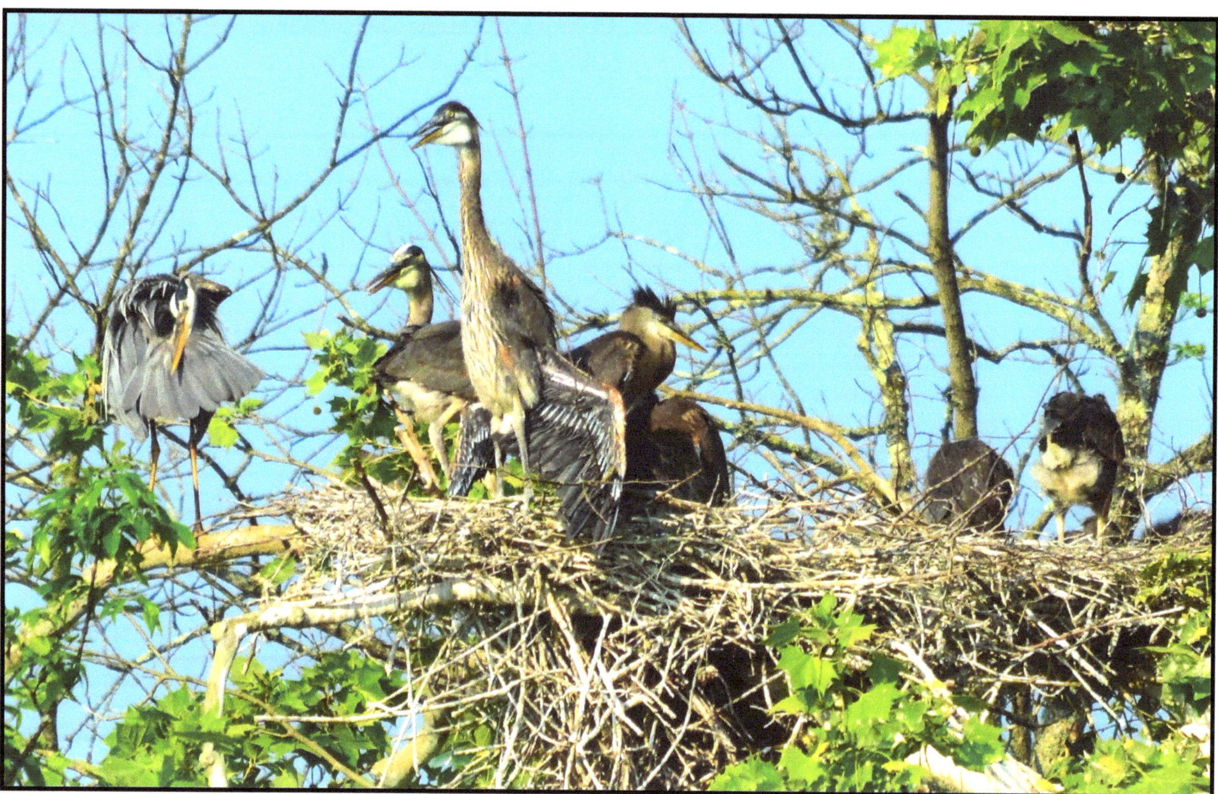

The top photo shows a typical Heron family. But, when the nests are close together, the older, more adventurous young will tend to gather in their neighbor's nest, also. If there's room, they always seem to be welcome.

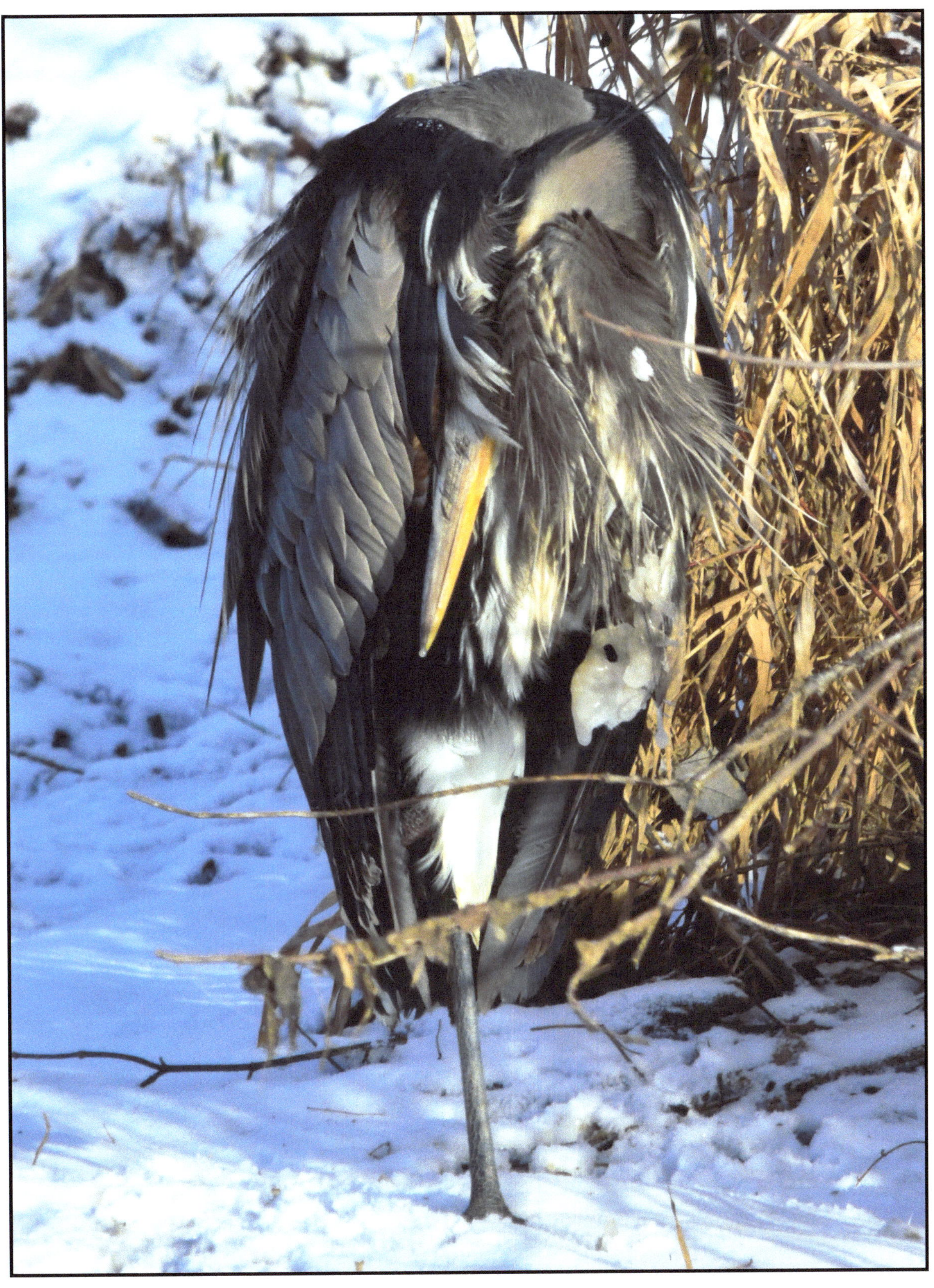

Great Blue Herons are tough birds. Even at 7 below zero and with ice frozen to its feathers, this bird survived the winter. In fact, a couple of weeks after this photo was taken, he was fishing as if winter had been nothing at all.

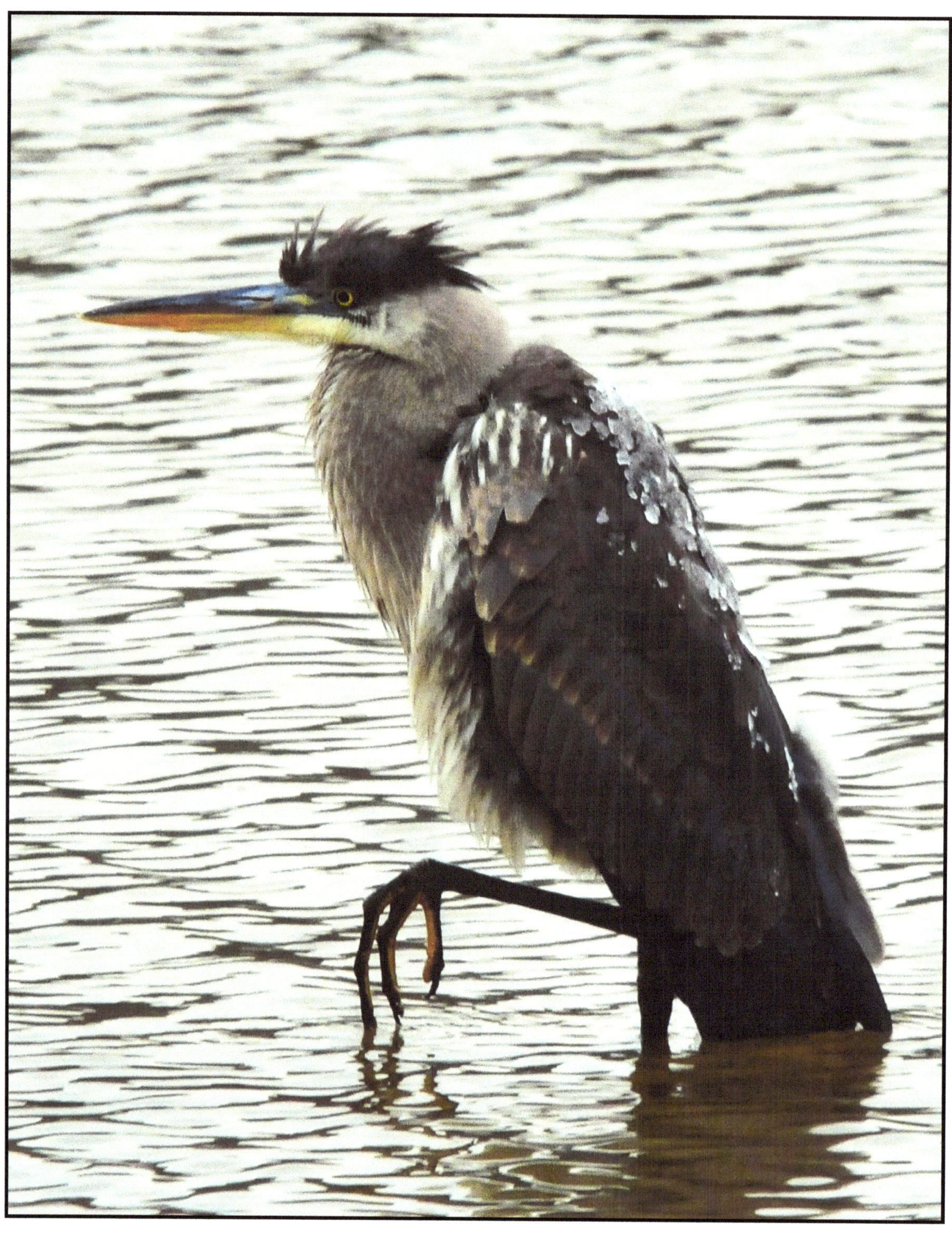

Here's that tough old bird again, still ice covered, but with his indomitable survival instincts still intact. Following are more photos of wintering over Great Blue Herons.

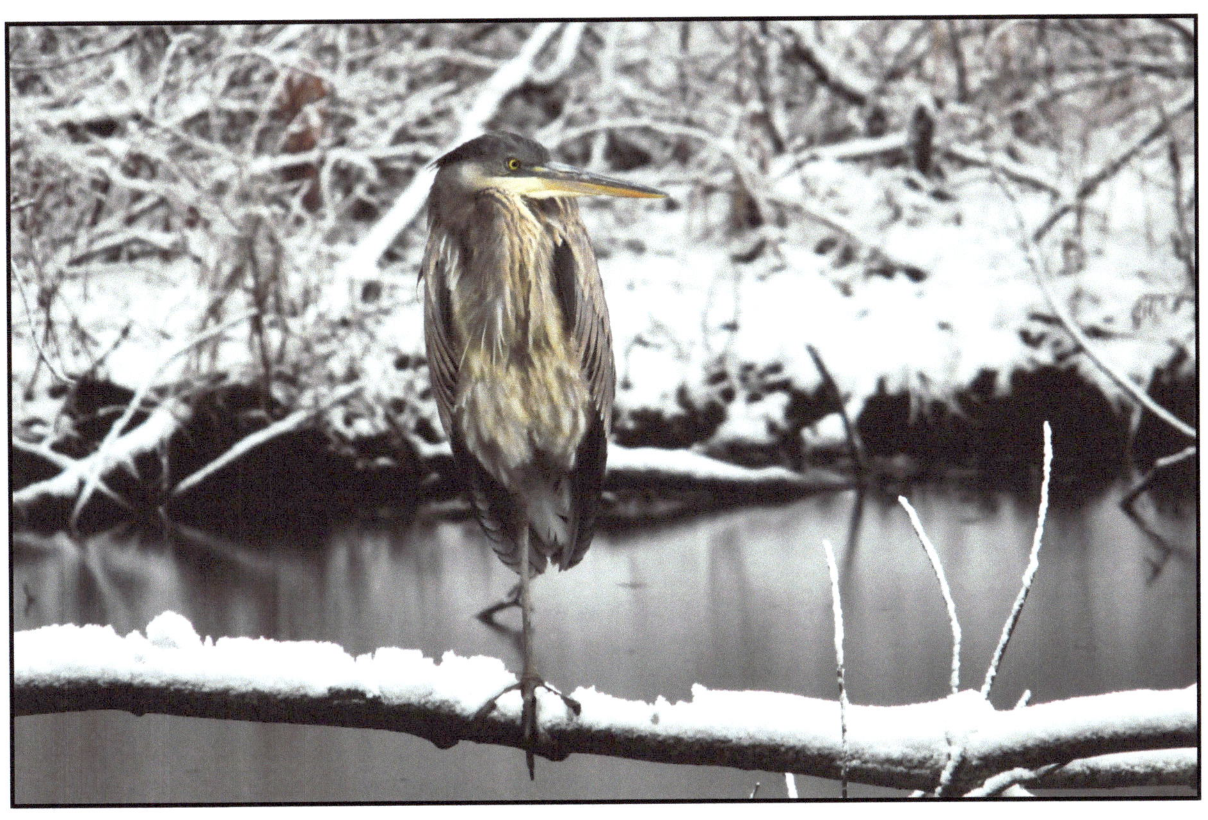

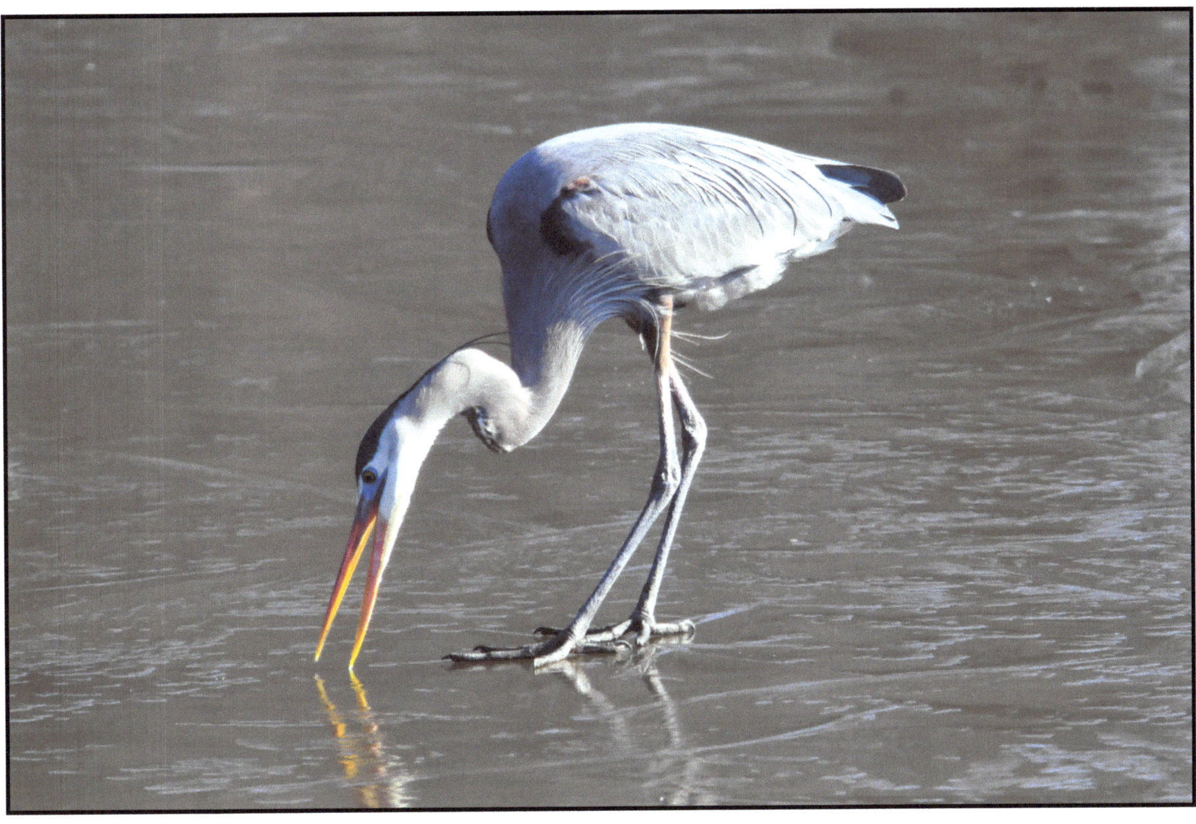

Bud Simpson

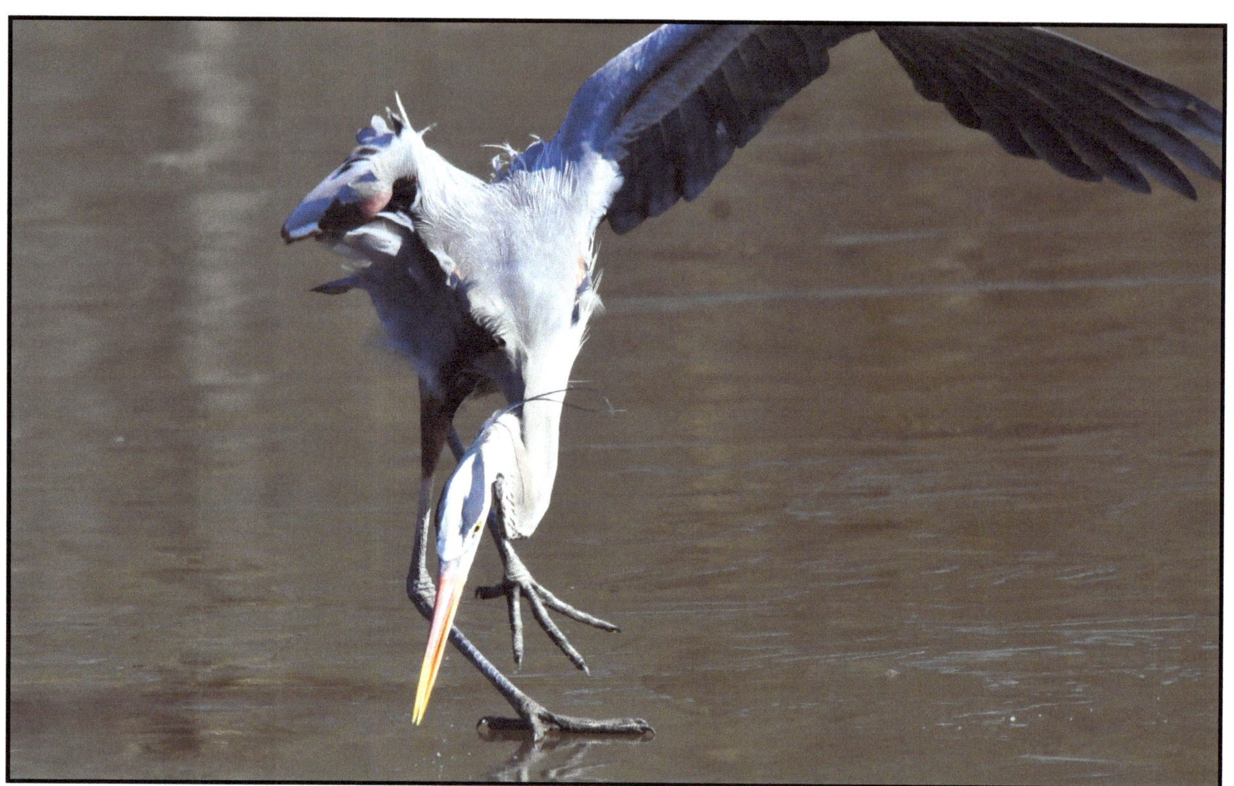

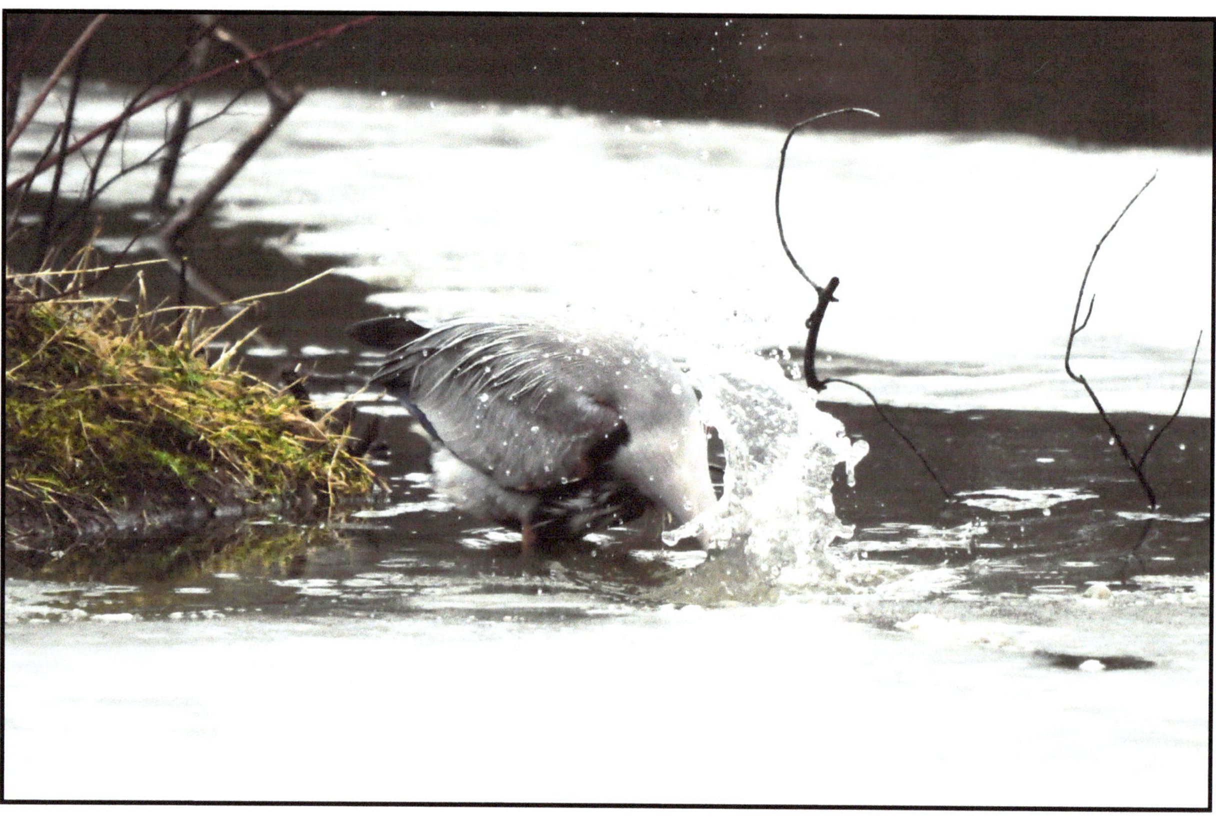

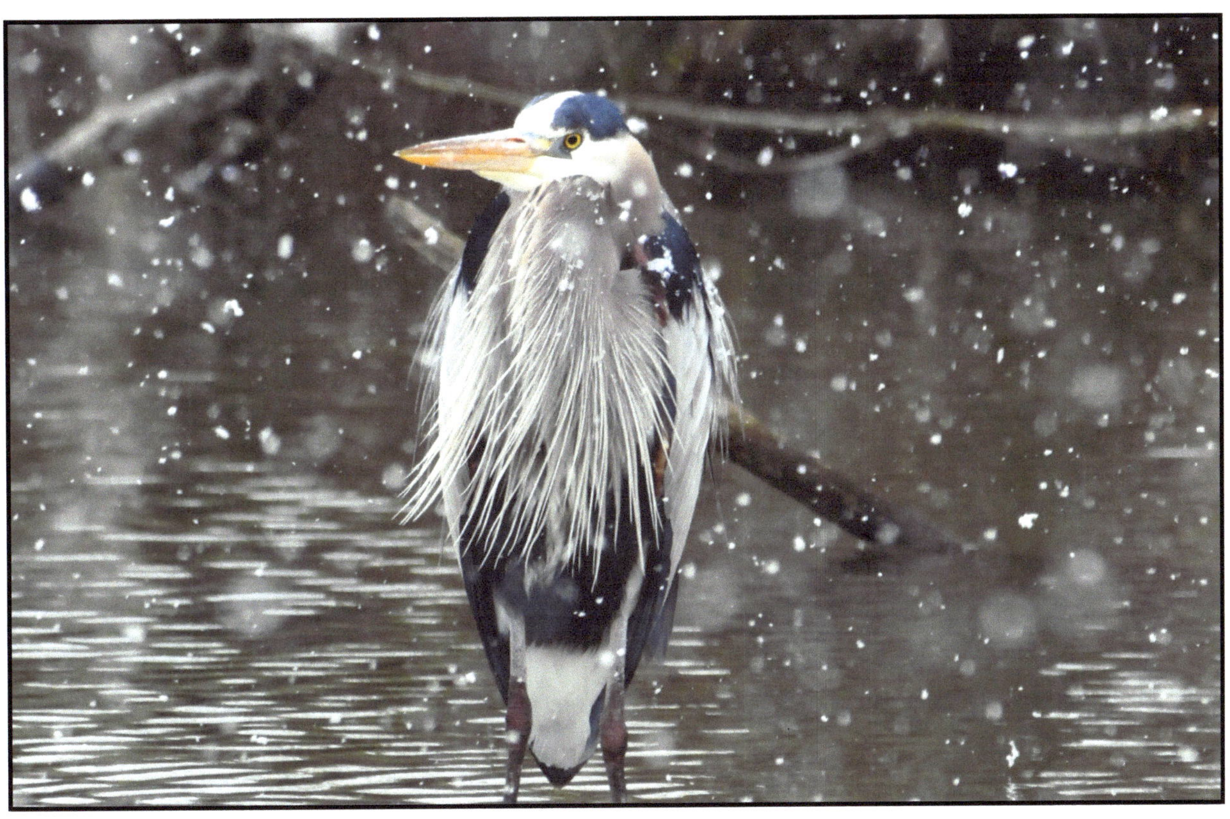

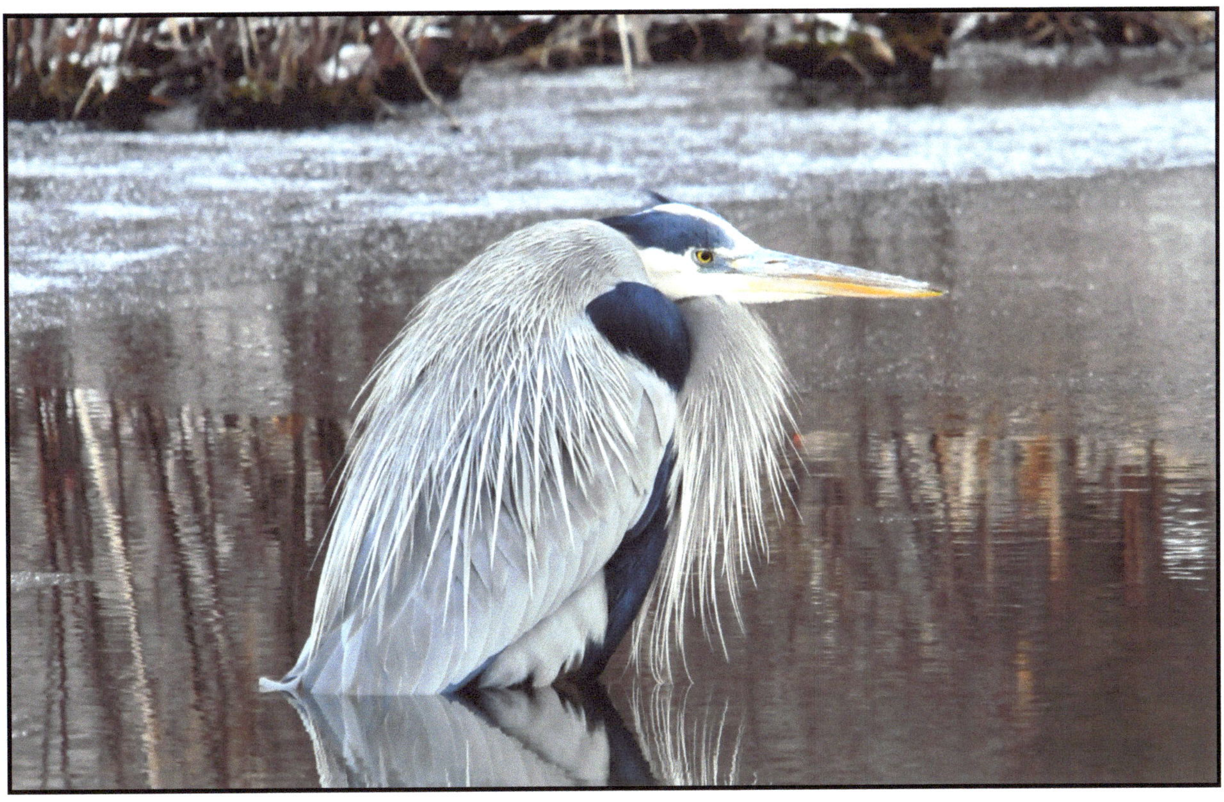

Bud Simpson

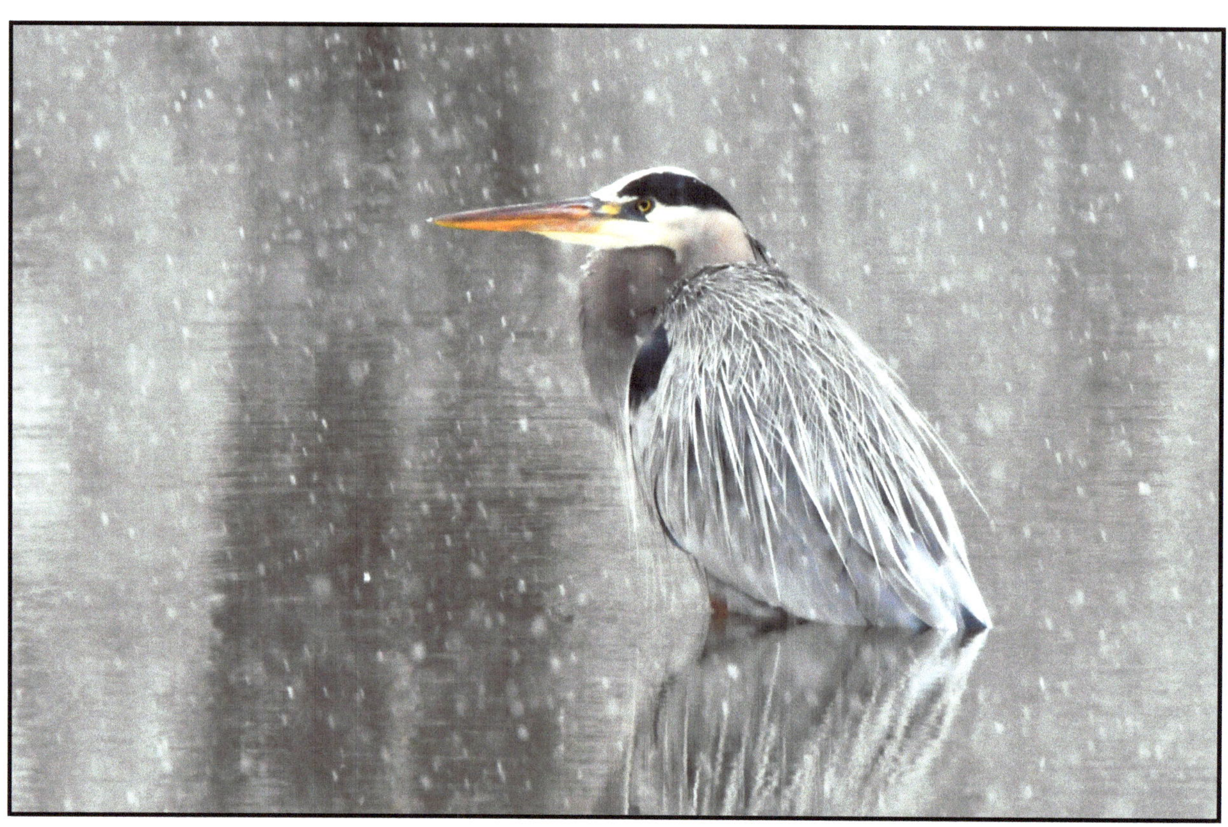

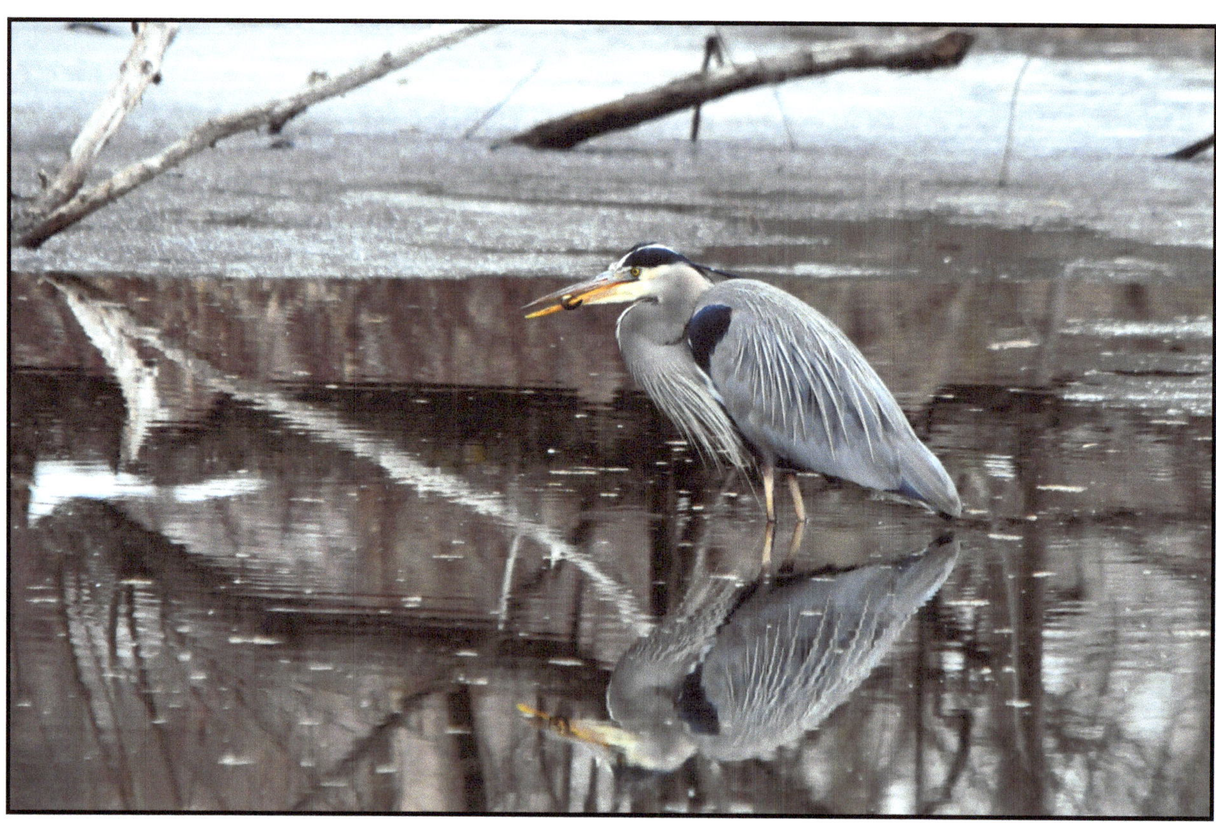

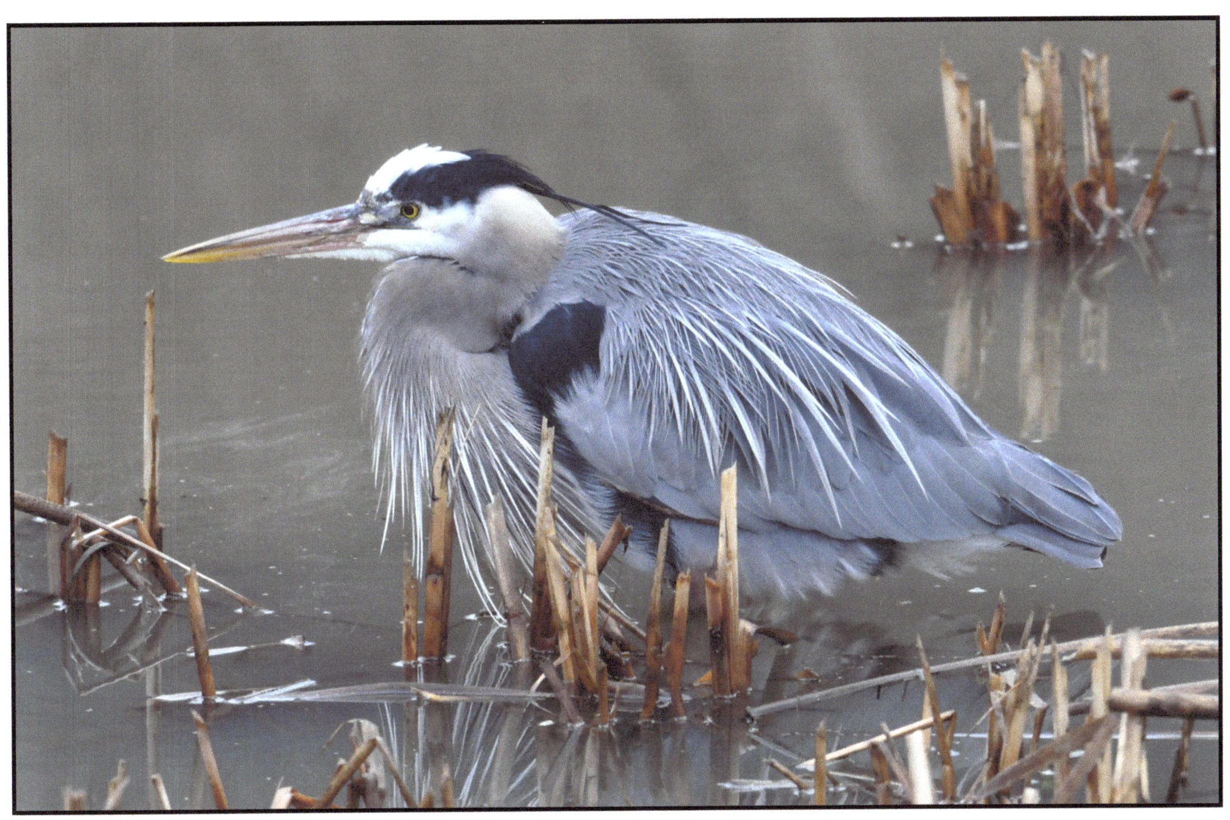

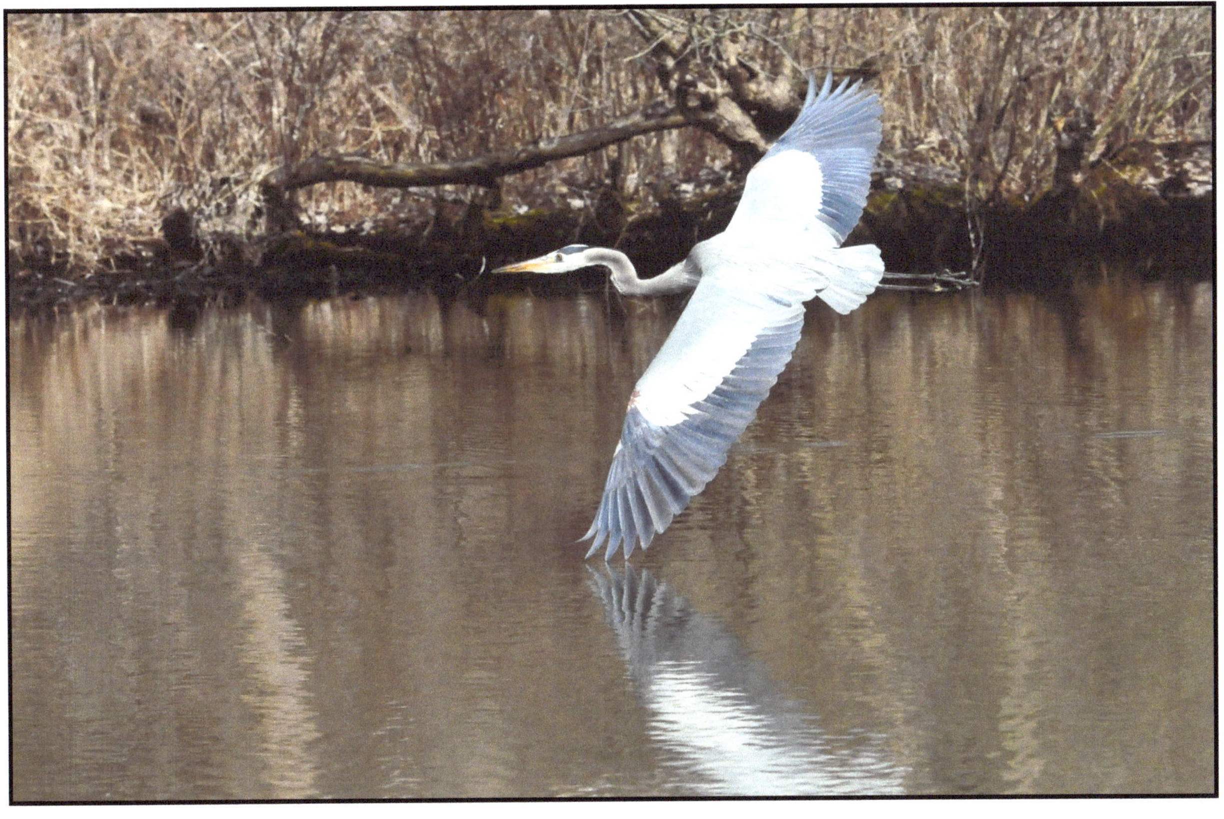

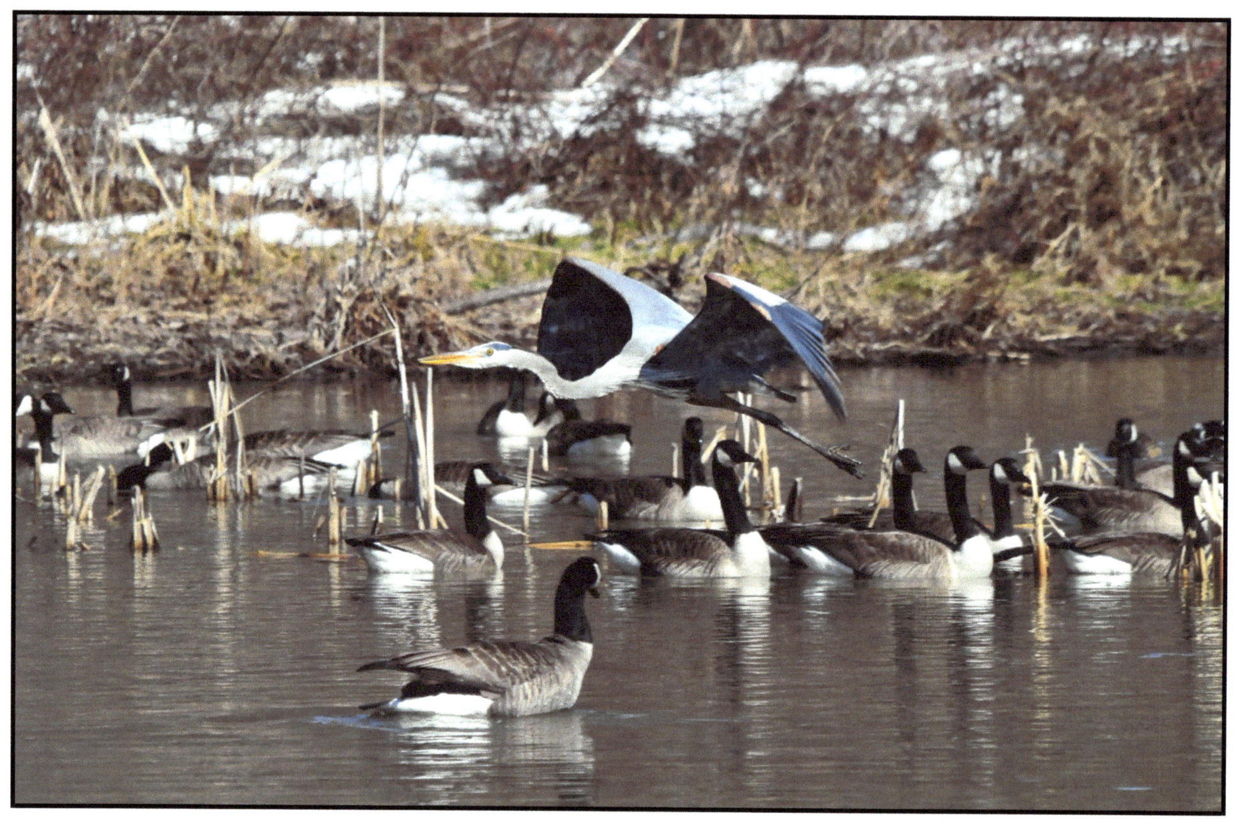

Spring at last!

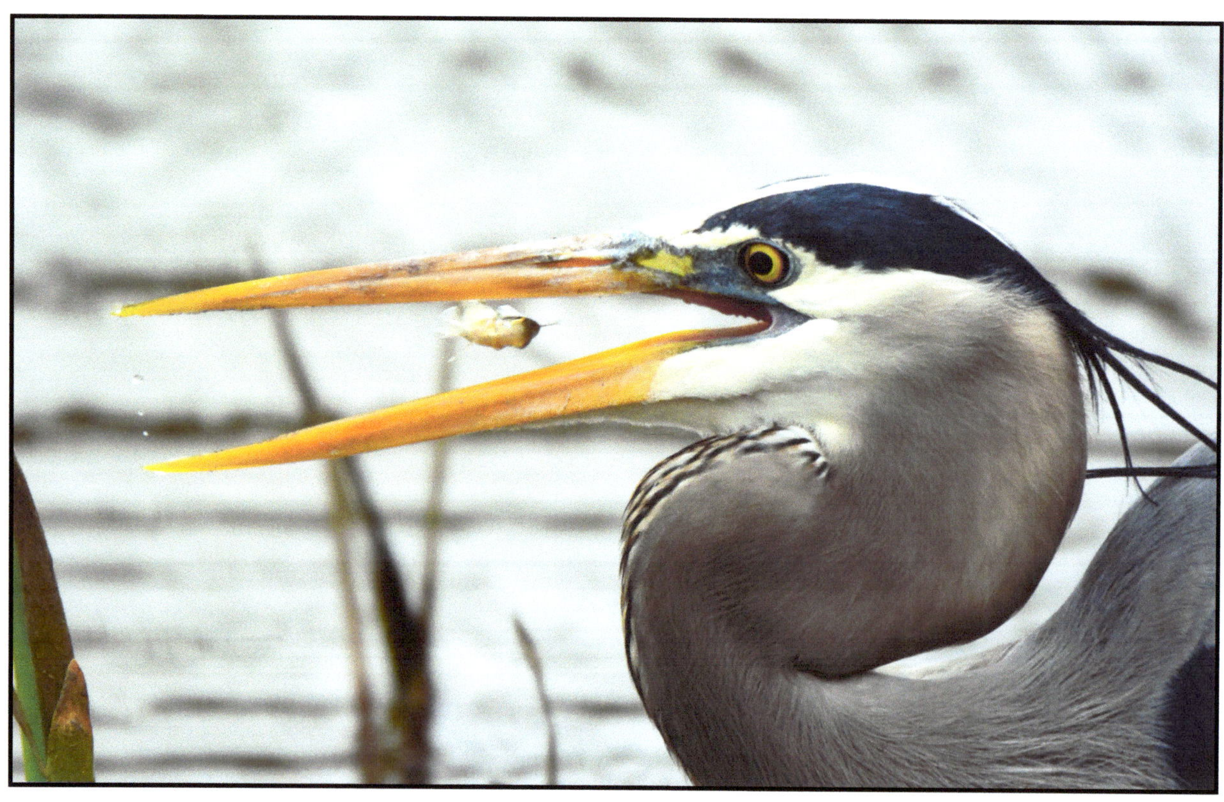

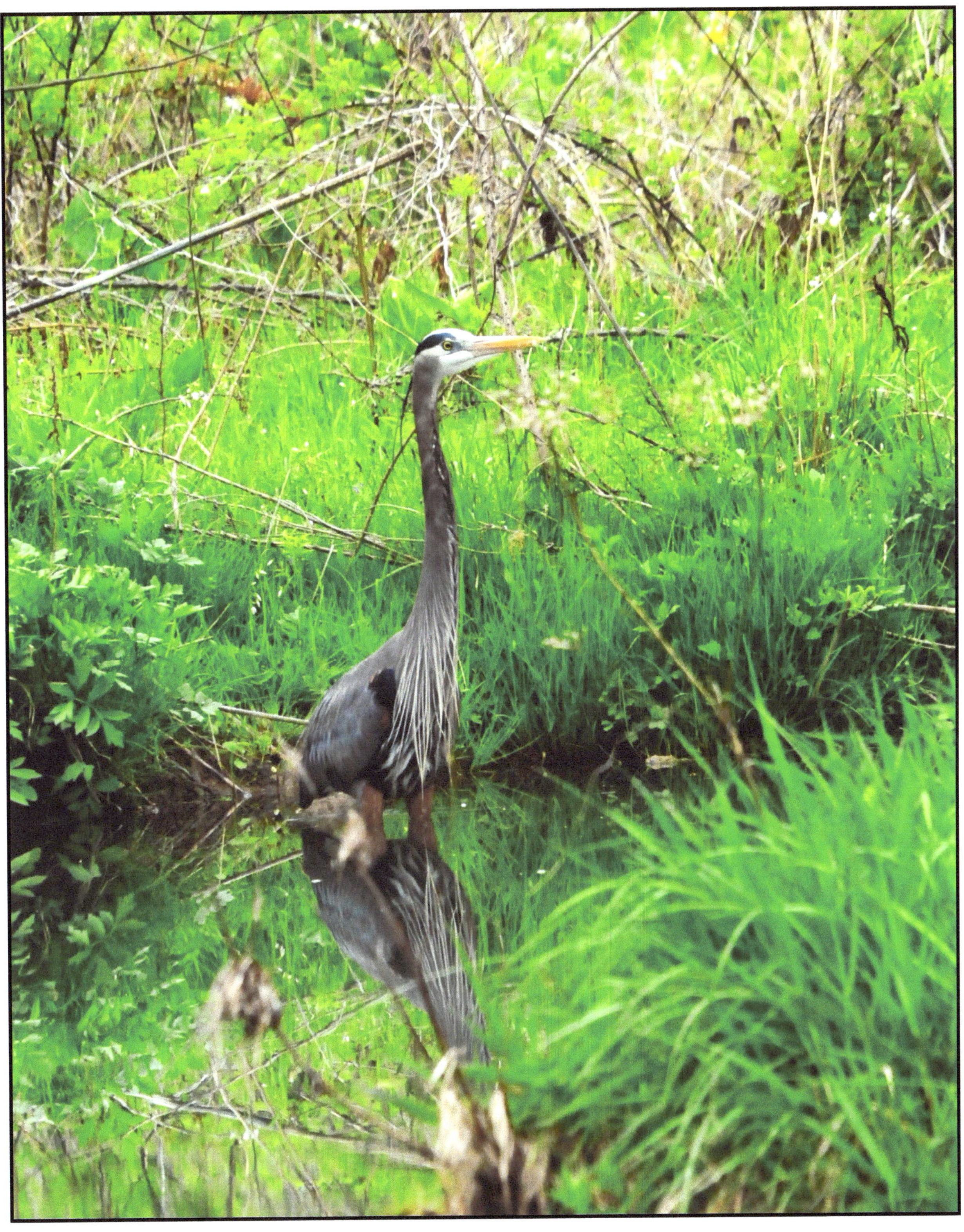

This Heron seems to be thinking, "This is much better than ice and snow."

WHAT DOES A GREAT BLUE HERON EAT?

What *does* a Great Blue Heron eat? The answer to that question is: It depends on where the bird lives. Their dietary habits are extremely adaptable. If they live near the oceans, they will eat crabs, fish, or nearly anything else that will fit into their surprisingly large maws. Here in Ohio, I have personally seen them catch and eat their primary diet of fish; any species will do. Other snacks may include young Red-Wing Blackbirds, voles, small turtles (even snappers), crayfish, and snakes.

Catfish give them special problems which they have adapted to overcome. The sharp, erect spines on a catfish's pectoral and dorsal fins could puncture their alimentary canal at any spot. Therefore, rather than give up a good meal, the Heron will puncture the catfish with its very sharp, pointed beak many times until it is dead, soft, and very limp. At the same time, it will try to break the spines close enough to the body to flatten them so they don't protrude outward. With these operations performed, down the hatch it goes like any other fish. This special treatment of catfish can go on for fifteen or twenty minutes if the fish is large, until the Heron is satisfied its meal can be swallowed safely.

Following are some photographs showing a Heron preparing a catfish for safe swallowing:

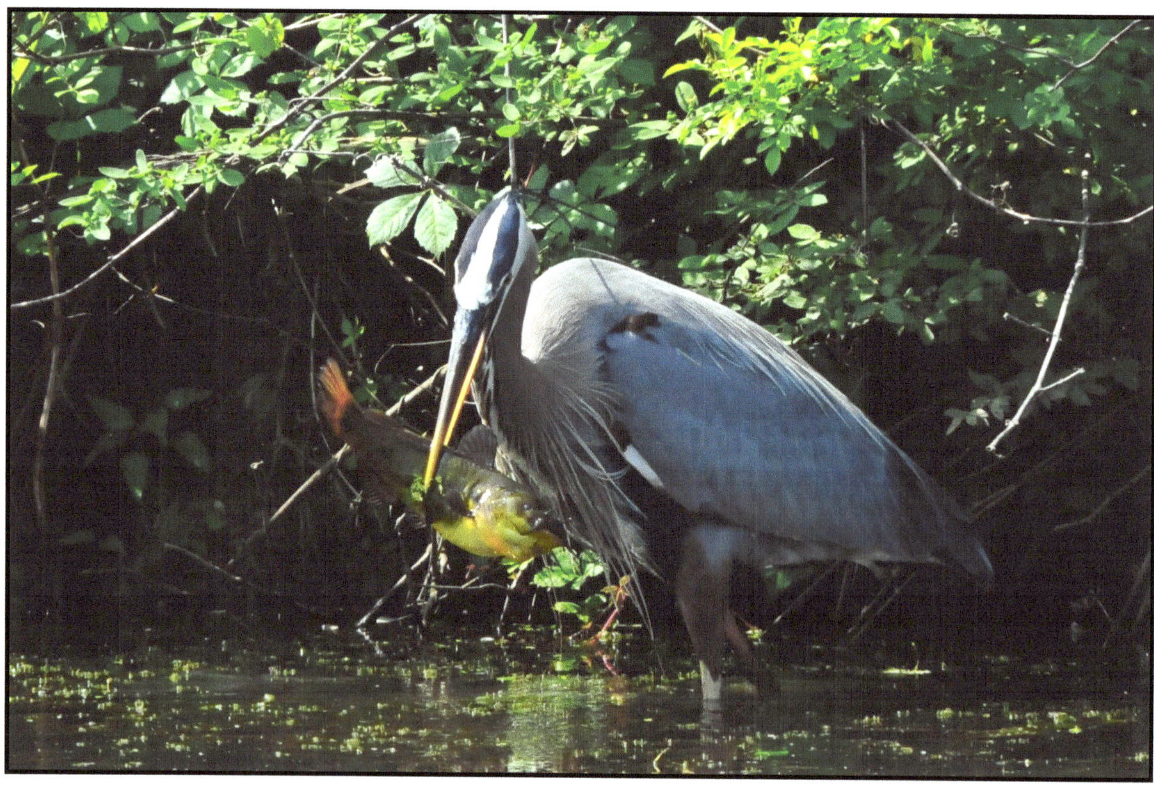

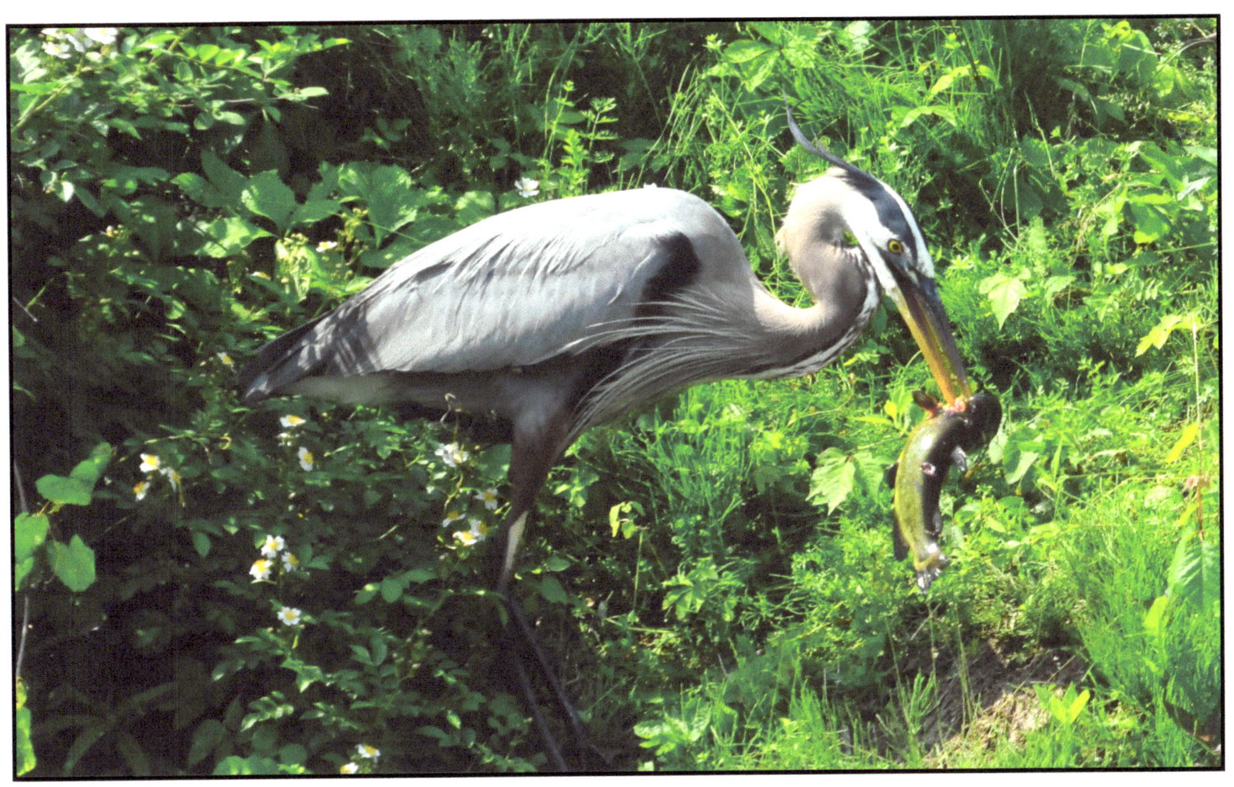

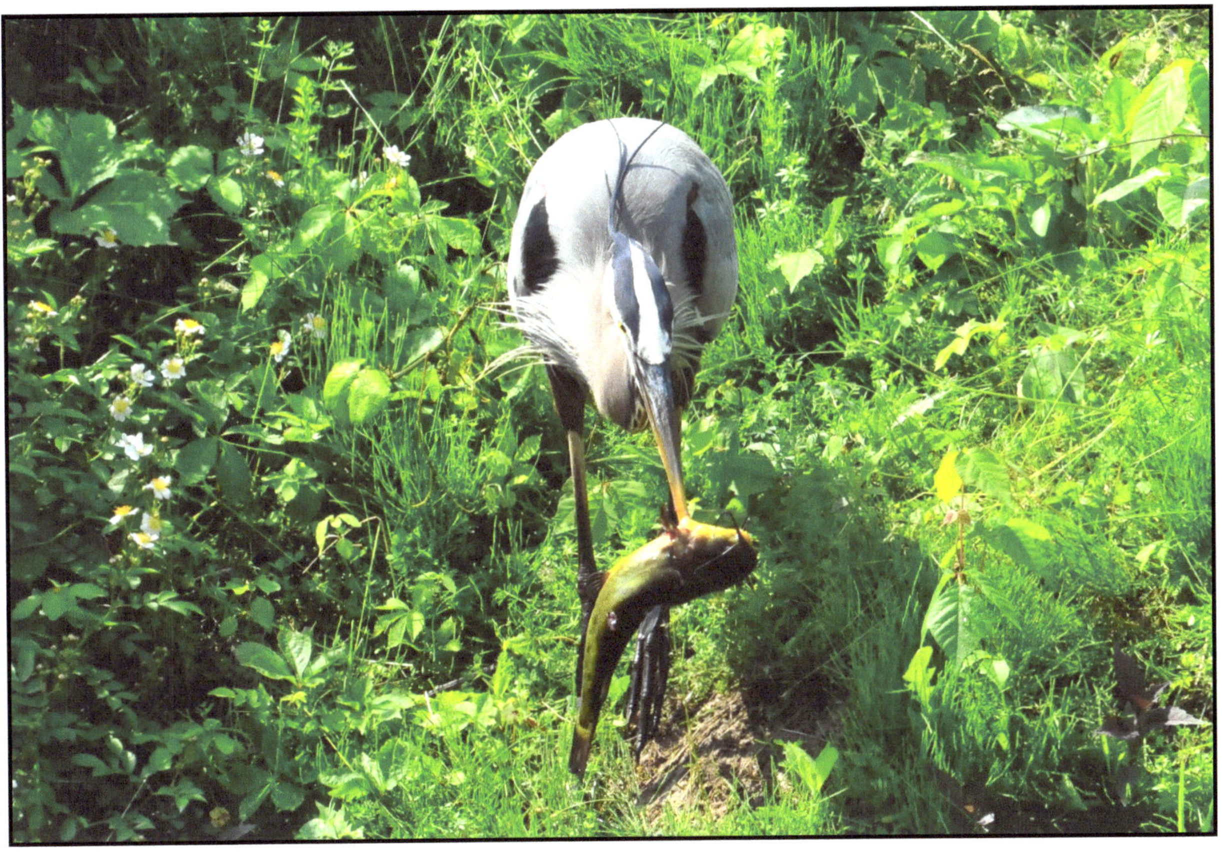

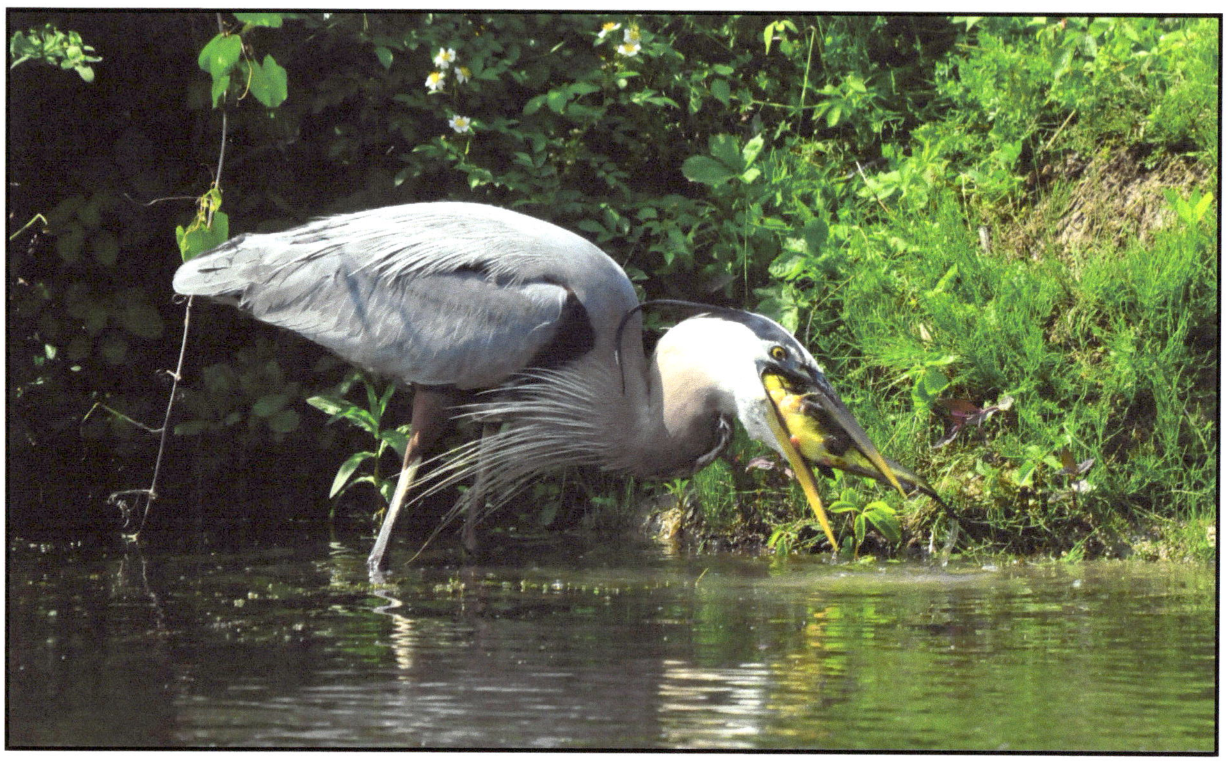

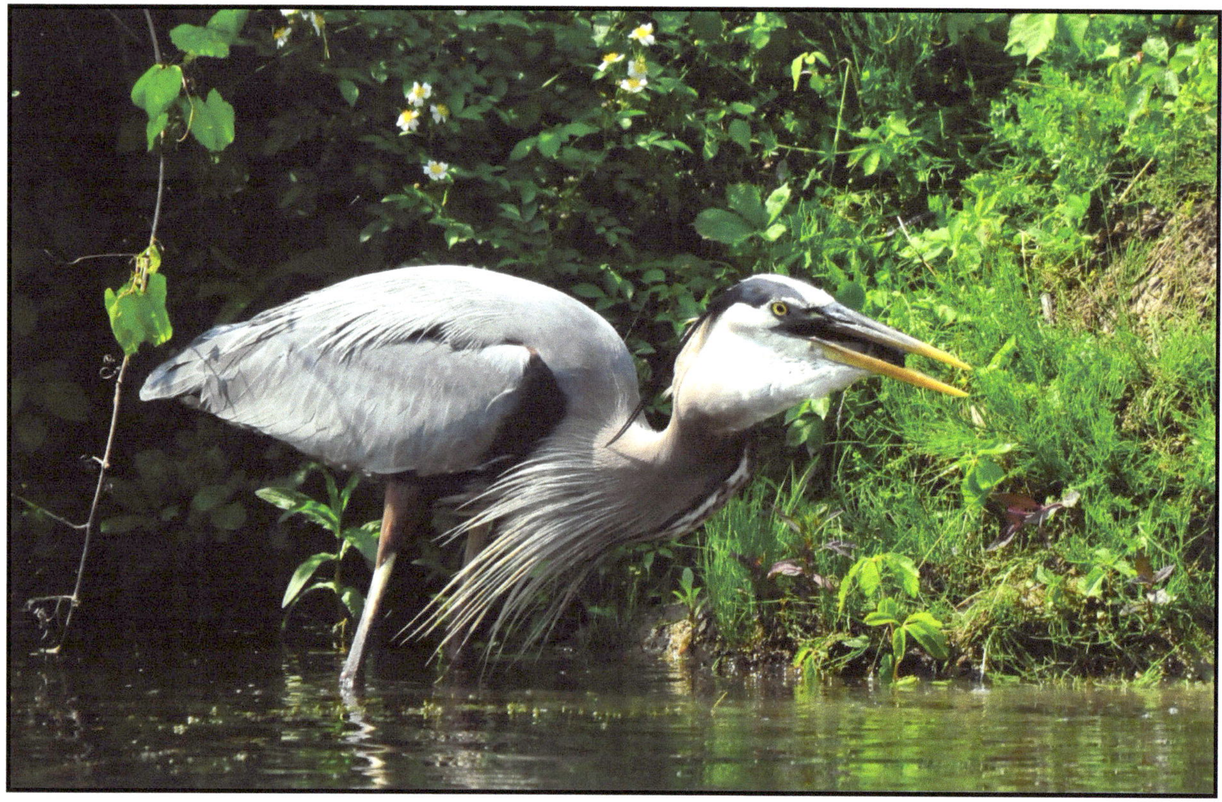

Finally ... Down the hatch!

HOW BIG A FISH CAN A GREAT BLUE HERON SWALLOW?

A Great Blue Herons can swallow a much larger fish than you would imagine, but there are limits. In fact, I have seen them swallow shockingly large fish. On a large fish, they will sometimes "soften them up" by spearing them many times as with a catfish. In the years I have observed them, the following three photos show the only times have I observed a Heron give up on a fish meal.

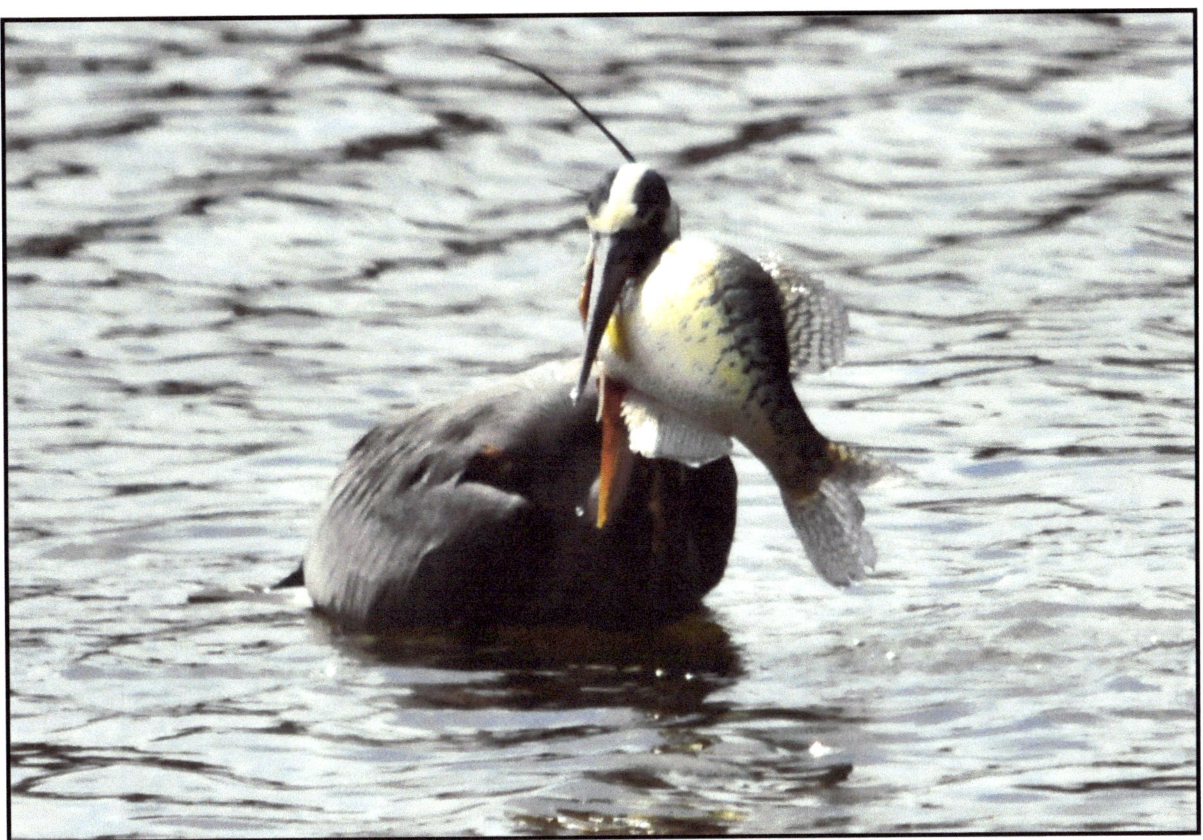

This Heron finally gave up trying to swallow this large Crappie. Any fisherman would have been proud of this particular fish. Its diameter was just too much for this Heron, though. The Crappie was still alive when it was dropped back into the water, where it leaped and dove like a porpoise. But, it died later from its harsh treatment. A Bald Eagle made an easy meal of its carcass the next day. Not much goes to waste in nature

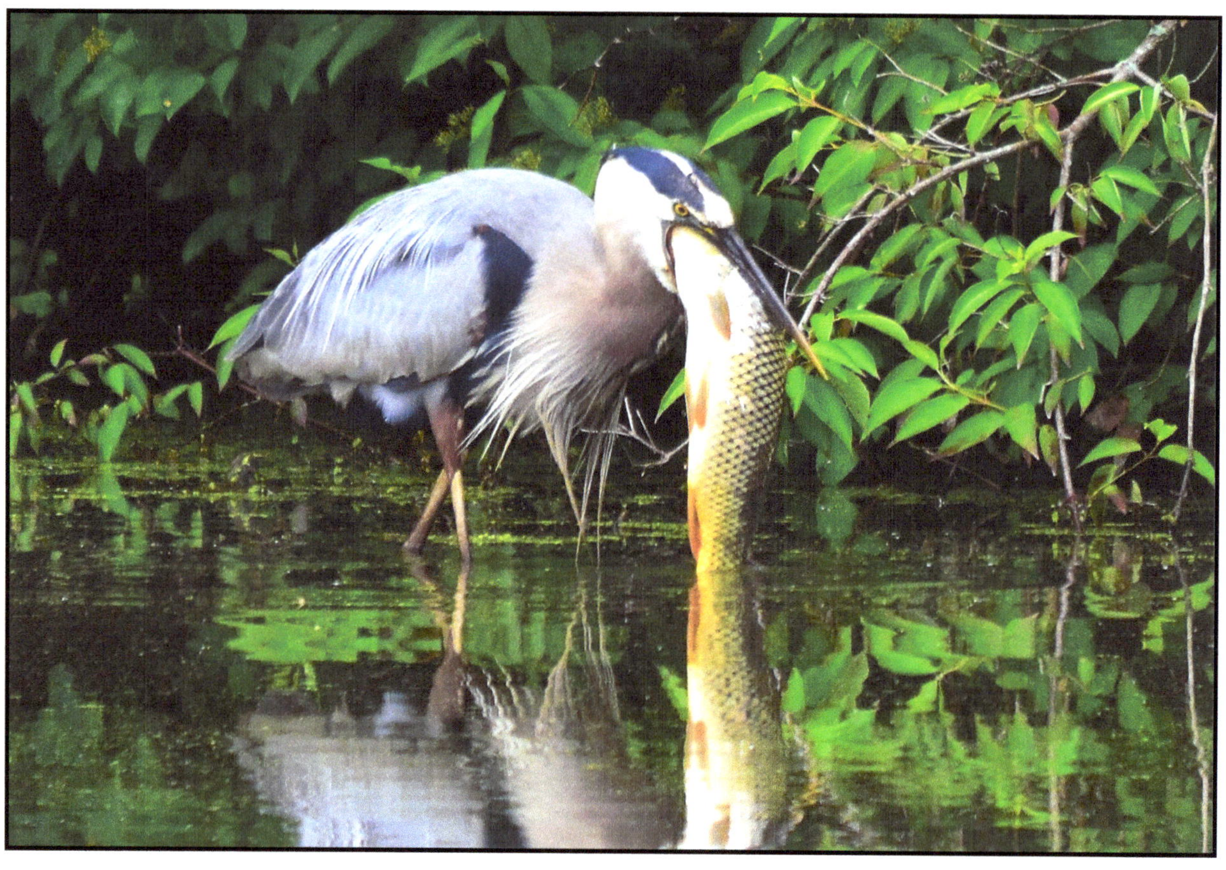

It's truly obvious as to why this Heron finally had to give up trying to swallow this Carp. It was *way* too big, but the Heron didn't give up trying. Below is another failure; a Gizzard Shad.

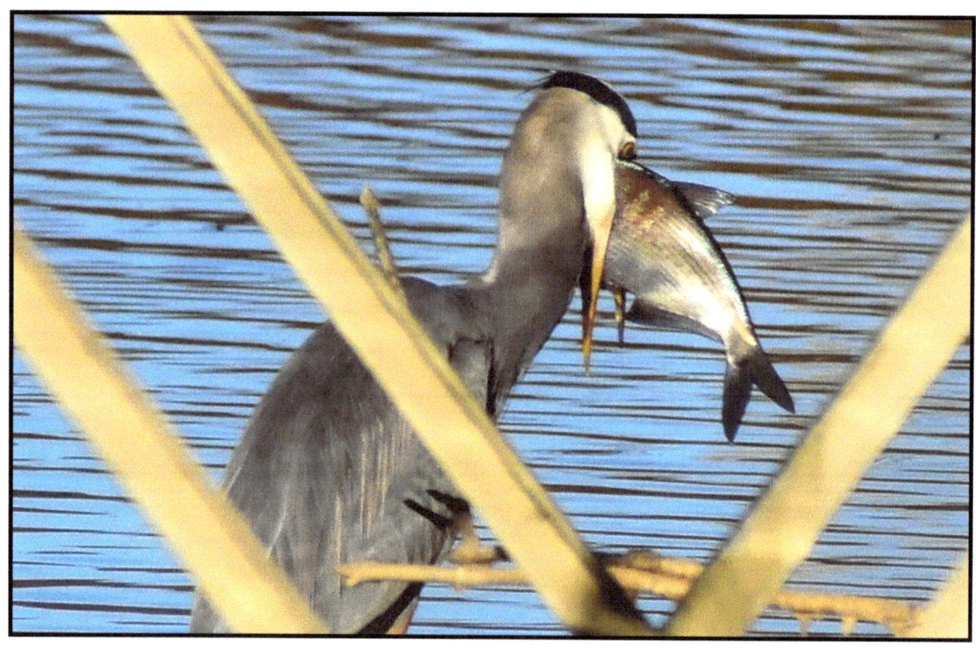

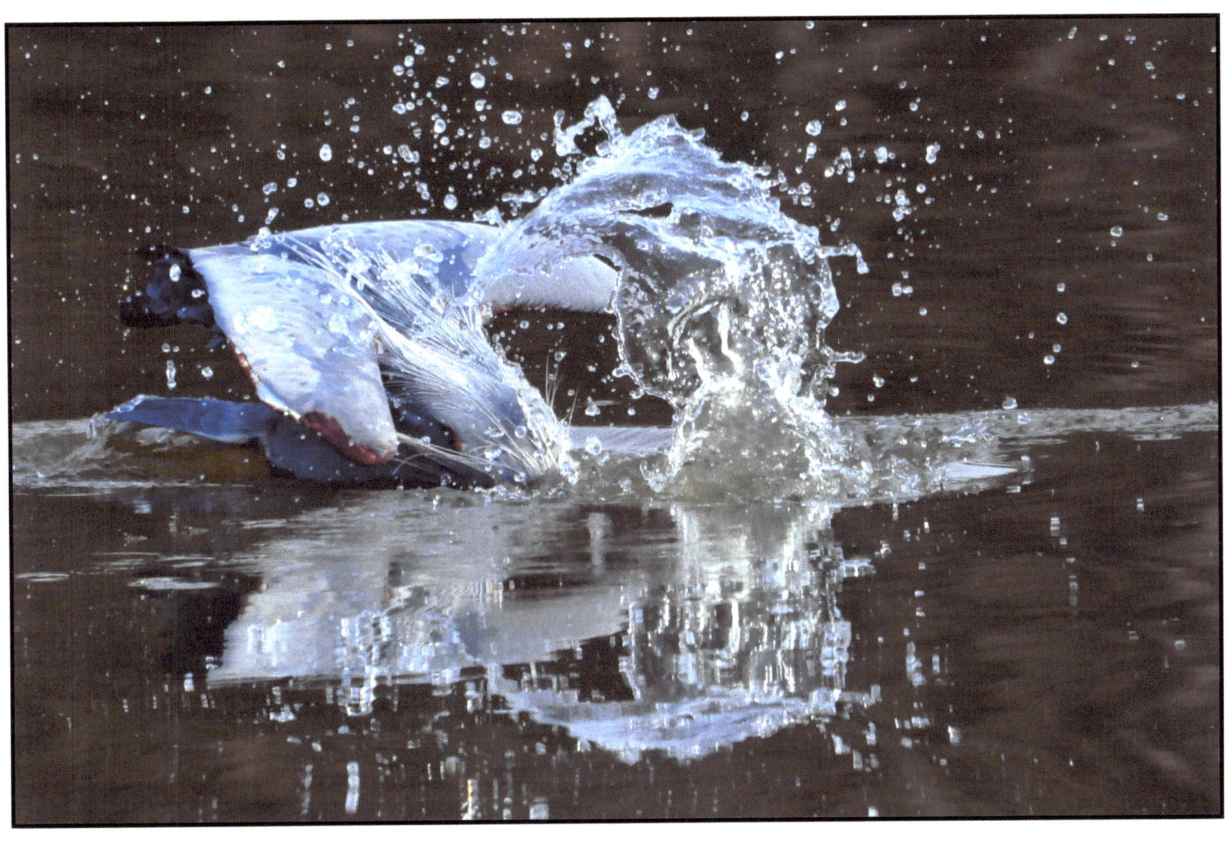

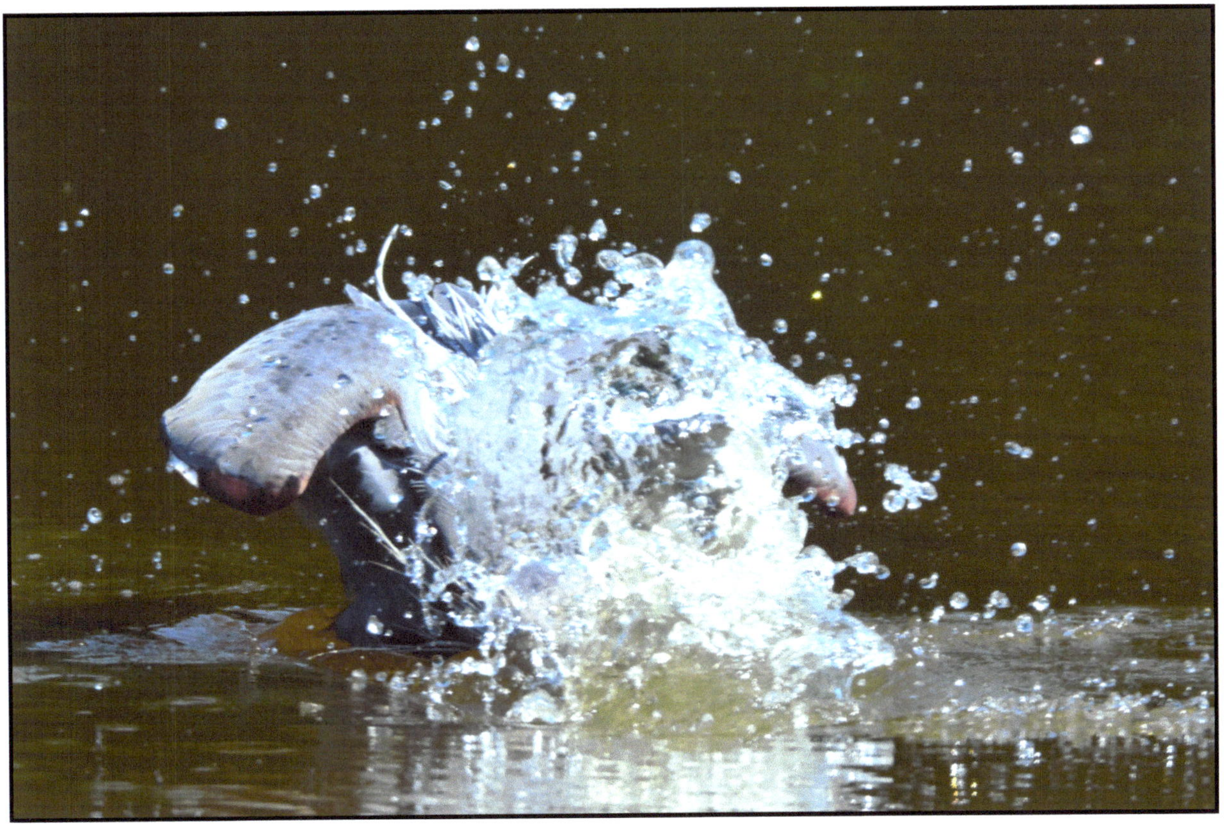

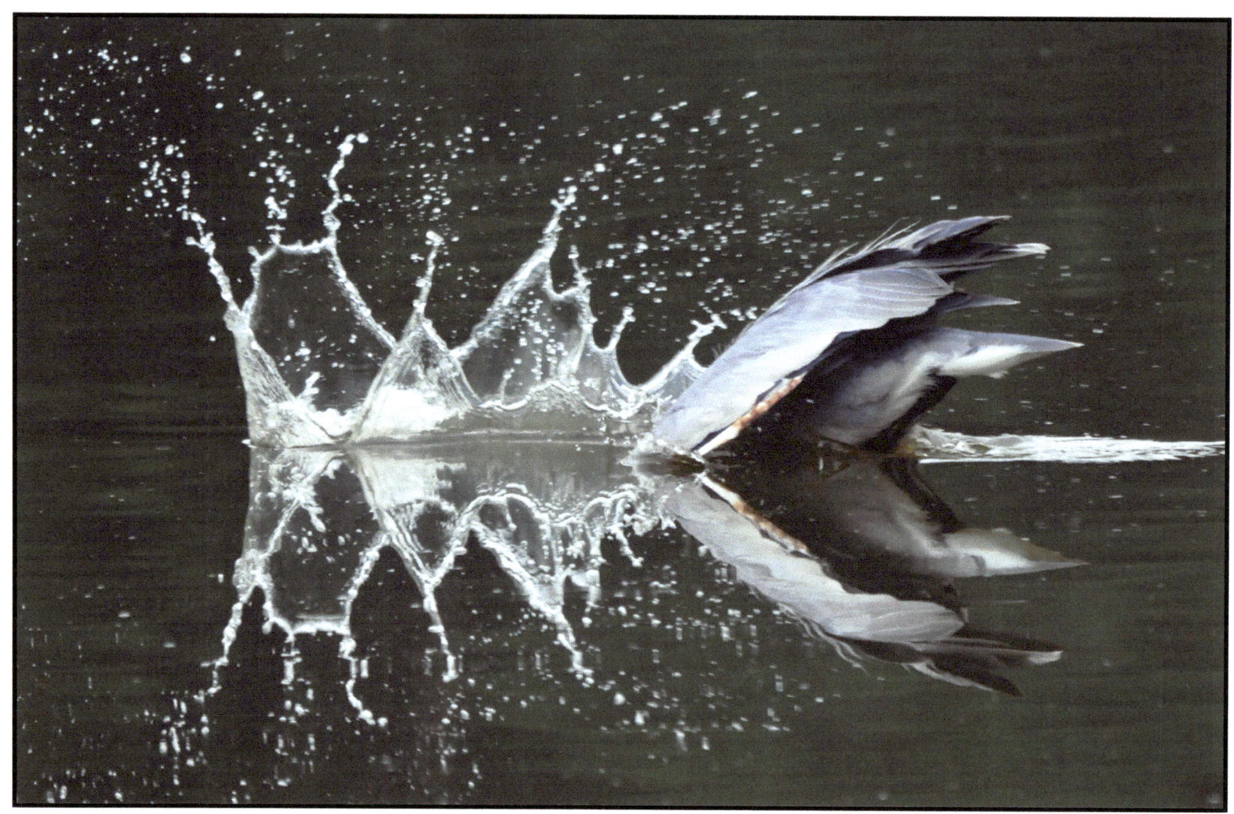

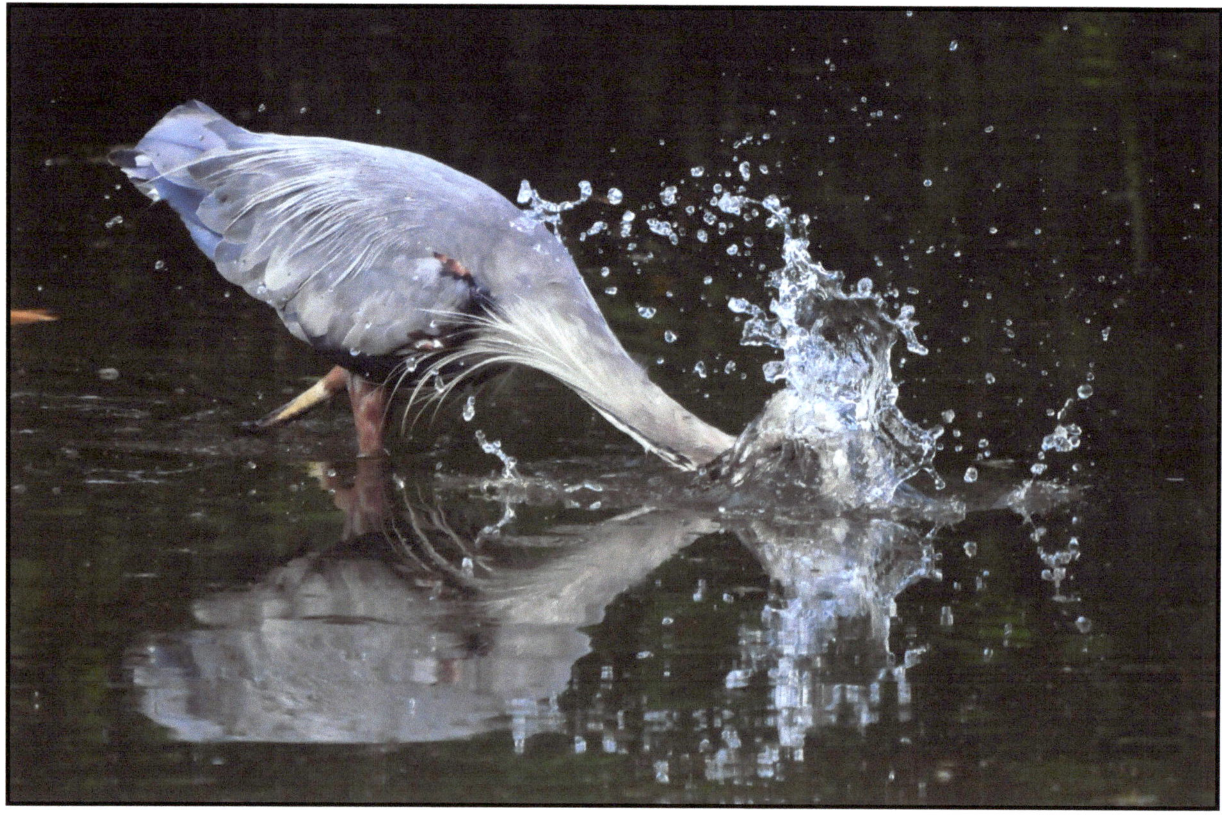

The four preceding photos show the sometimes spectacular splashes made as Great Blue Herons attempt to catch their meals. As might be expected, every splash is not always rewarded with a catch. Some Herons are better fishermen than others, but their luck seems to improve with experience. I have seen young herons miss as many as eighty percent of attempts, as older birds succeeded three out of four times. If they are perpetually inept, the survival of the fittest factor kicks in and they don't live to a ripe old age. Fortunately, most learn quickly. Following are shown some of the successful catches. The size of their catches vary from tiny to almost gigantic.

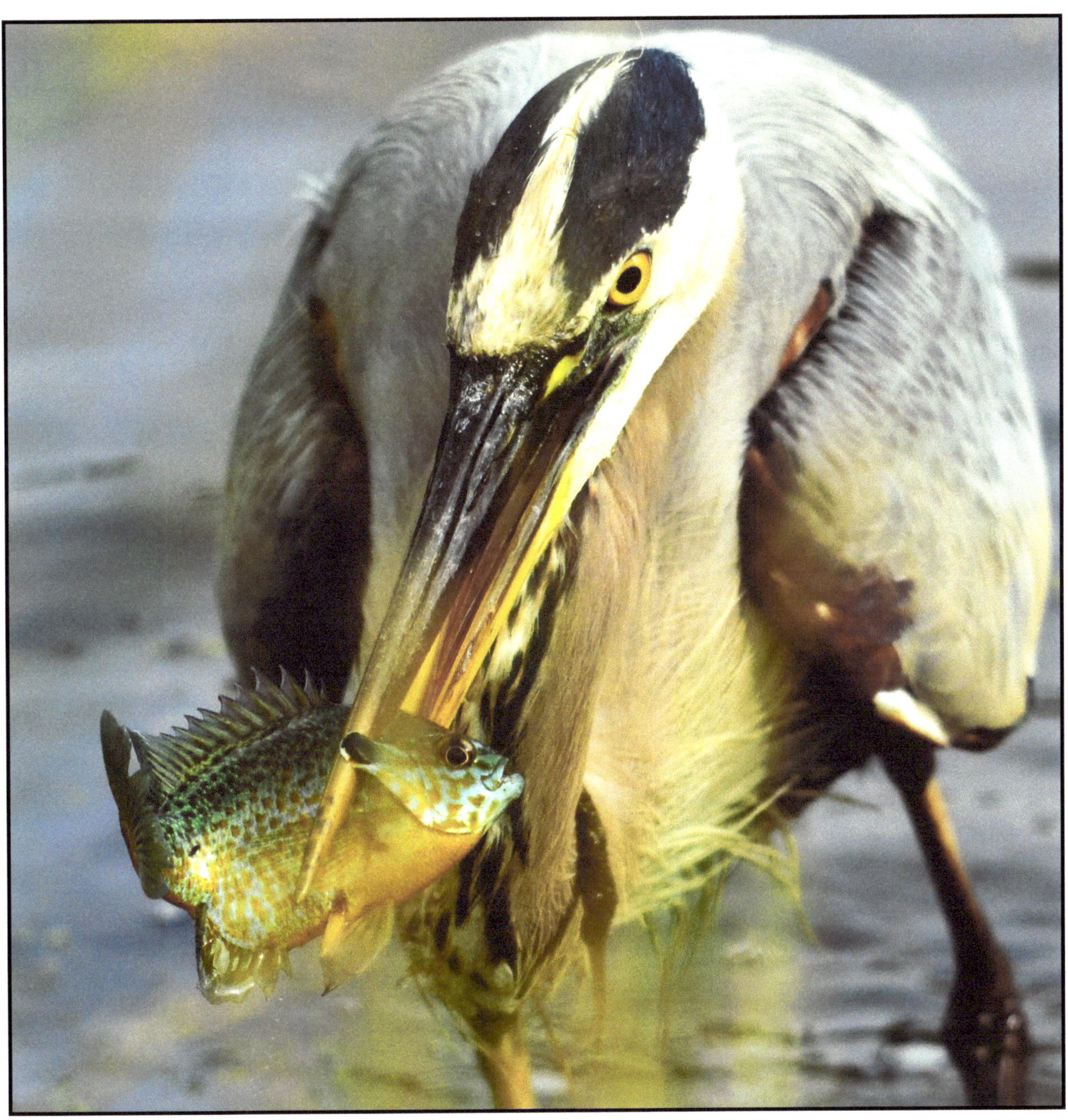

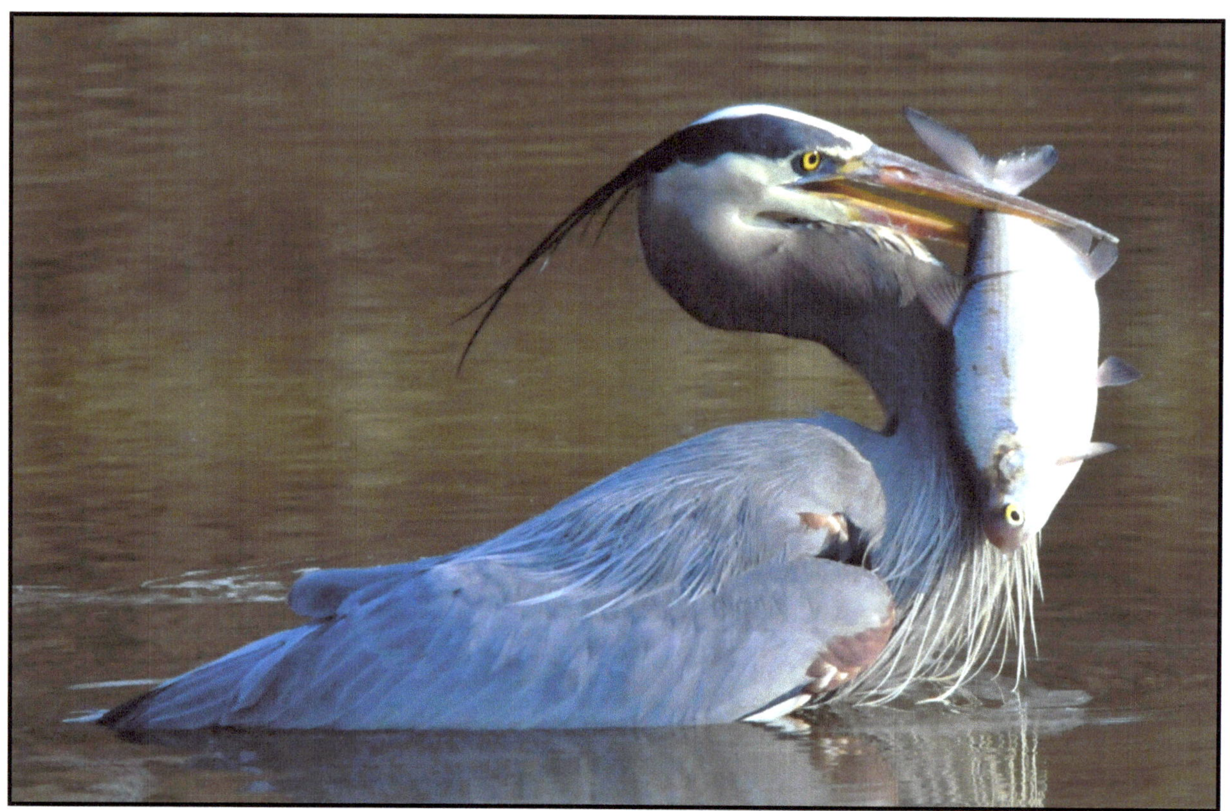

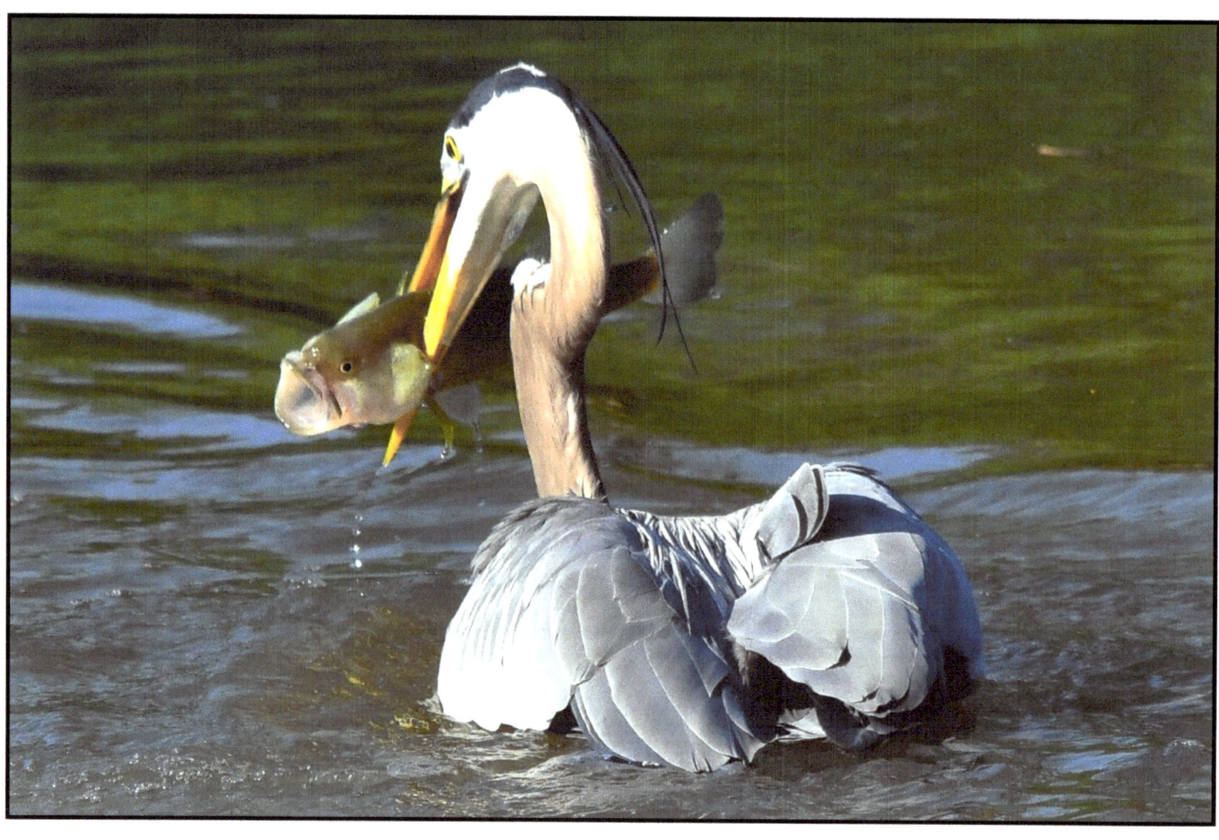

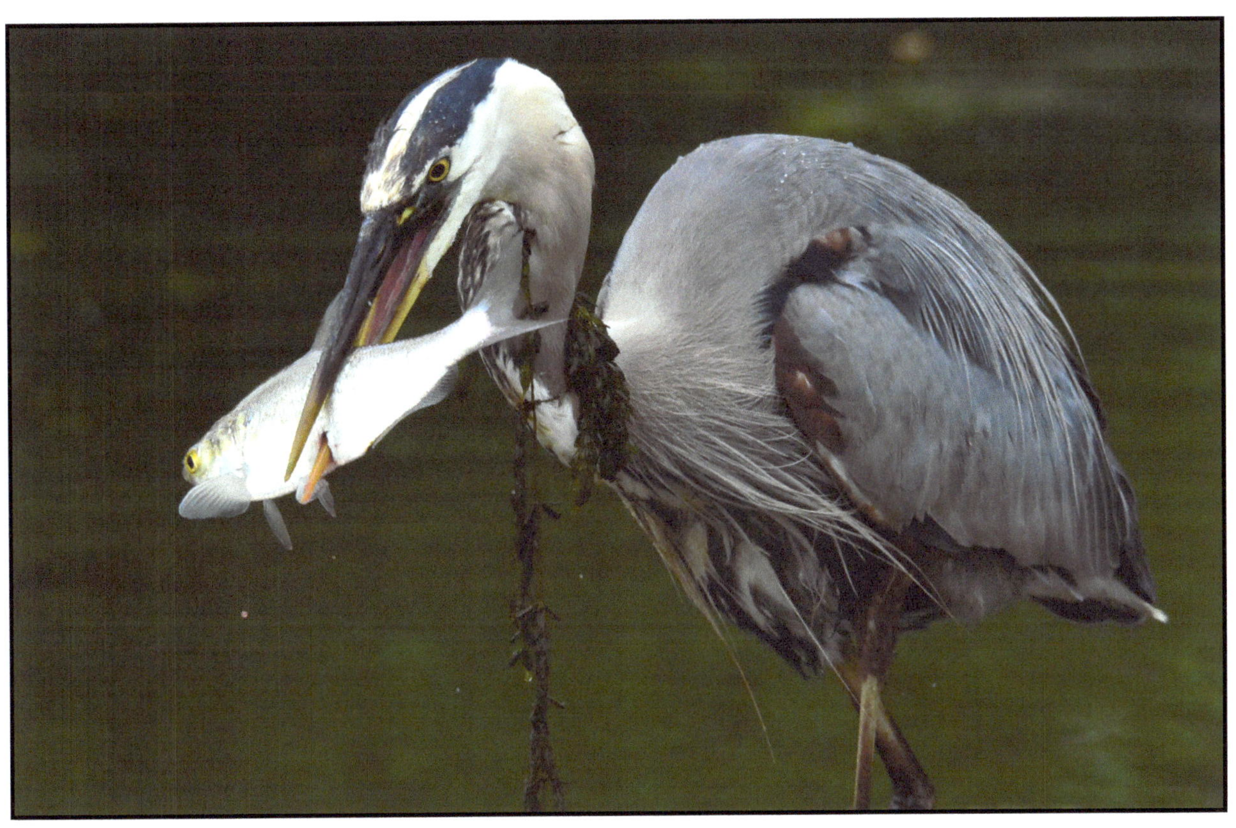

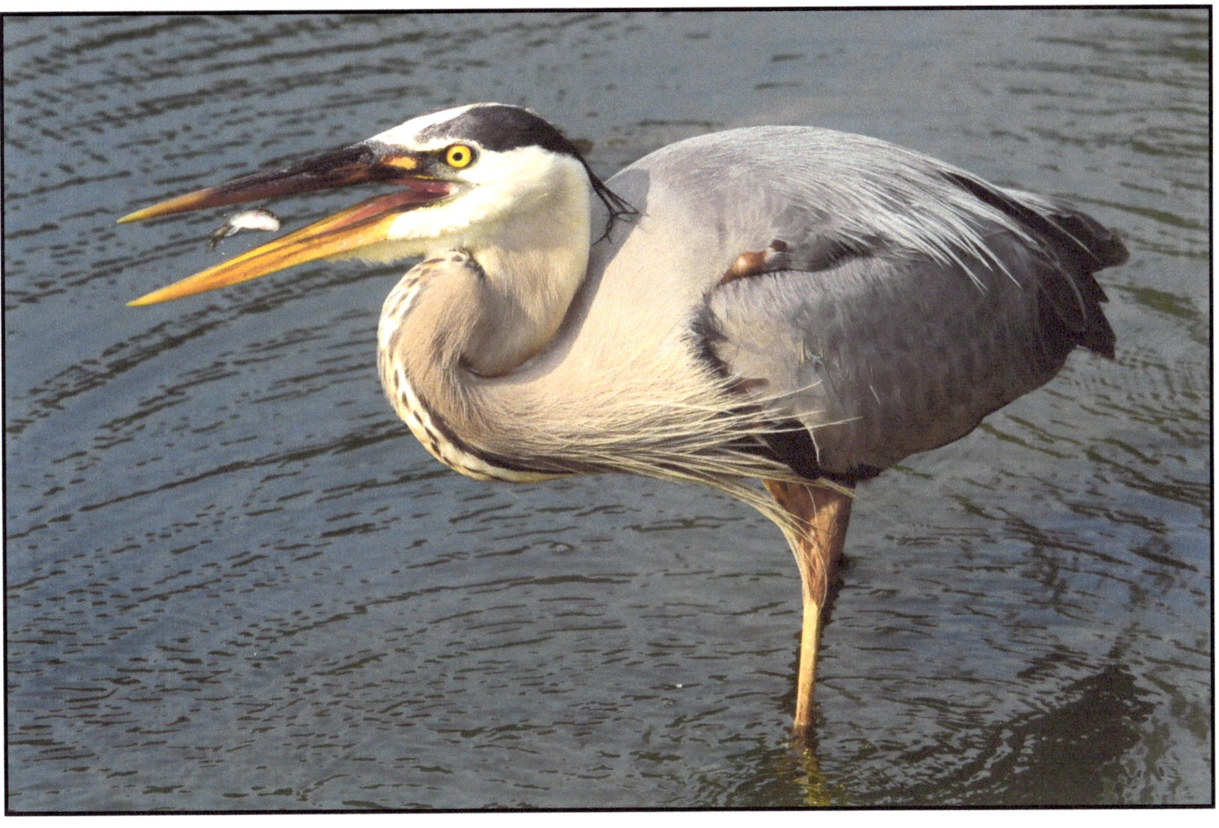

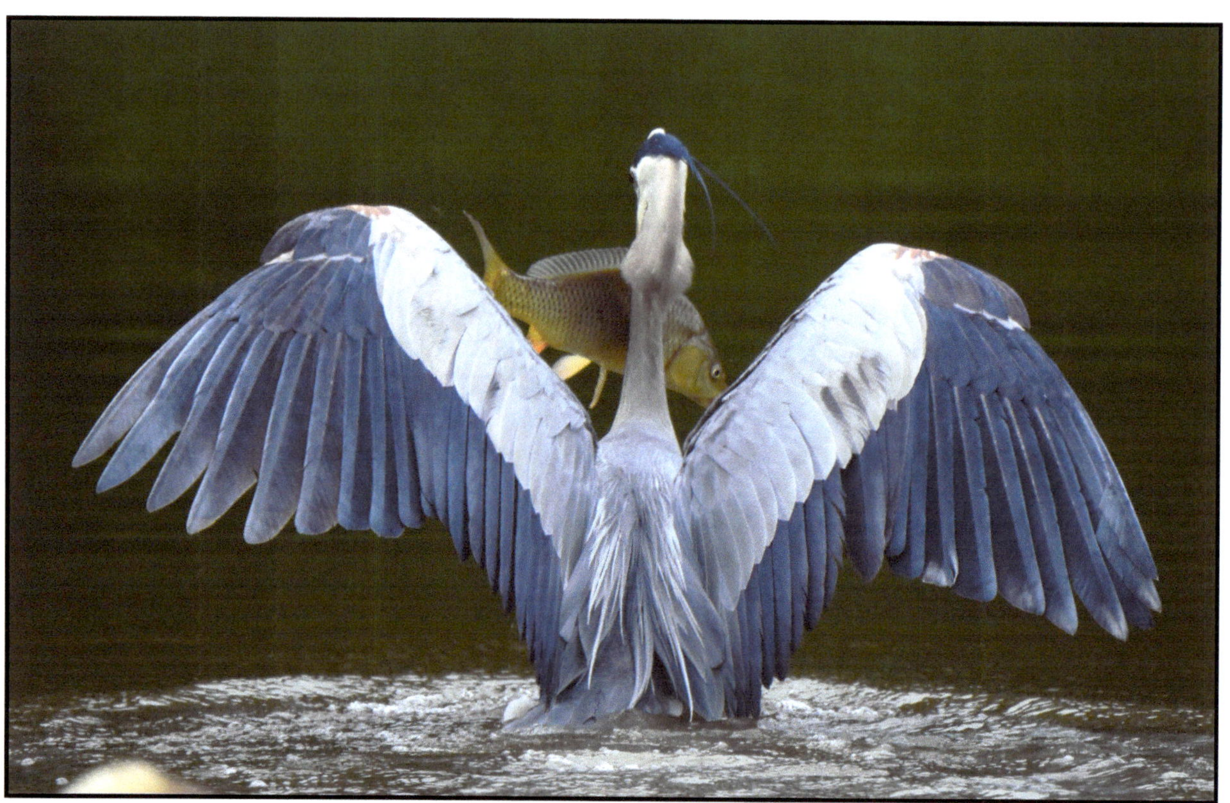

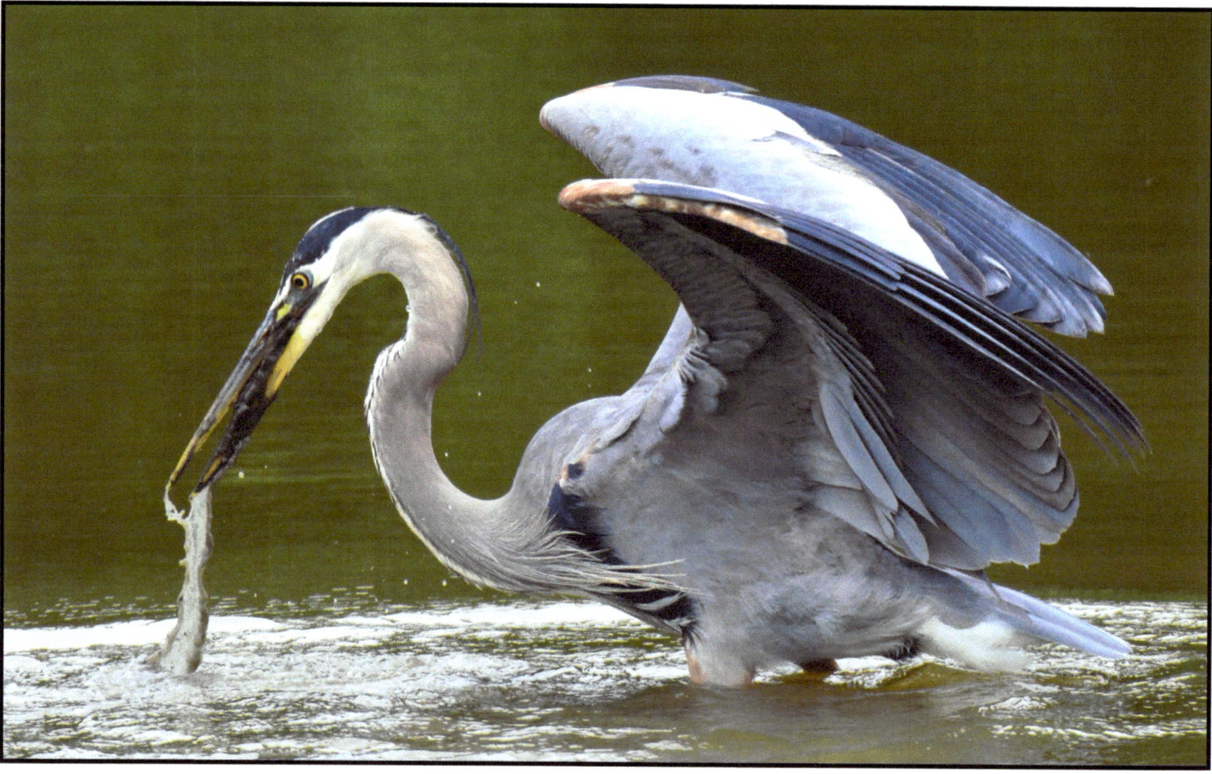

Fish are not the only thing that will fill a Heron's bill. Sometimes a bit of the muddy lake bottom finds its way in, too. This Heron missed his prey and drove his bill much too deeply into the muddy lake bottom. A few shakes of his head, and he was back in business, though.

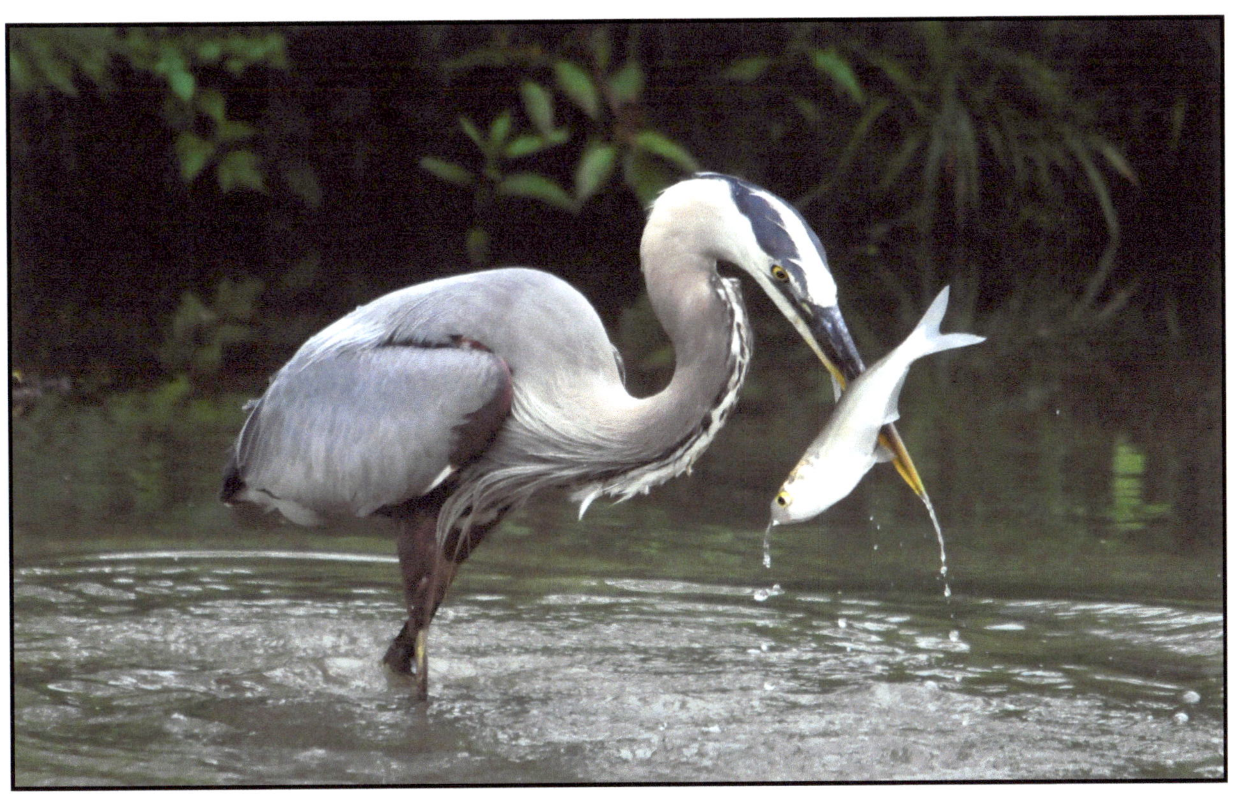

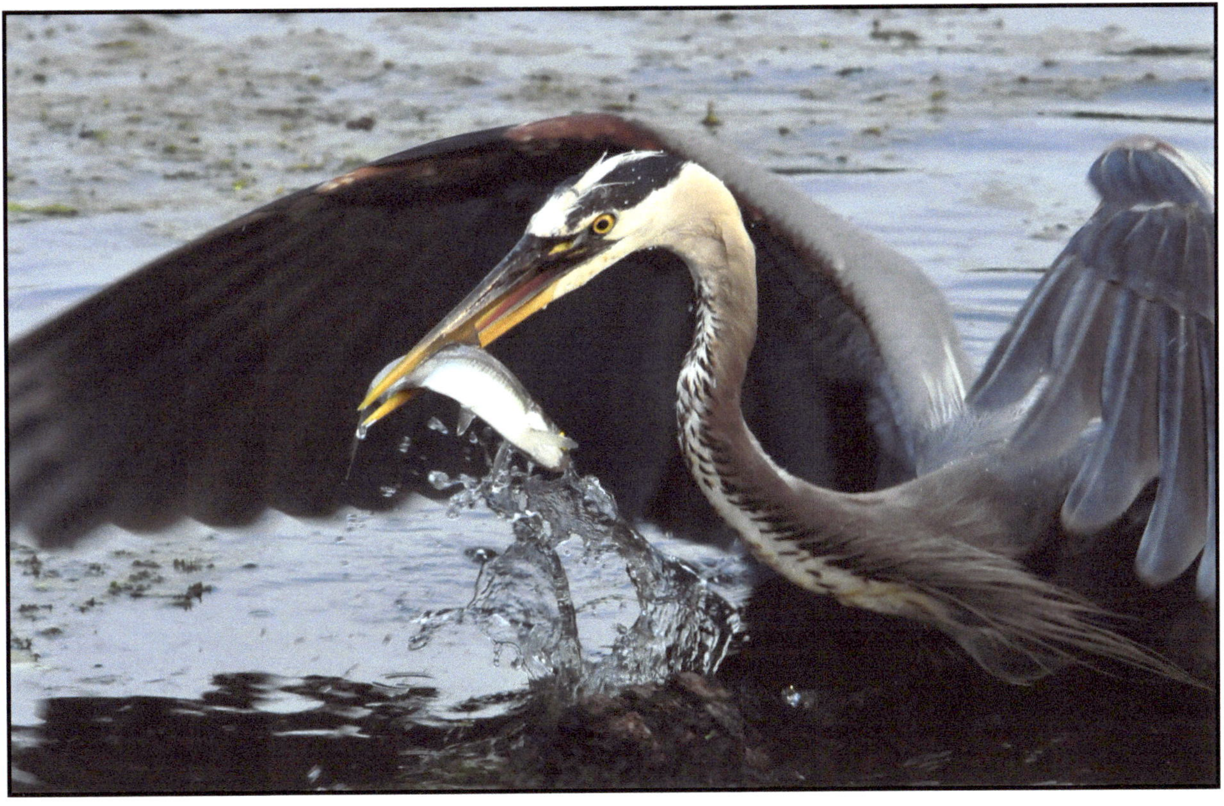

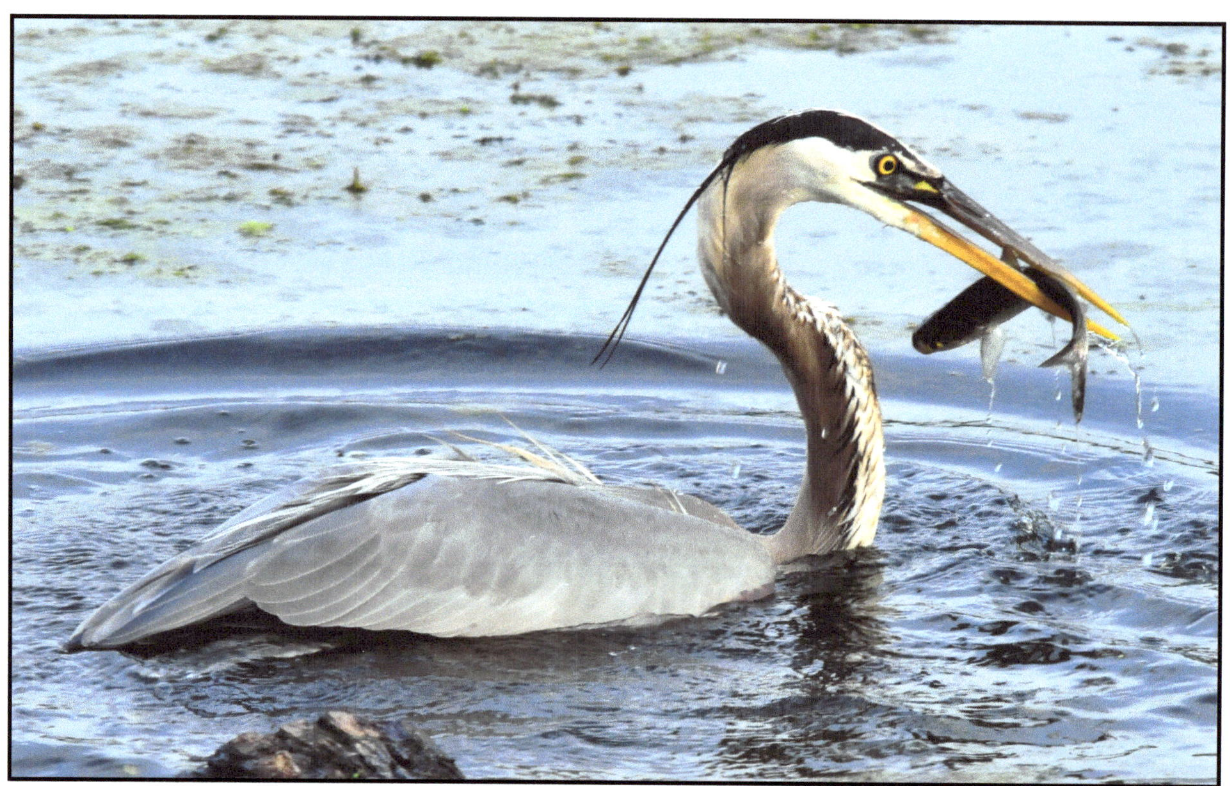

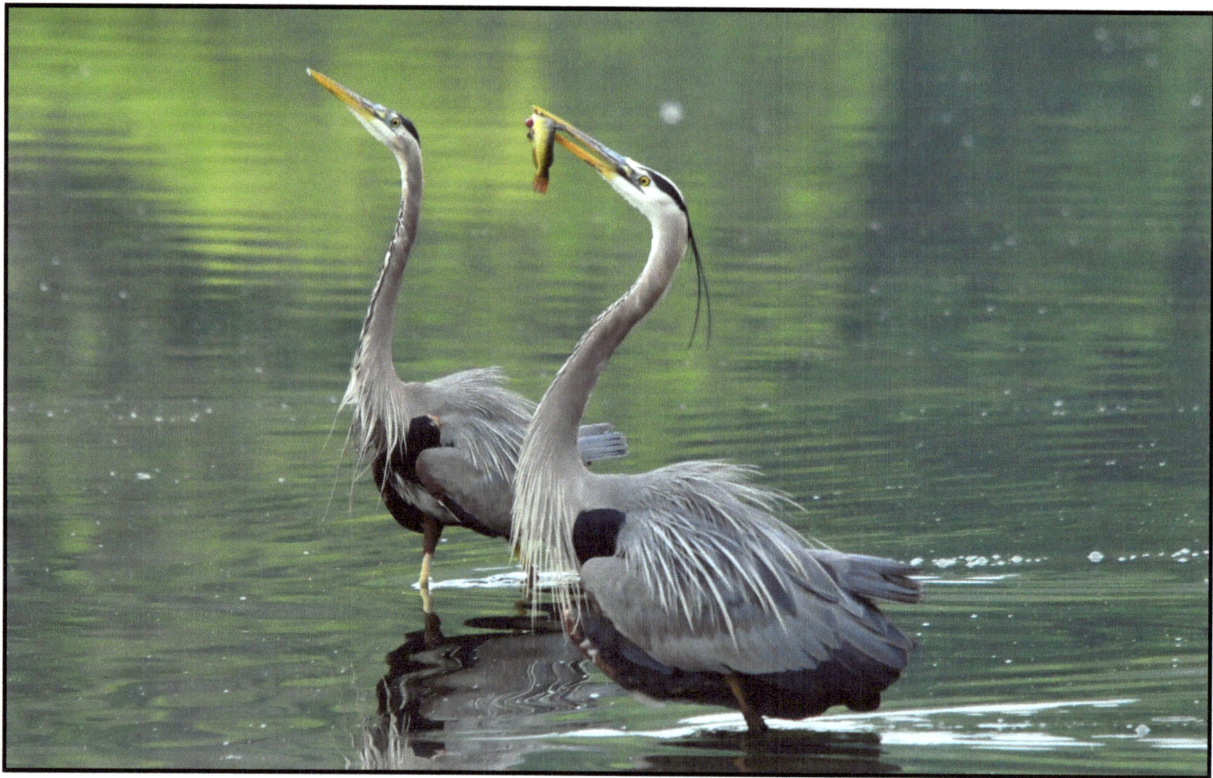

This Great Blue Heron seems very proud of his small catfish. He caught a much larger one later.

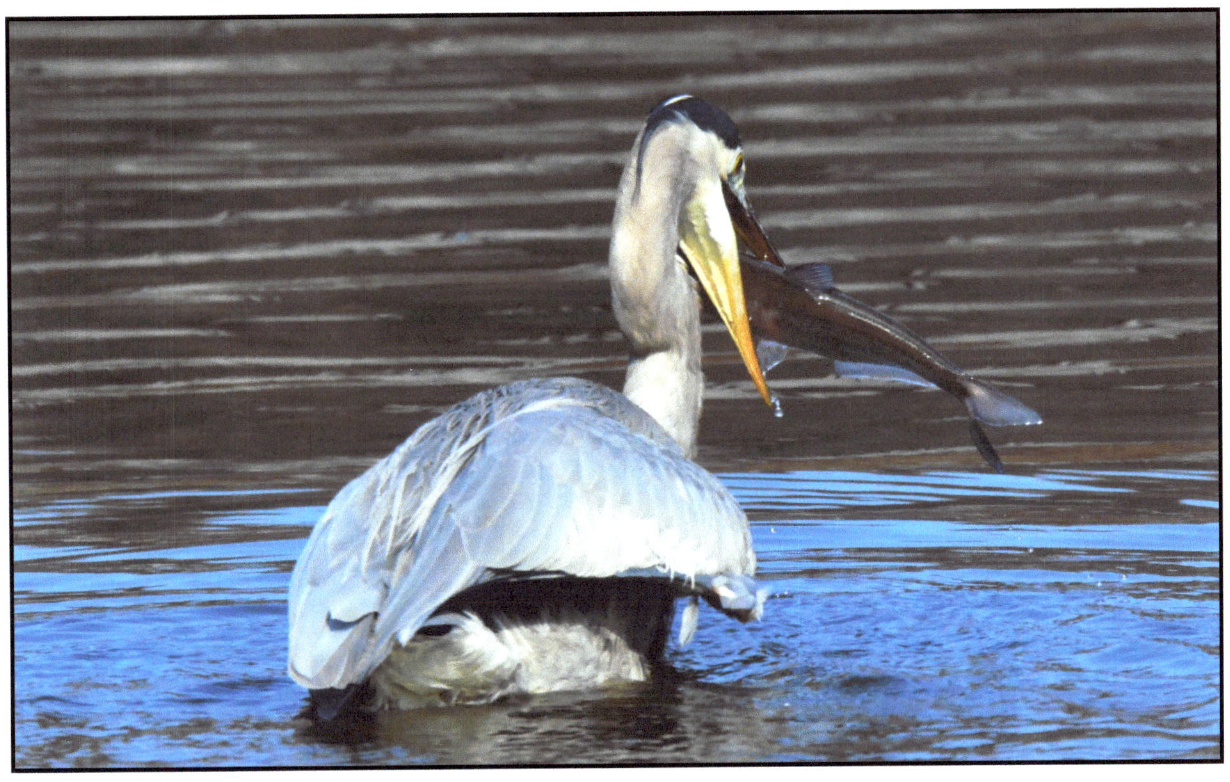

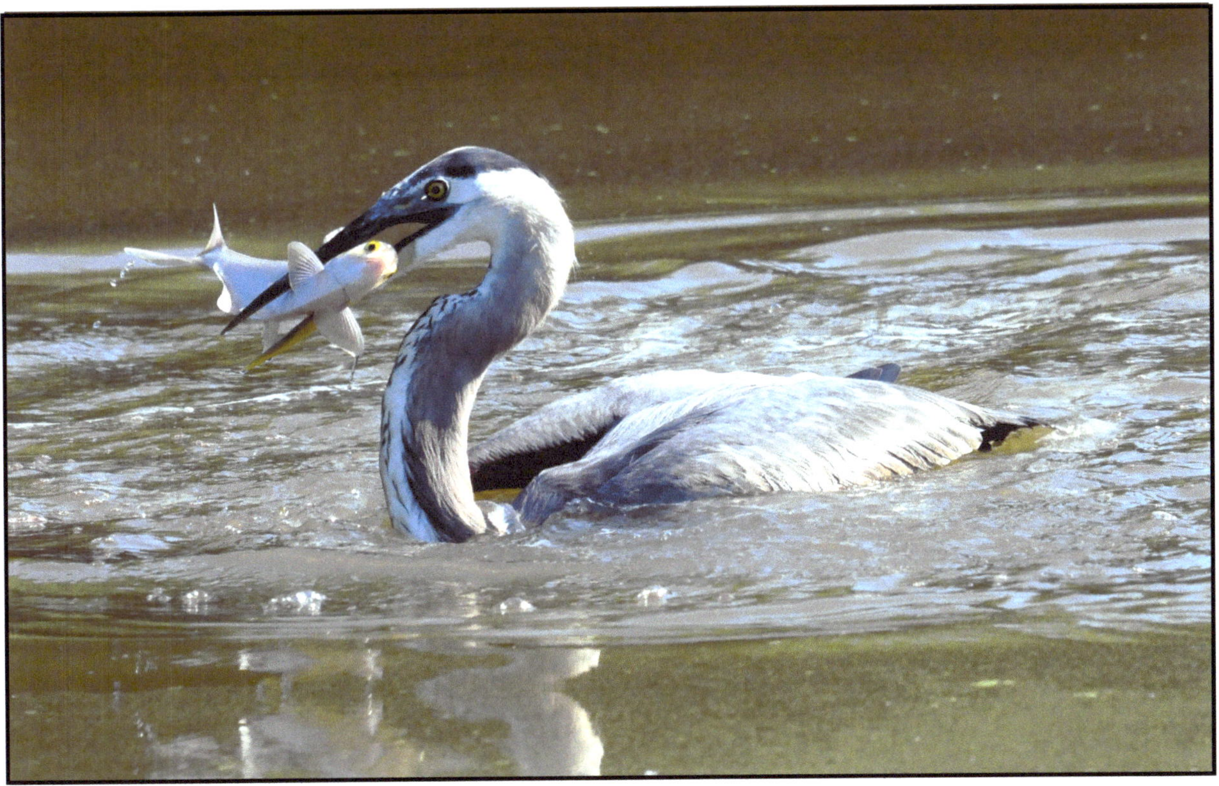

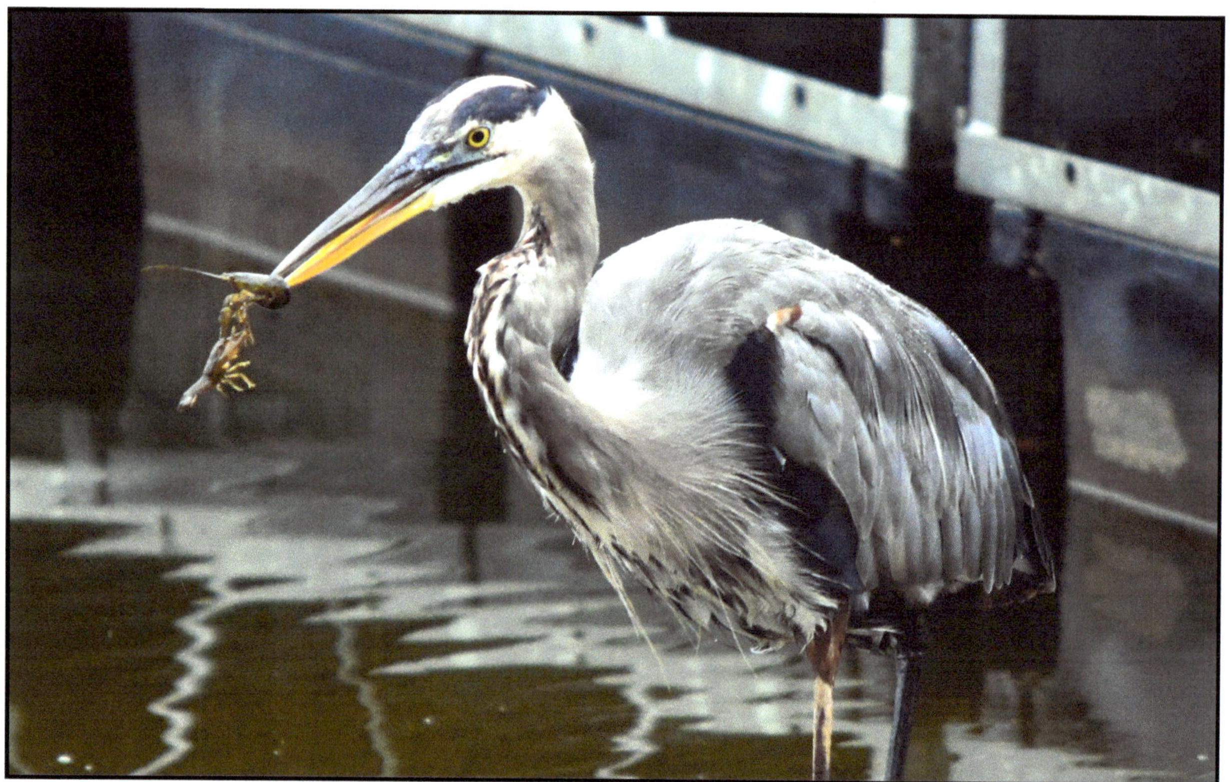

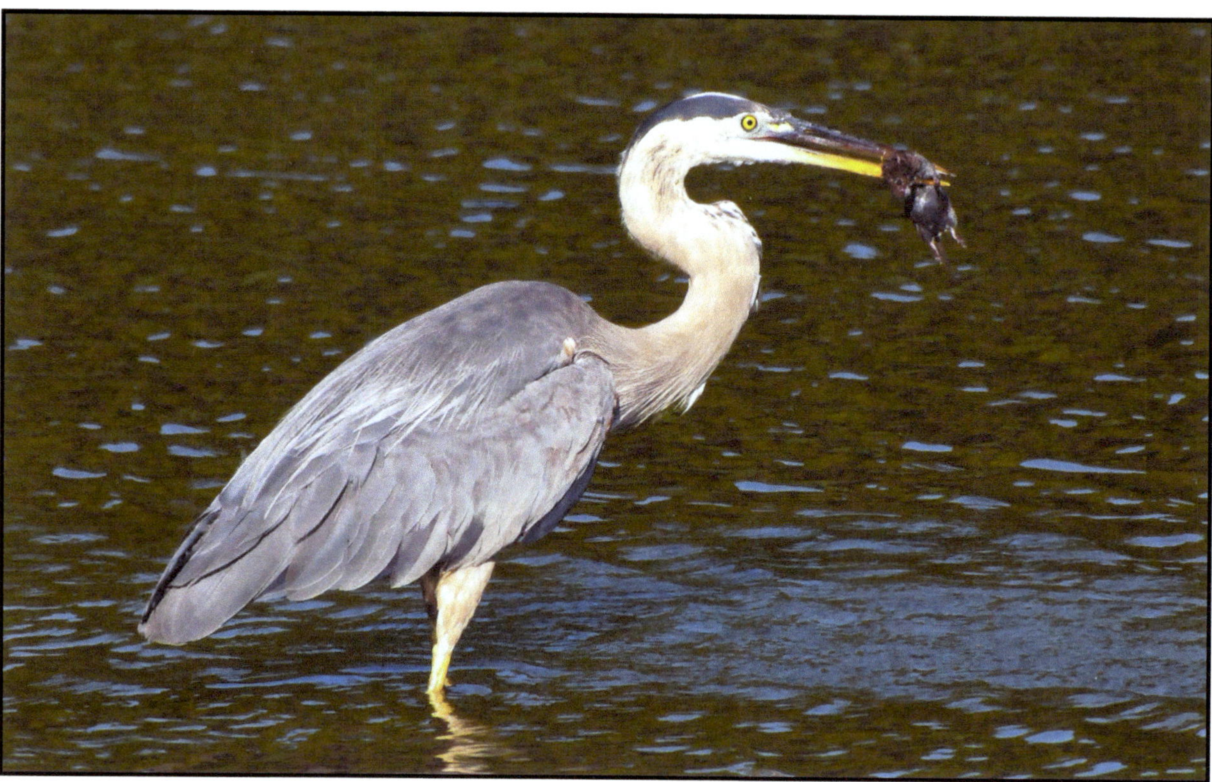

Top photo shows a Heron with a pair of crayfish in its bill. The bottom photo show one with a vole he has prepared for breakfast by stabbing it repeatedly with his beak and drowning it.

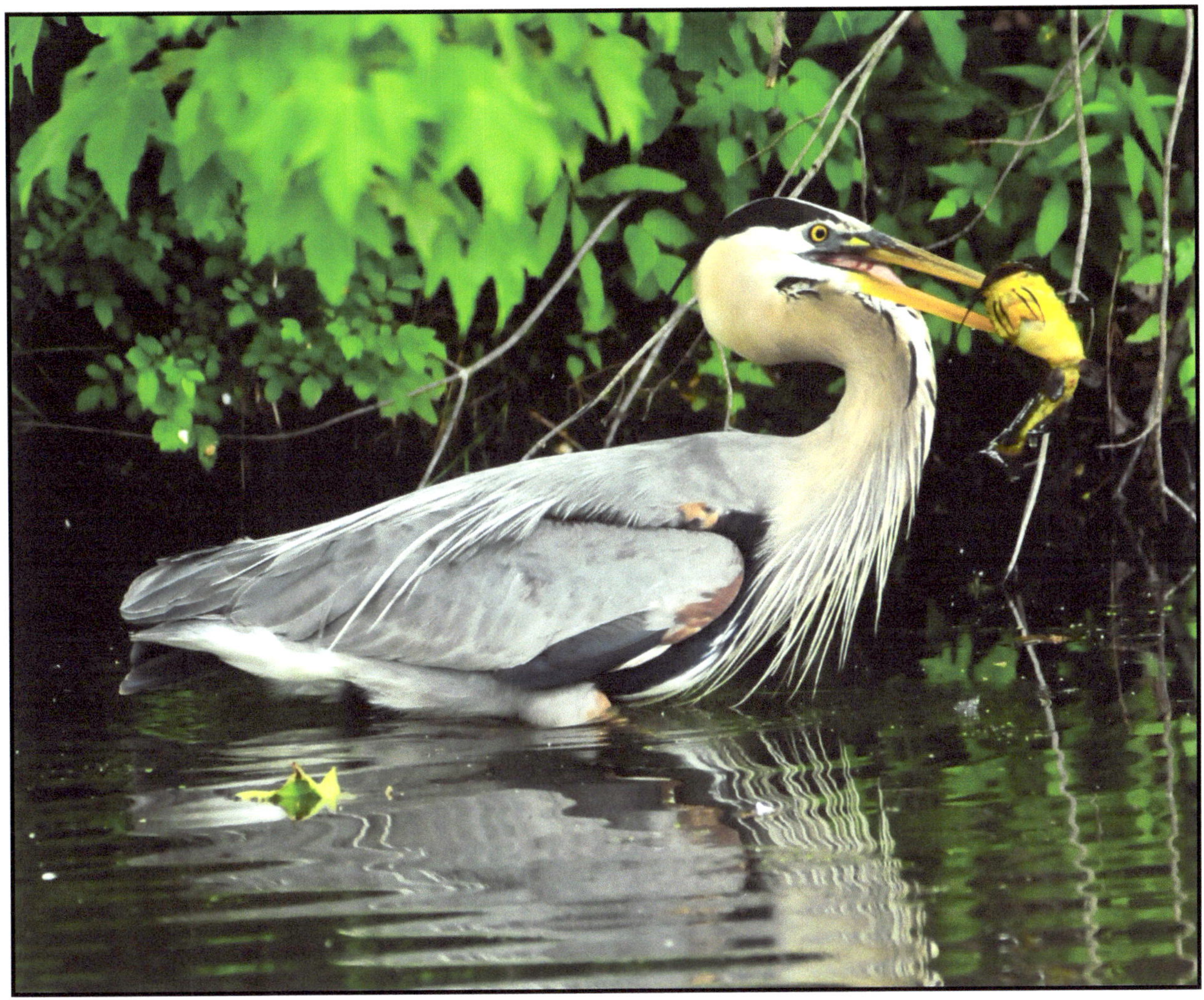

Here is a beautiful, immaculately coiffed, Great Blue Heron starting his workday. Seemingly, not a single feather is out of place. But, it takes a lot of grooming to keep up this appearance. As with any bird species, the Herons must work at it for a good portion of each day. If they did not keep their feathers in good condition, it would leave them open to the vagaries of weather, and that is what would eventually kill them. Their feathers are as important to them as the shingles on your roof are to you. An un-maintained roof lets the weather and moisture into your house and, eventually, your house will be destroyed because of this lack of maintenance. Maintenance, in the case of Great Blue Herons, is a daily routine of preening; making sure each feather is in good condition and in its proper place. Following are some photos of Great Blue Herons tending to their feather shingles.

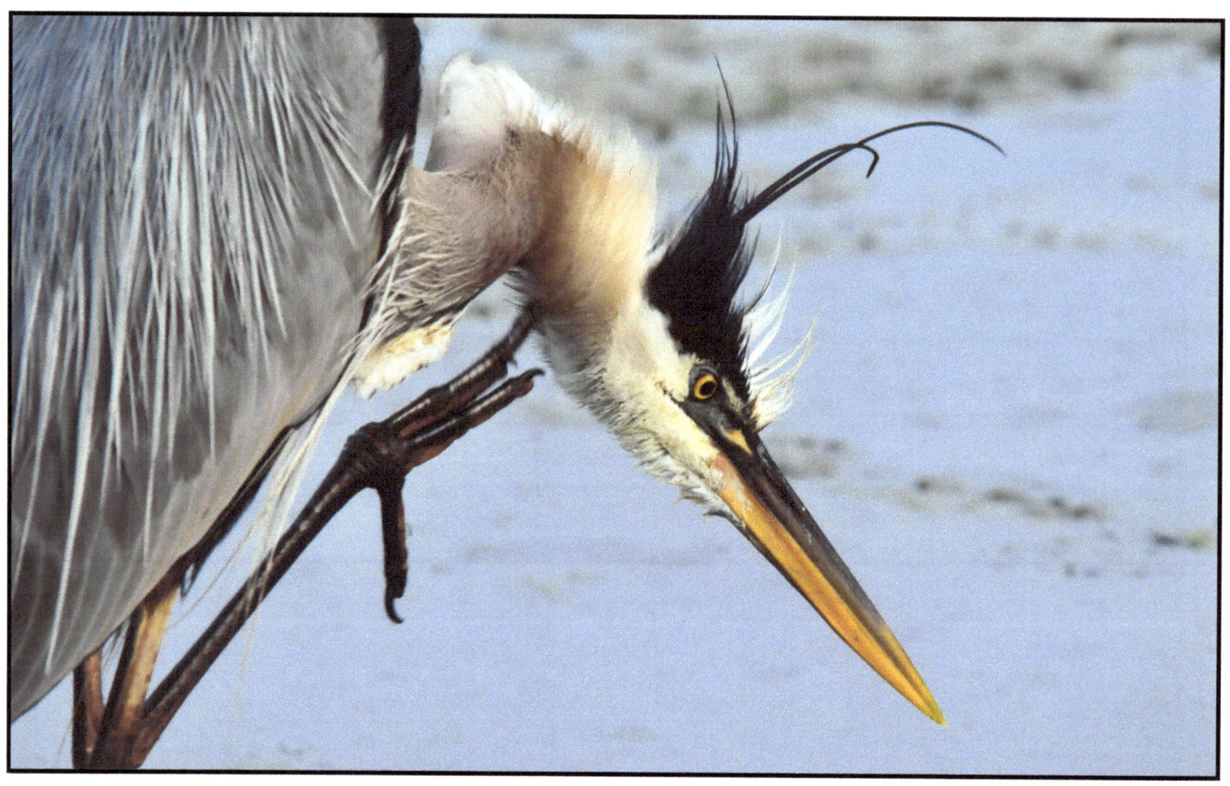

First, a little scratch. Herons always scratch a lot. An awful lot!

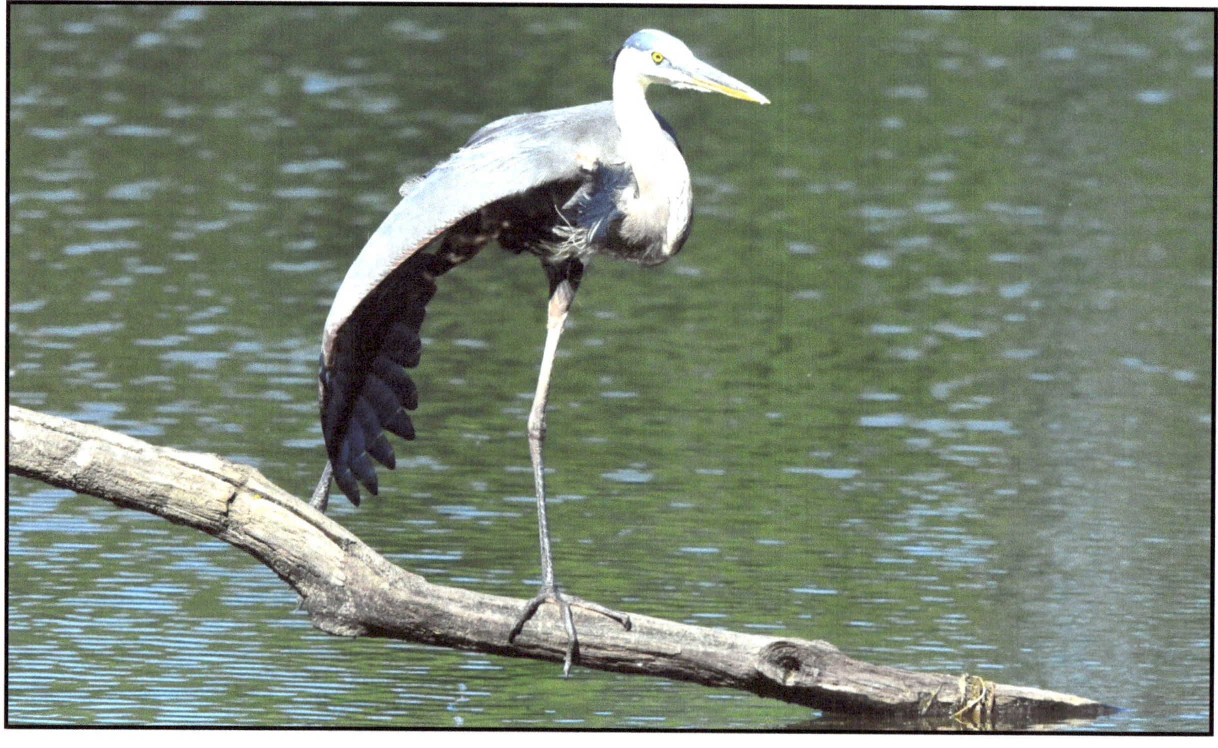

Then ... a little stretch. Maybe the other wing, too.

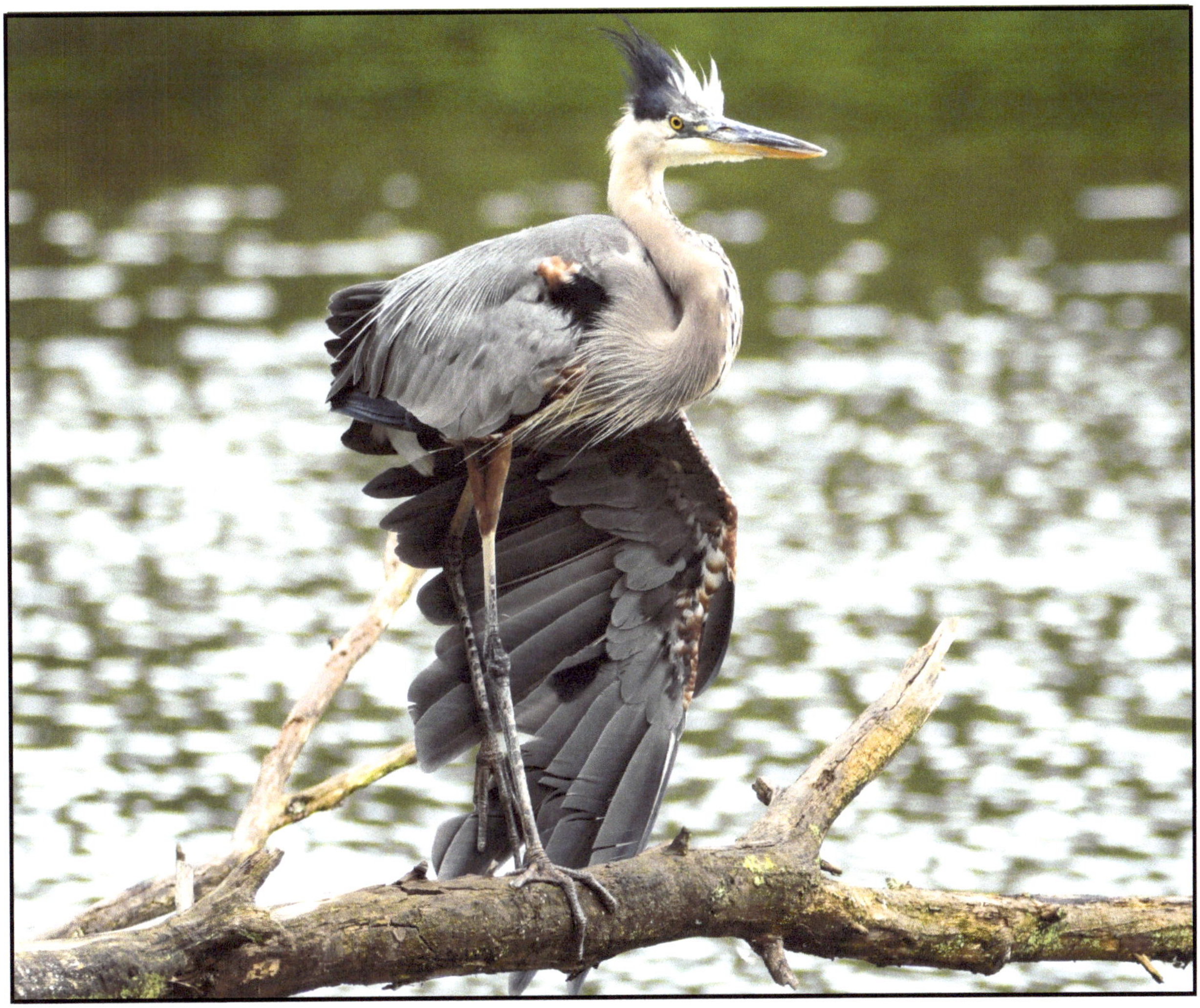

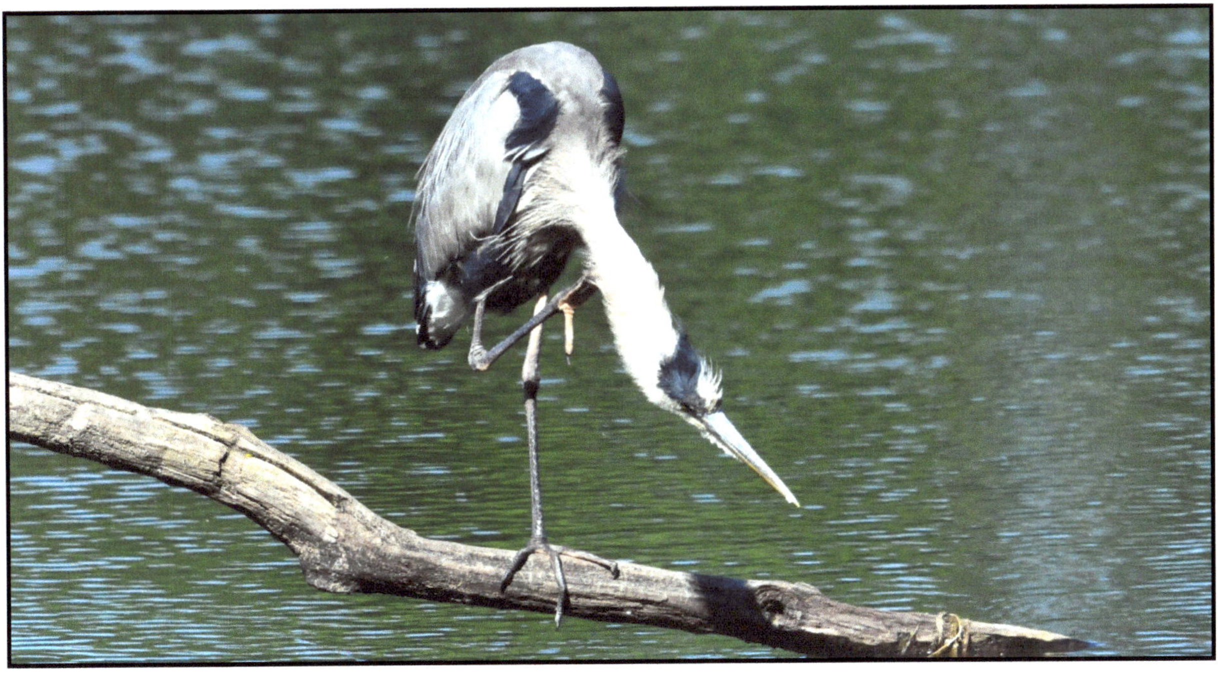

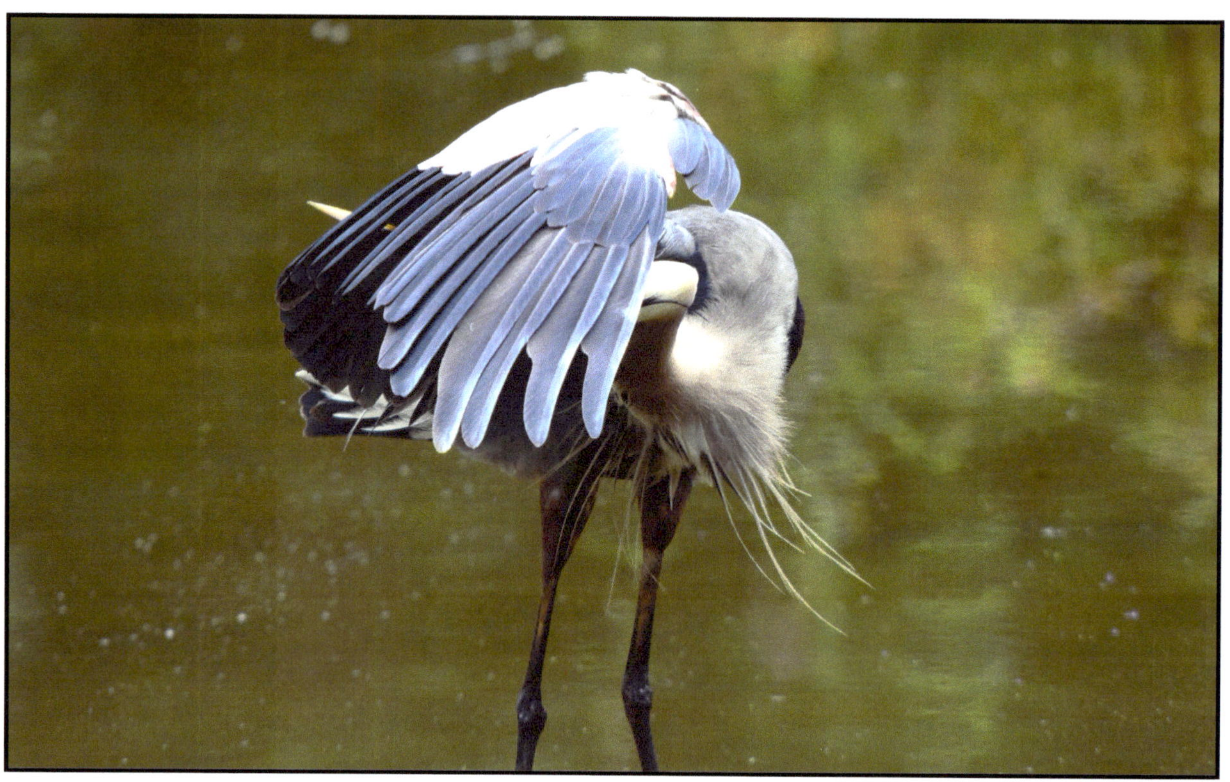

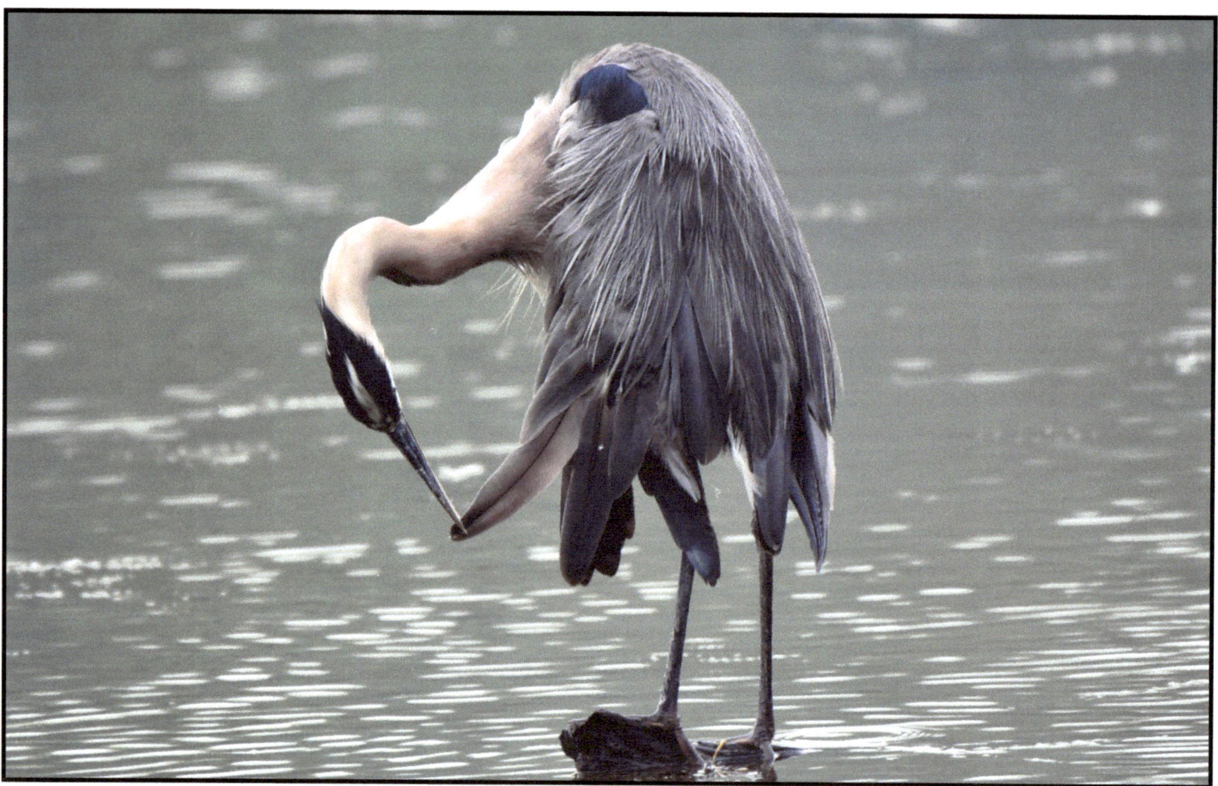

Each individual feather is as important as any other. Preen and check: sometimes visually.

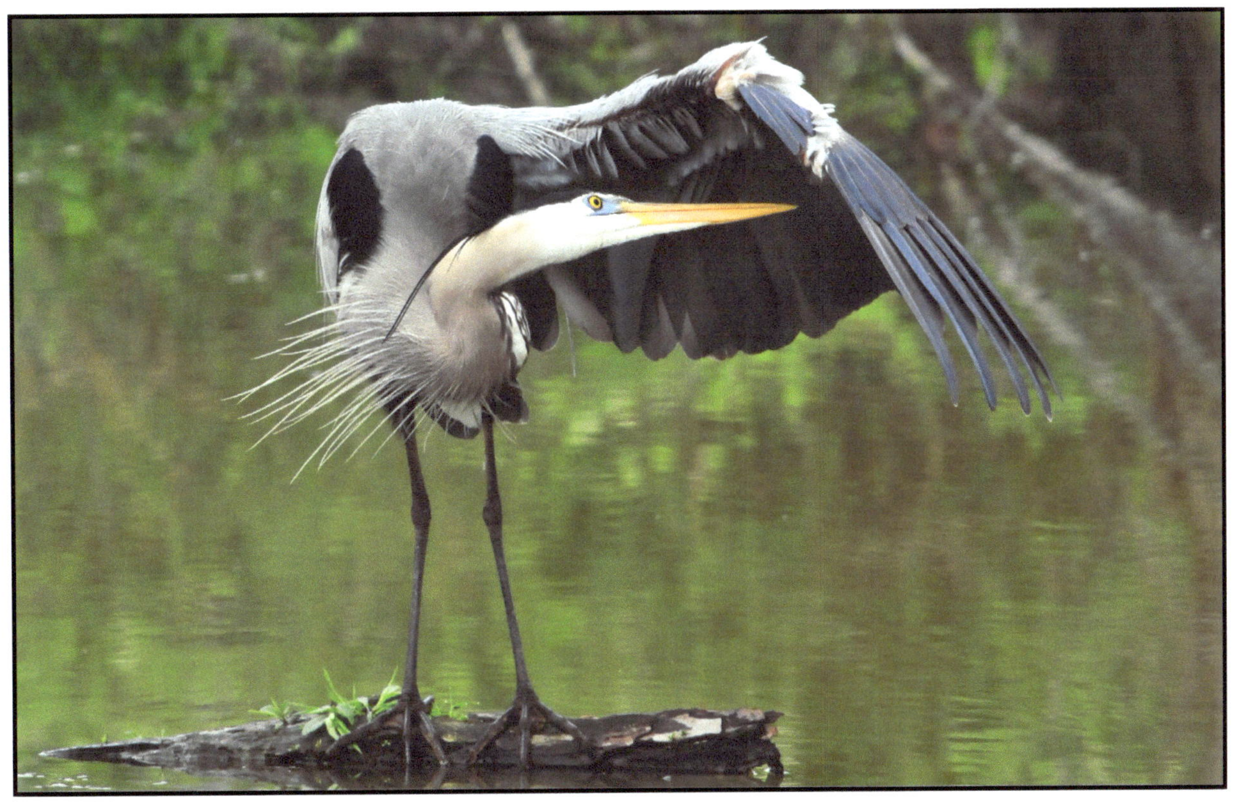

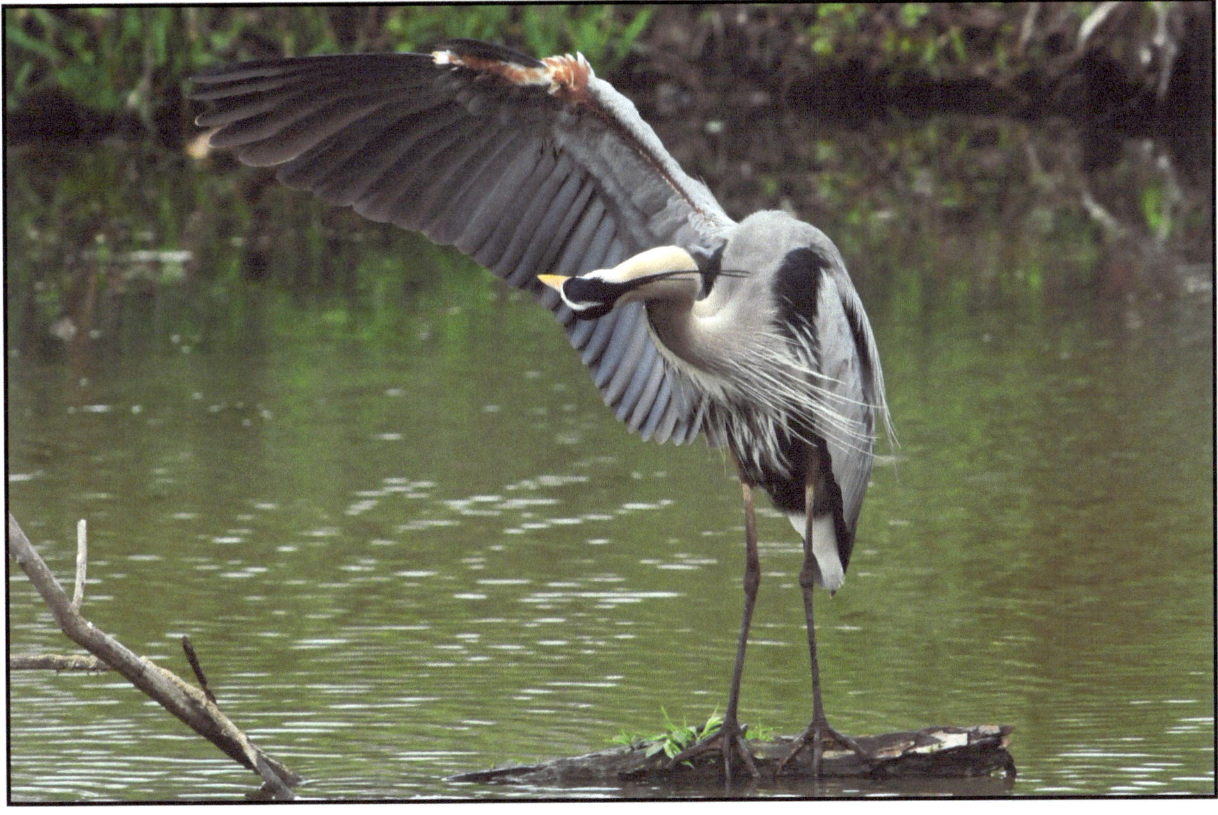

Hmm! A final check. Everything looks good to go.

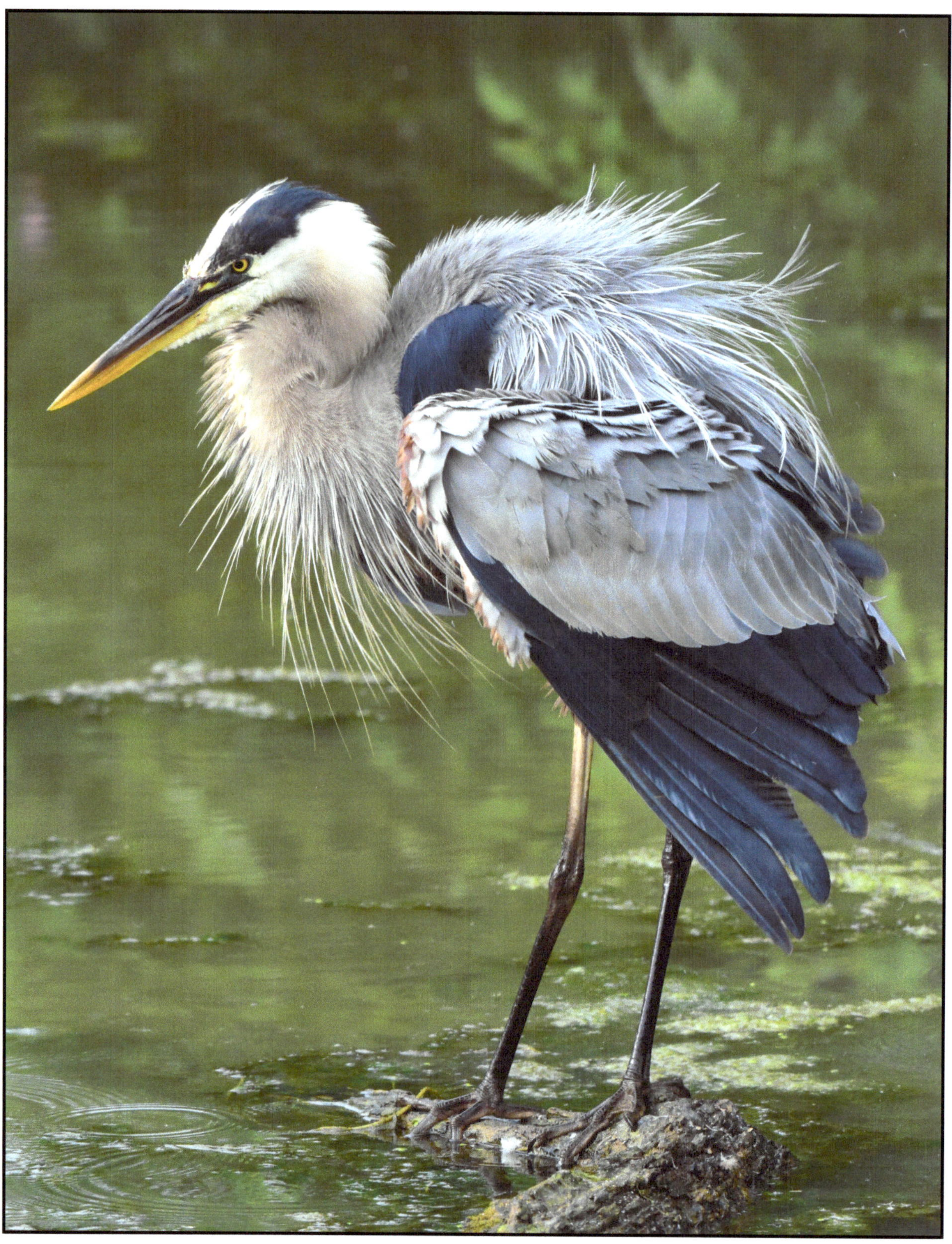

Okay! Fluff 'em all up; shake 'em around a bit; settle 'em back in place.
Looks like I'm ready to go again

How do these large, predatory birds get along with their neighbors? Most disputes arise while a Heron is feeding and another Heron is too close. These disputes are usually settled when the more dominant one flies at the other bird and drives him away, sometimes spectacularly .

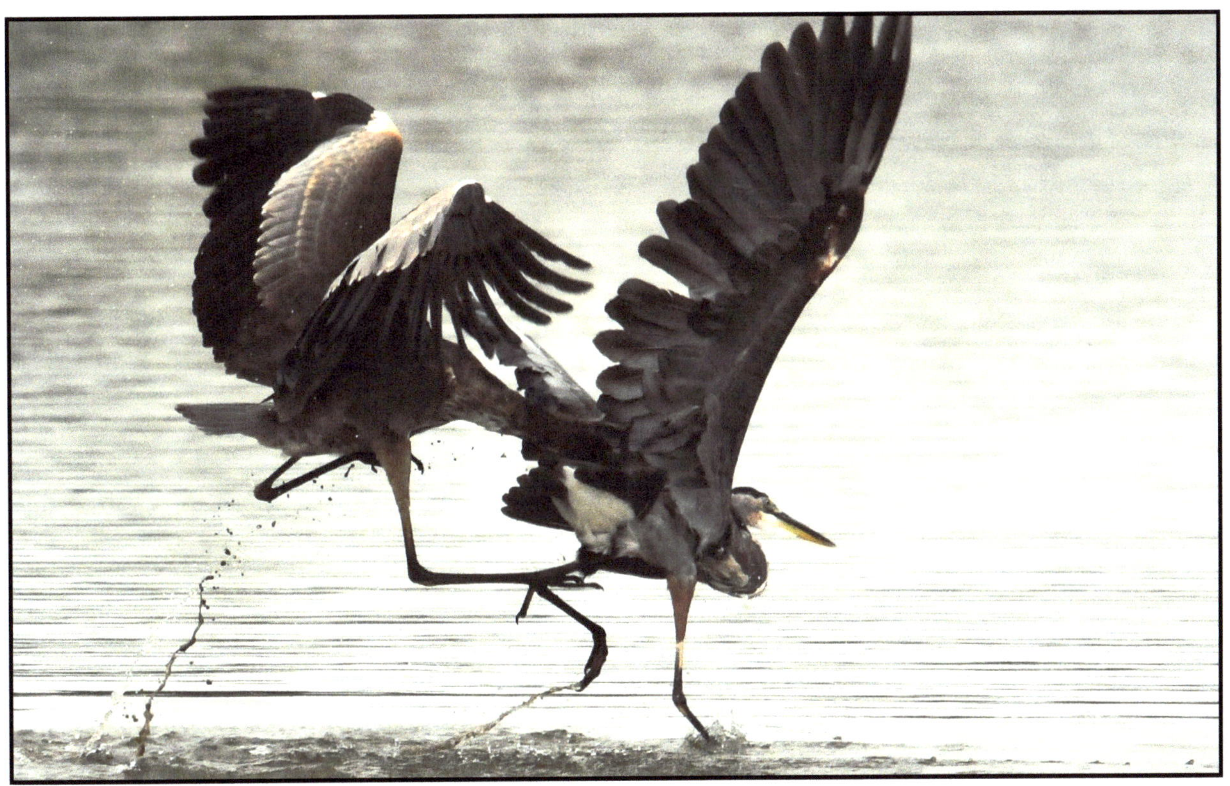

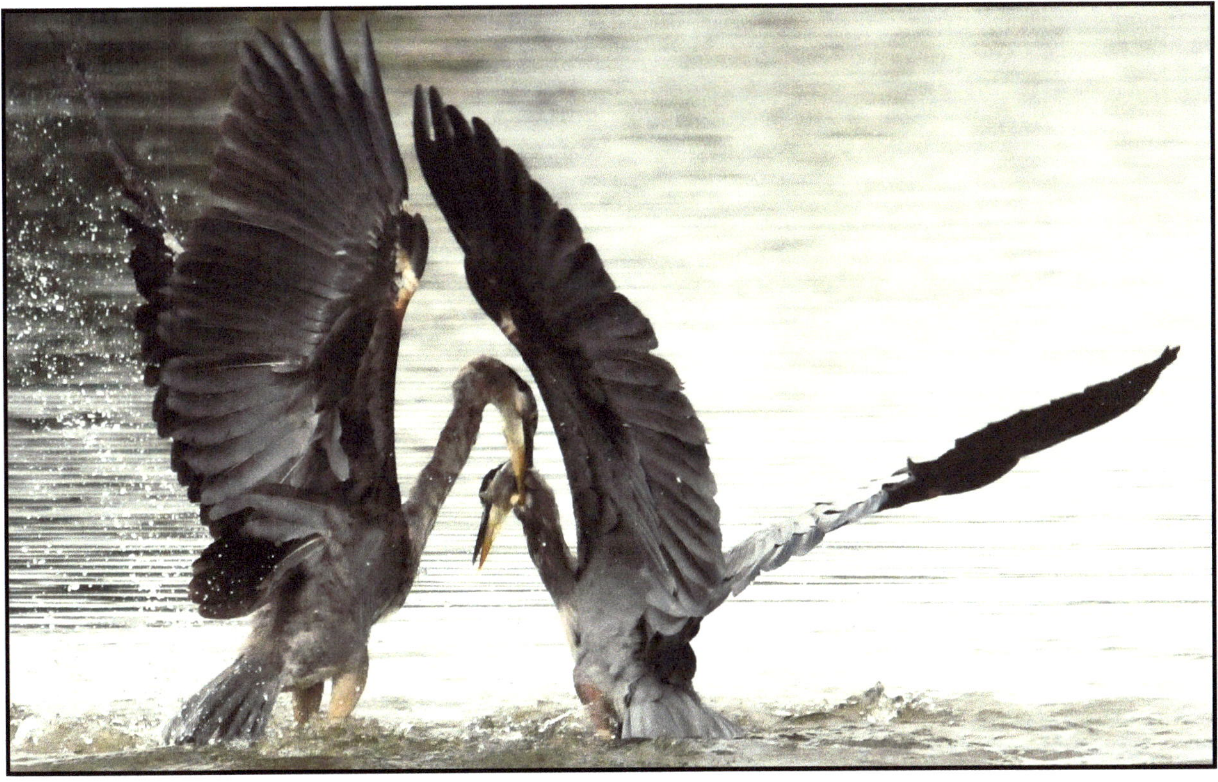

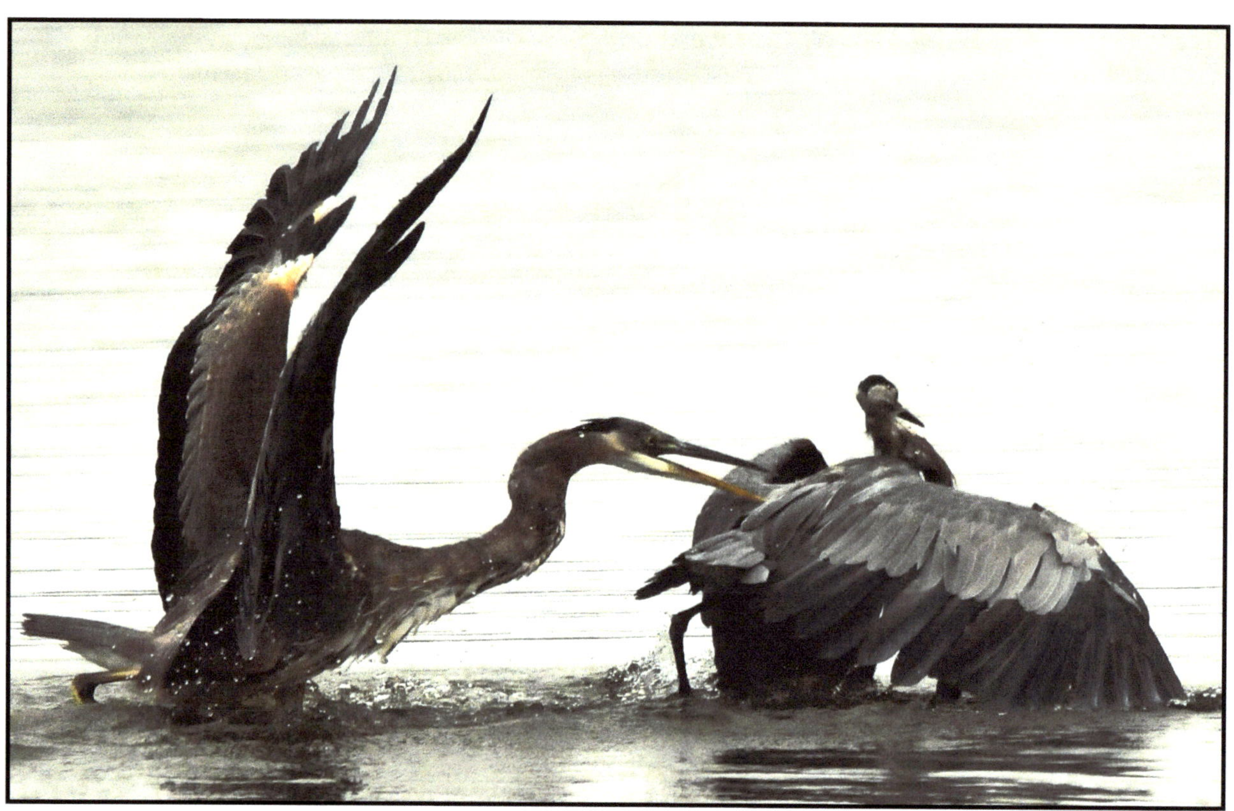

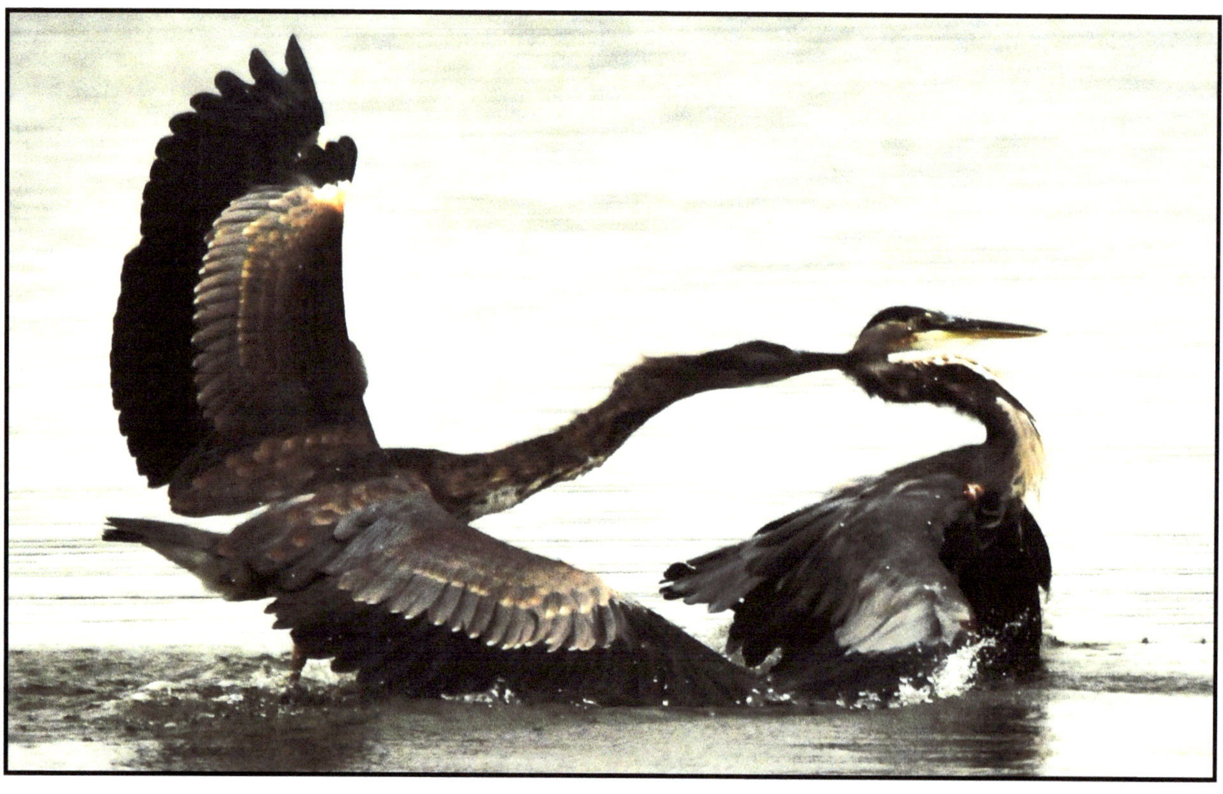

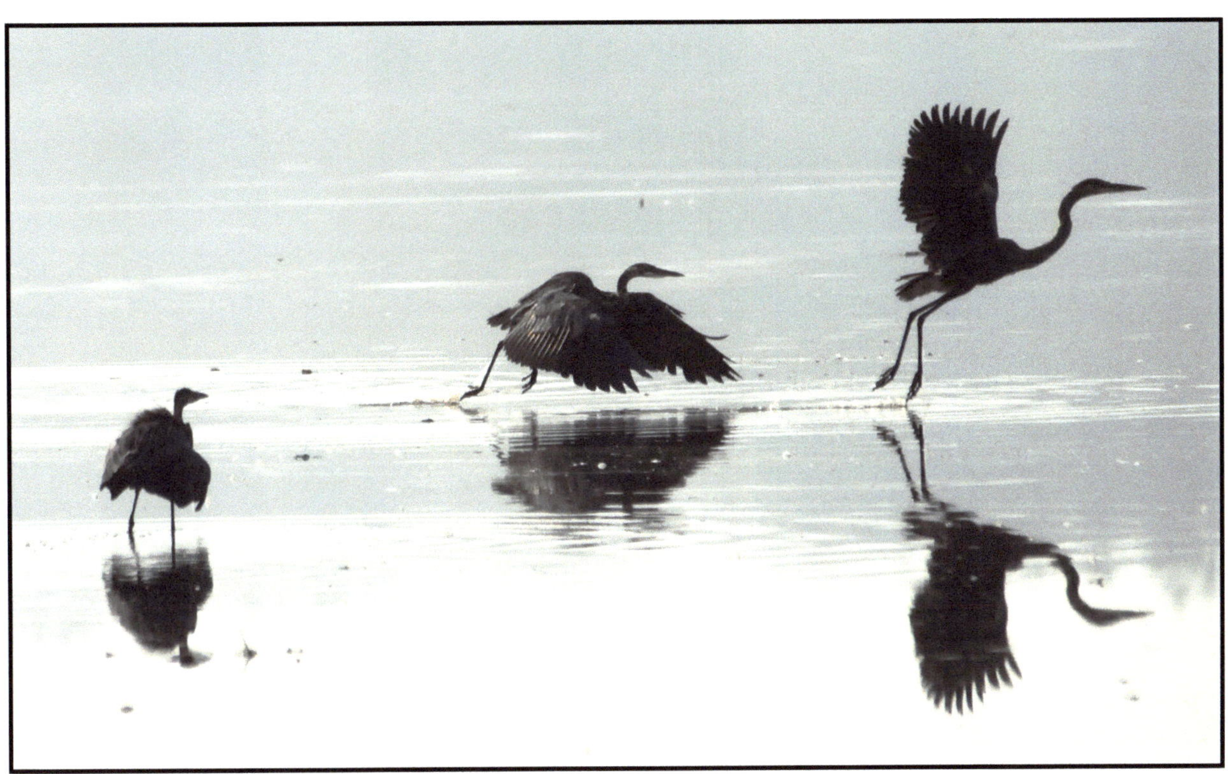

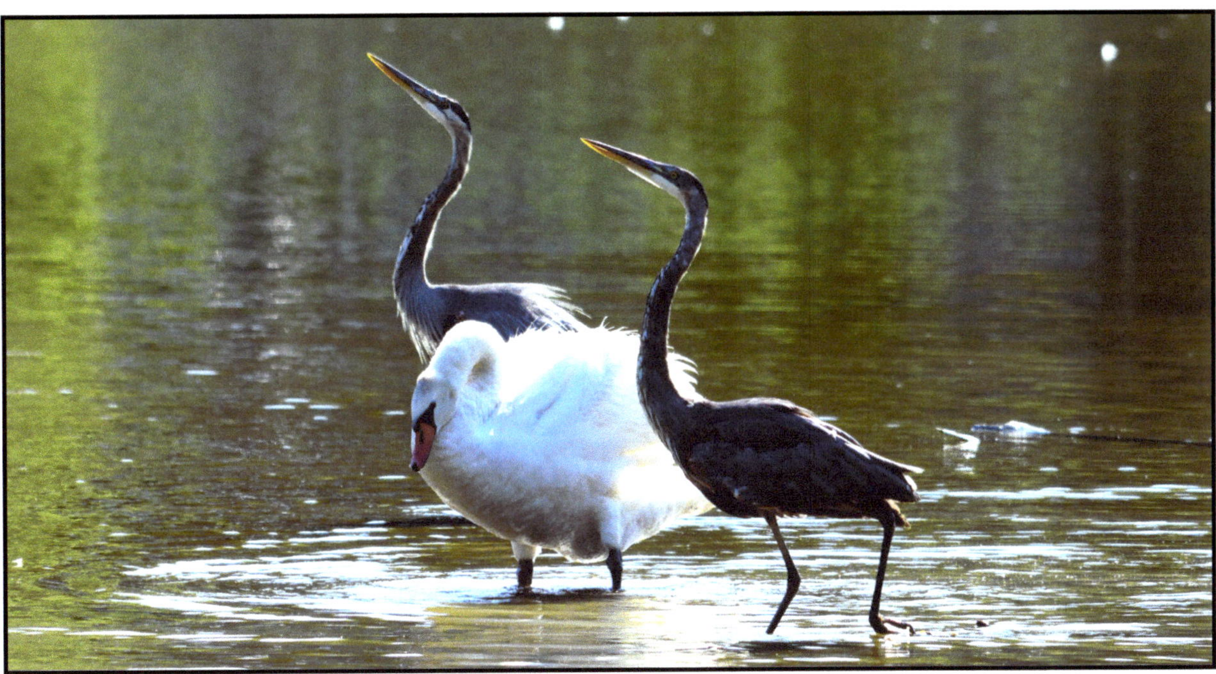

The Mute Swans are the largest birds on the lake. Herons don't intentionally bother them, but if the Swans feel the Herons are too close to the swan's young, they assert their size difference and chase the Herons away.

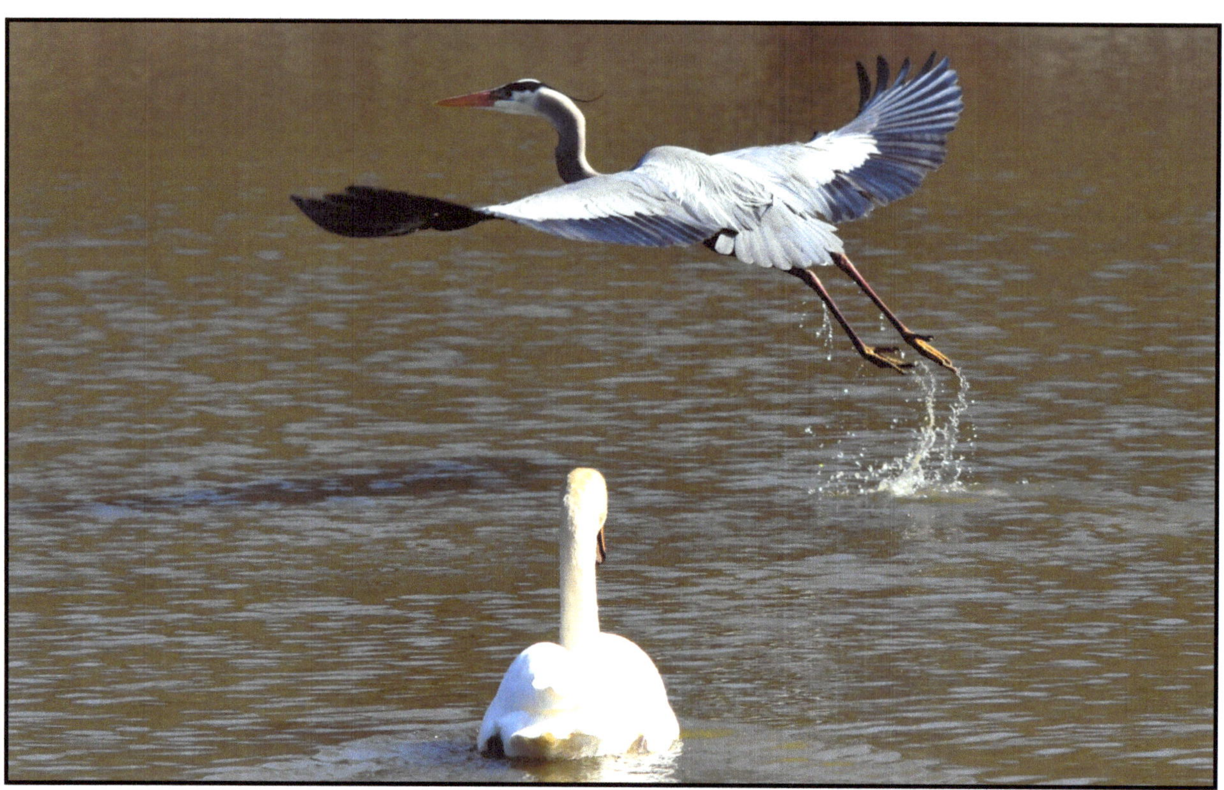

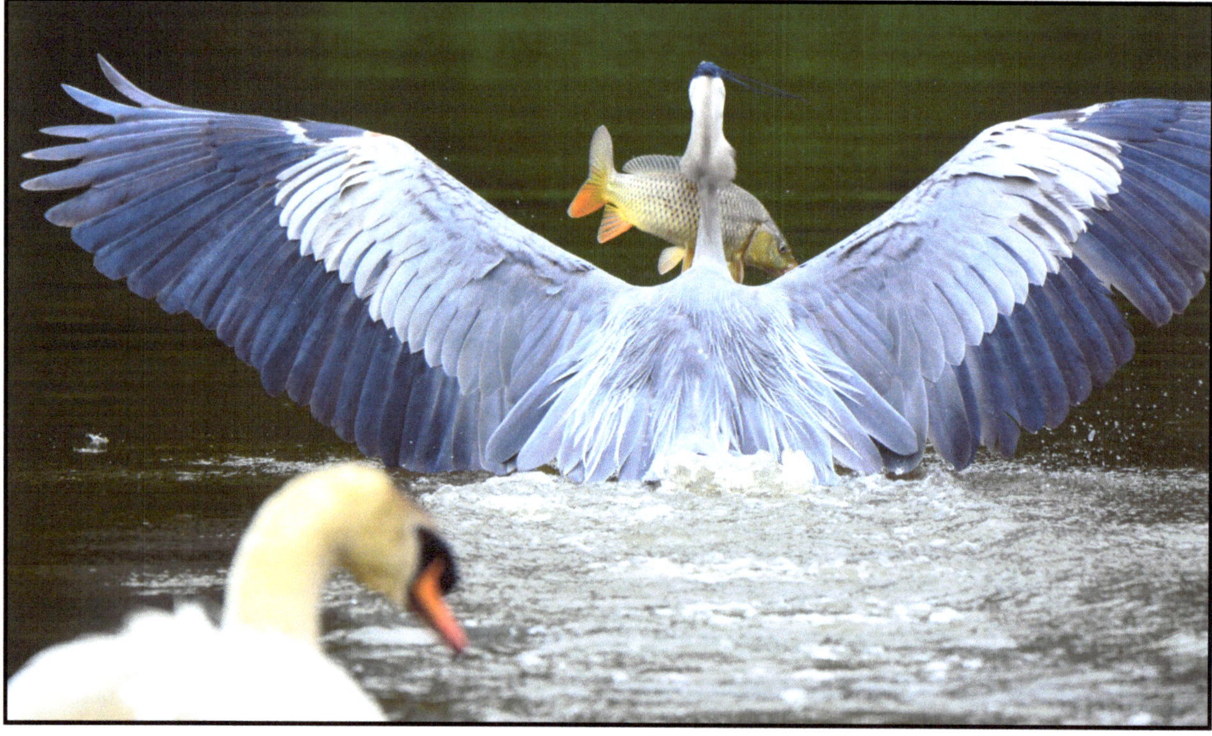

This Great Blue Heron didn't allow the swan to scare him away until it had caught this large Carp from almost under the swan's belly. The swan then turned against the Heron.

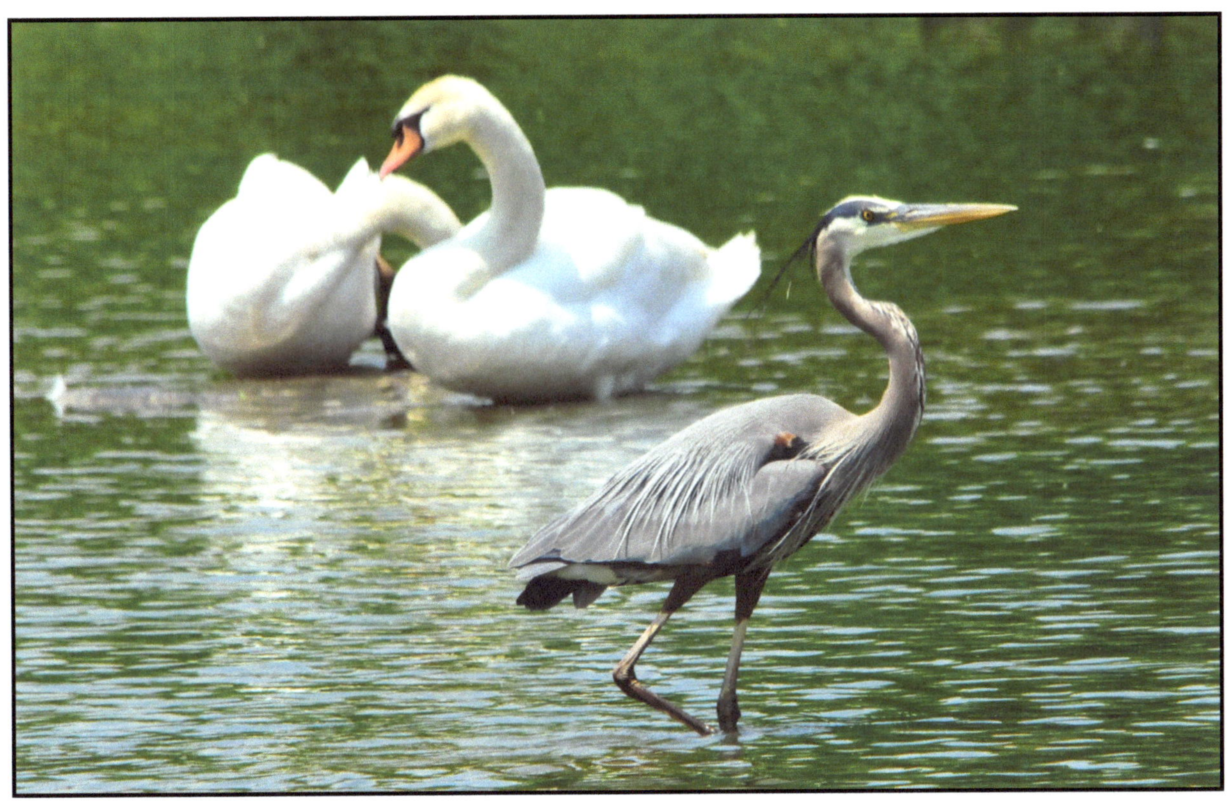

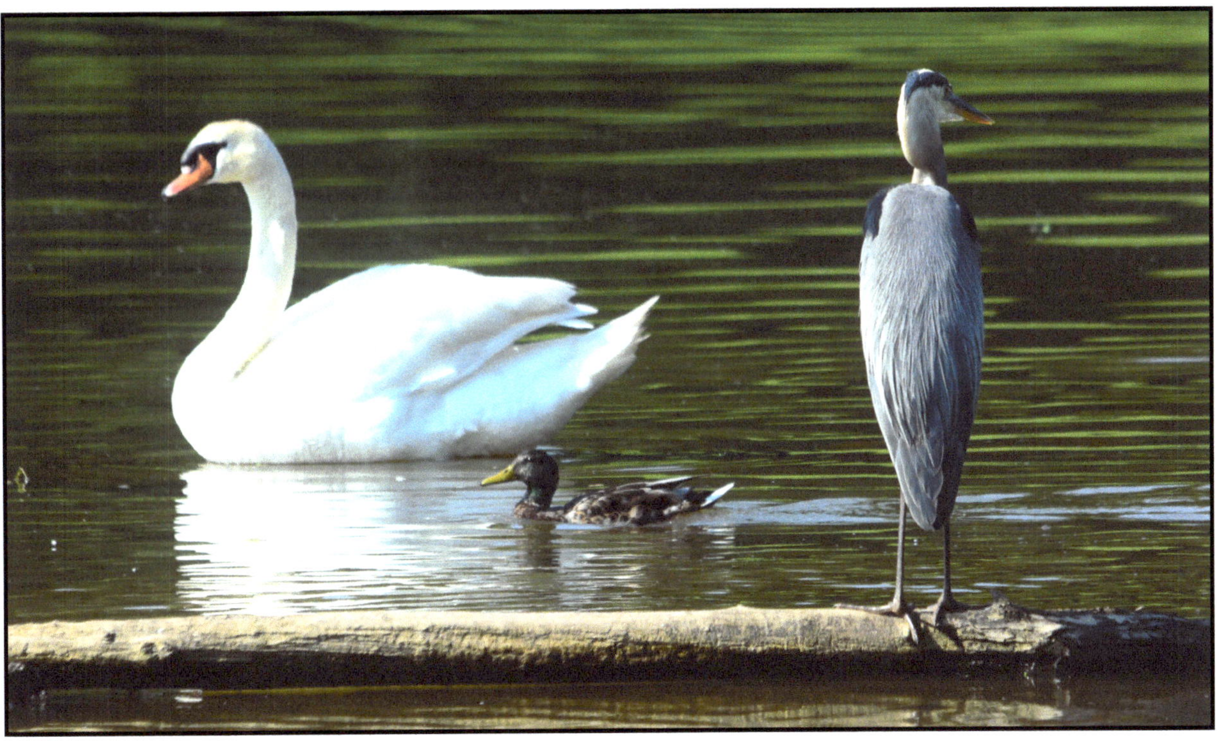

Peace reigns for the most part between the majority of bird species at the lake.

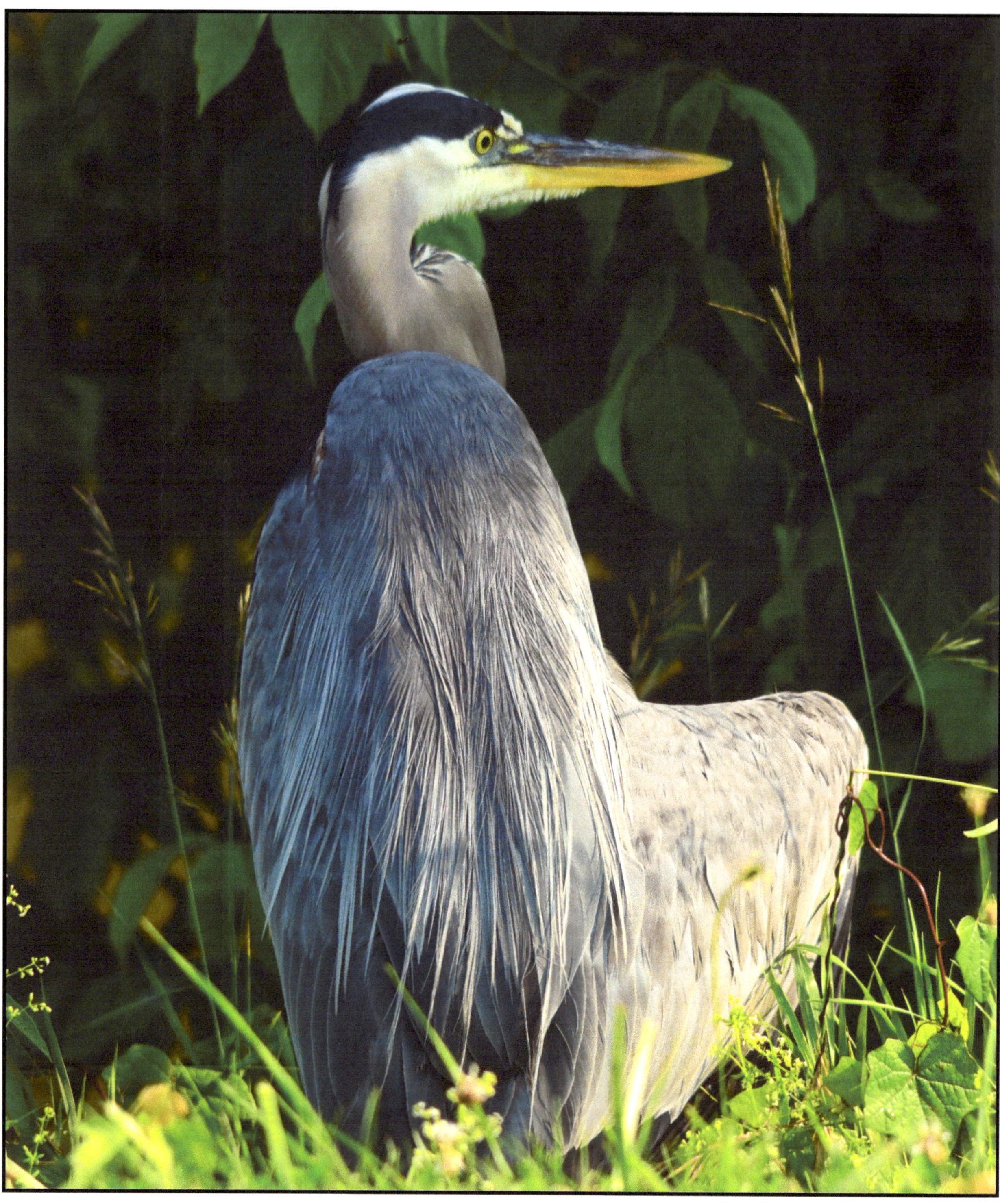

Early one morning, I found this great Blue Heron hiding under a tree by the edge of the lake. His wing was injured and he couldn't fly. I herded him back into the lake so he could feed himself.

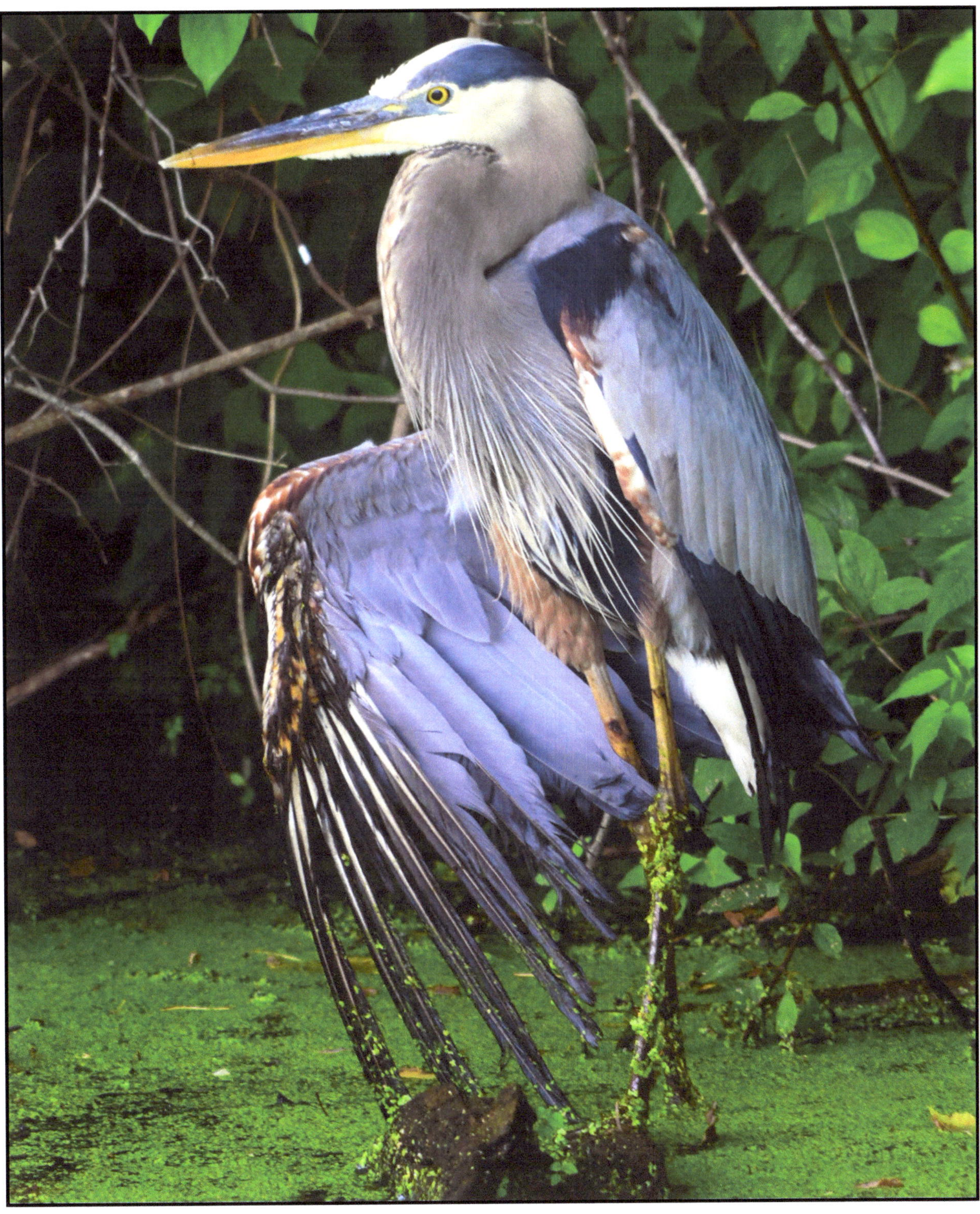

It was about a week before he stopped hiding under brush along the lake's edge. Finally, he came out and started feeding in the open. It was the first step in his ultimate recovery.

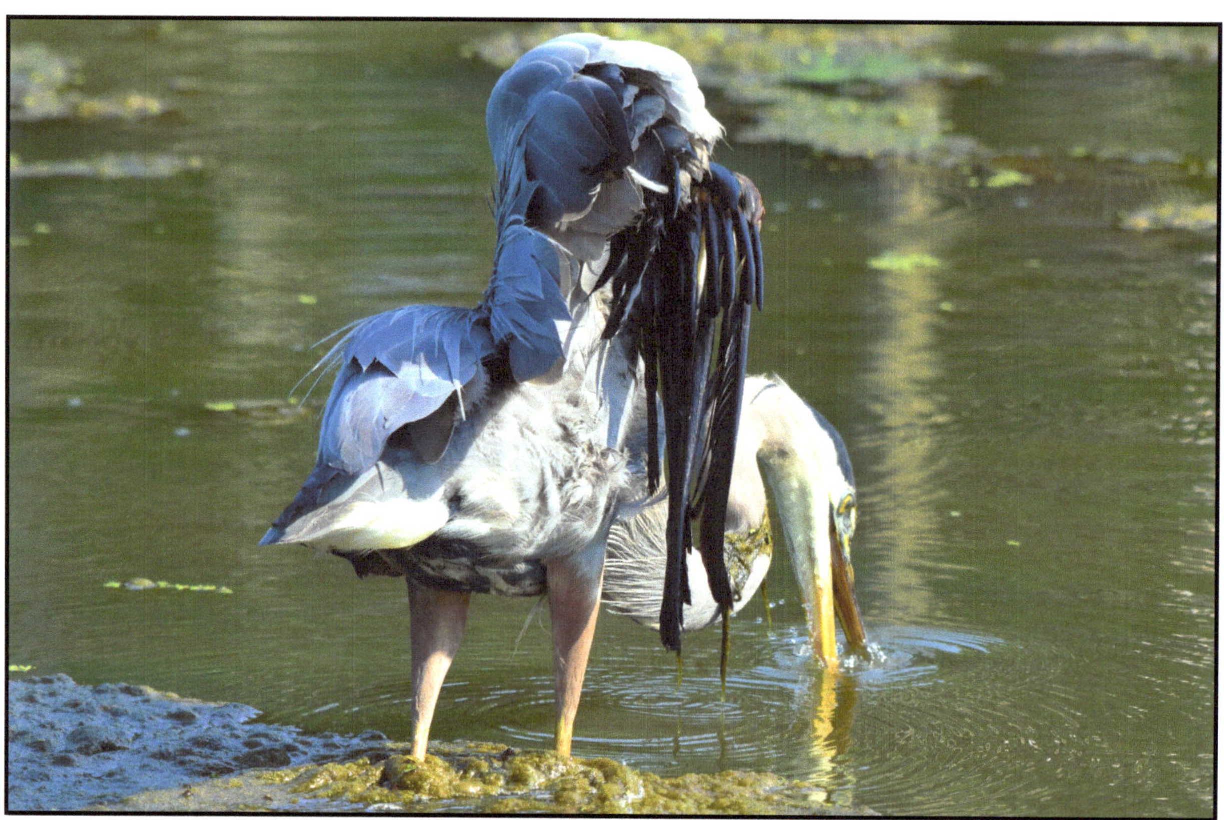

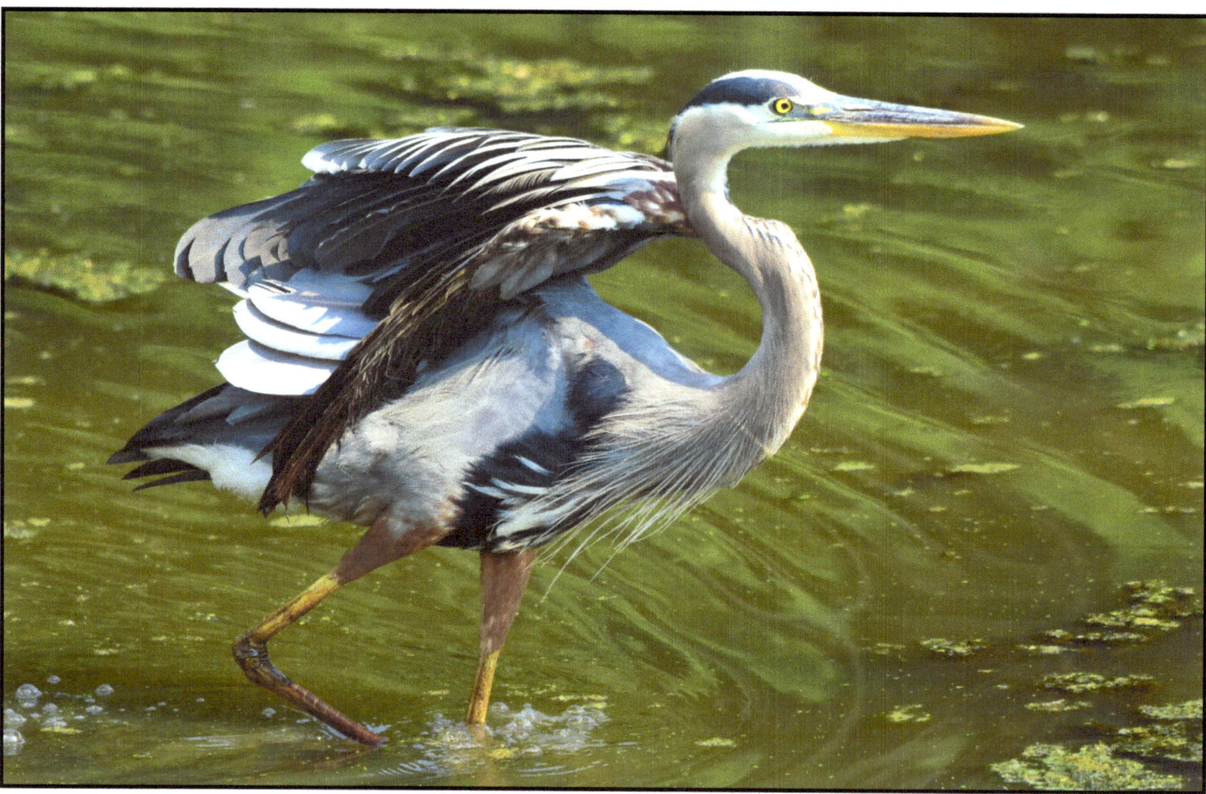

He learned to carry his injured wing over his back to keep it dry. Keeping the feathers dry, daily preening, and resting the wing, slowly made the wing useful again.

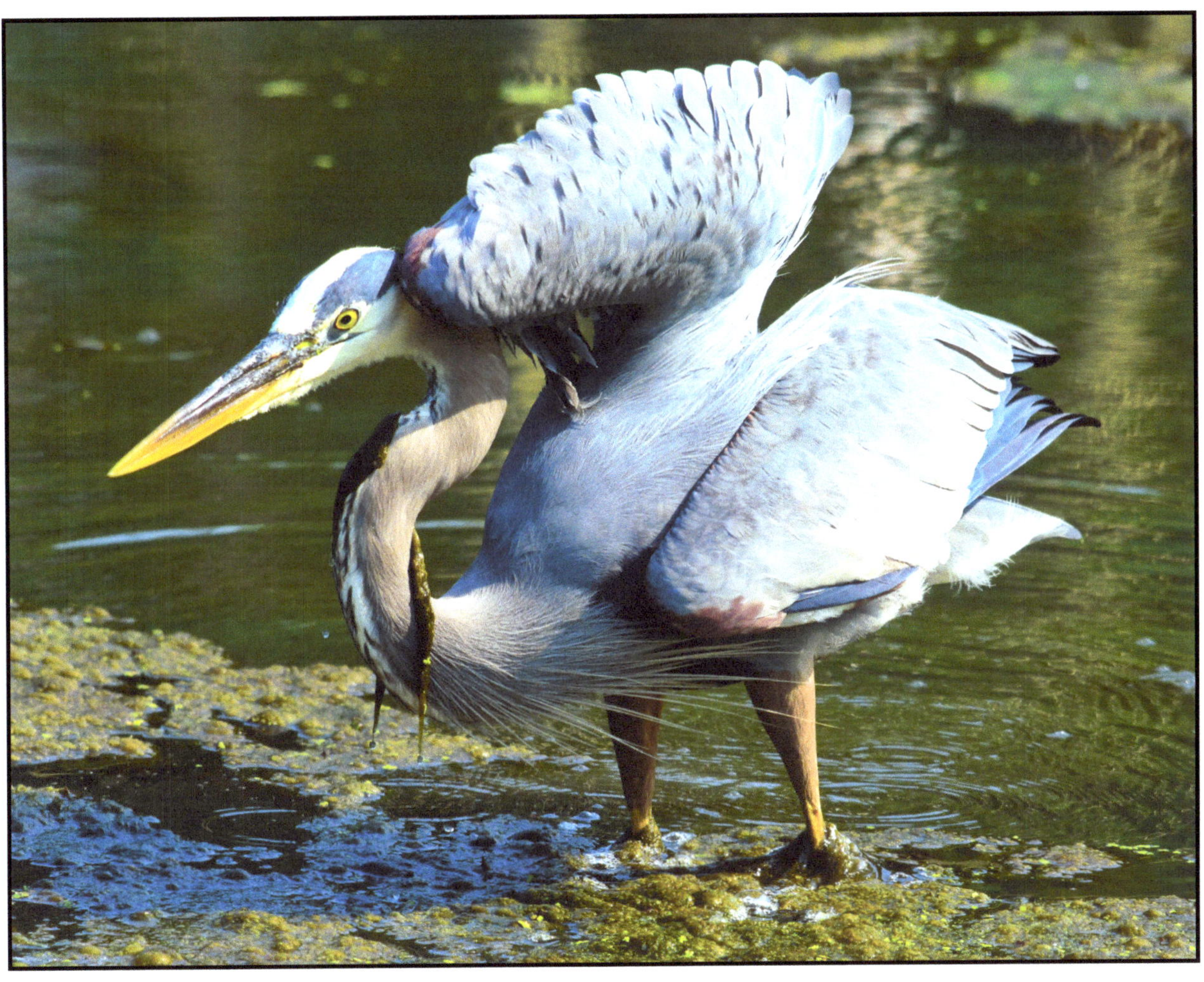

He was injured in the middle of June, but by carrying his wing high, as seen above, it eventually mended to the point where, in August, he was able to cover more territory. By that fall, he could actually fly up into the lower branches of lakeside trees to roost. He is fully recovered now and I can't tell him from many other Great Blue Herons on the lake. As I have said before, these Great Blue Herons are very tough birds. Following photographs are a photo essay of the everyday goings-on in the lives of the many Great Blue Herons on the lake.

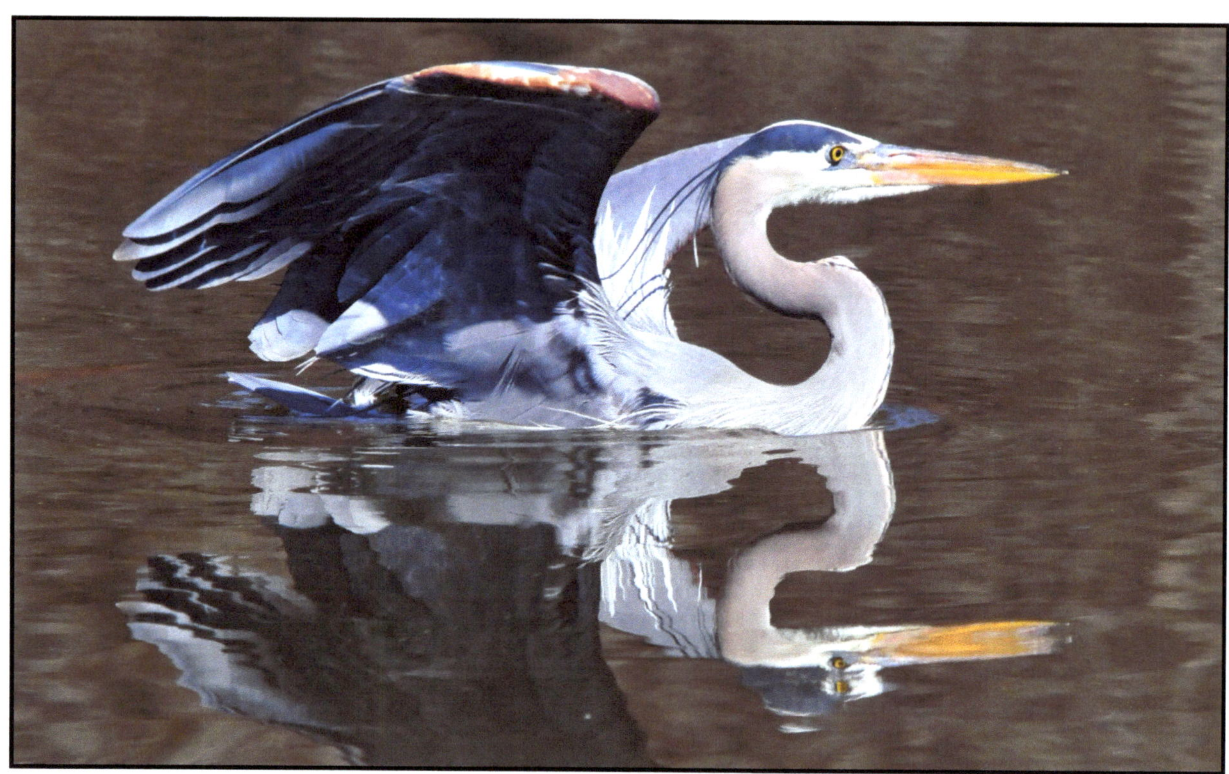

Most people would be surprised to know that a Great Blue Heron can actually swim. Not as gracefully as true waterfowl, but enough to get by when the need arises. I have actually seen these great birds dive into the water while flying over it, and, much like a Kingfisher, spot easy prey near the surface, dive in, and catch it. (above and below)

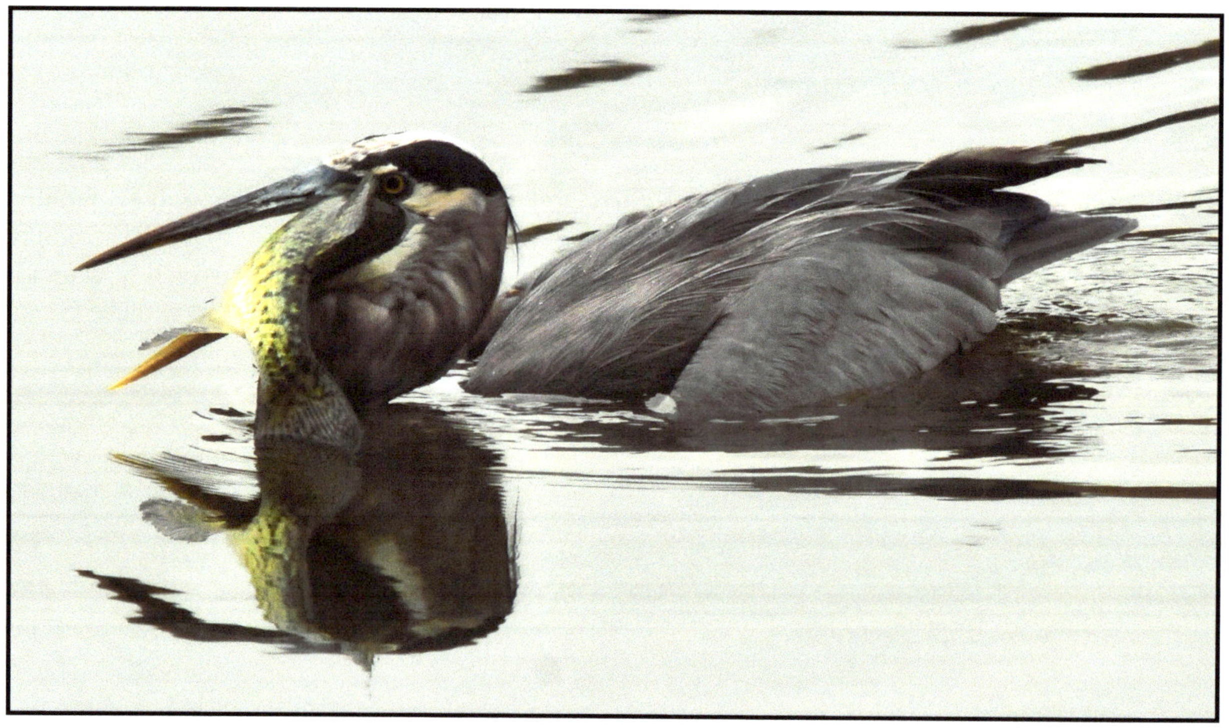

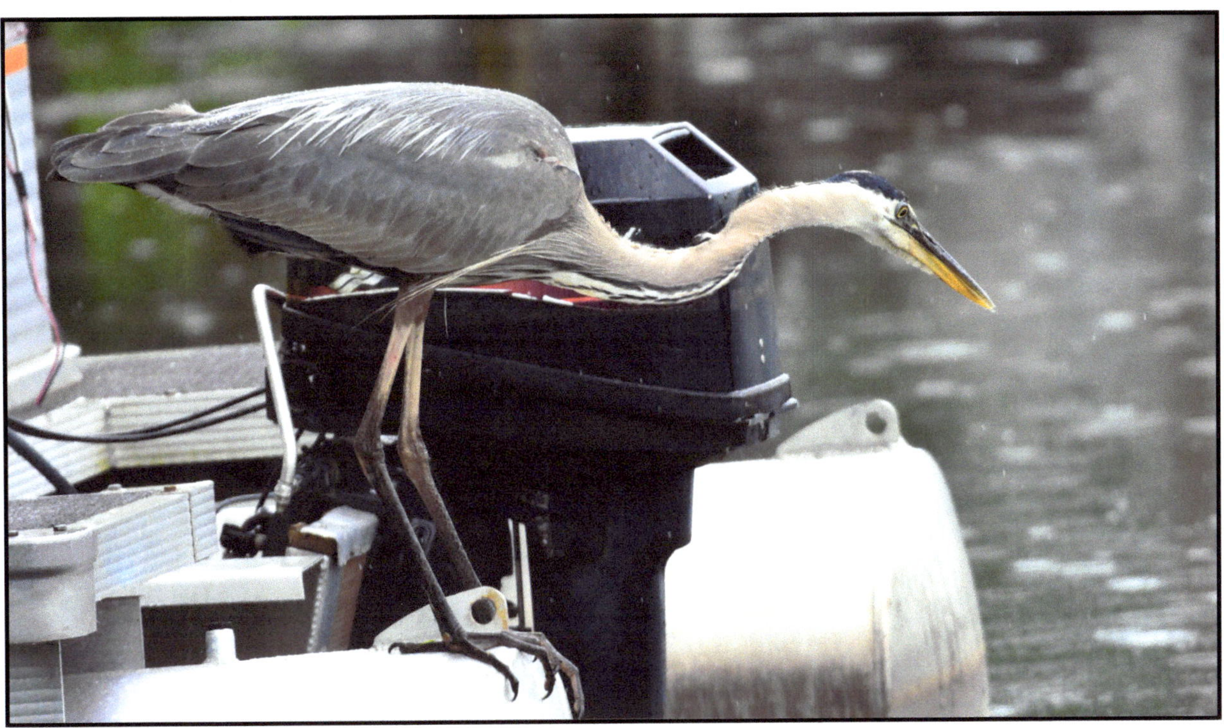

So, it follows, that diving from a platform and catching their daily rations is comparatively easy; as the following photographs show.

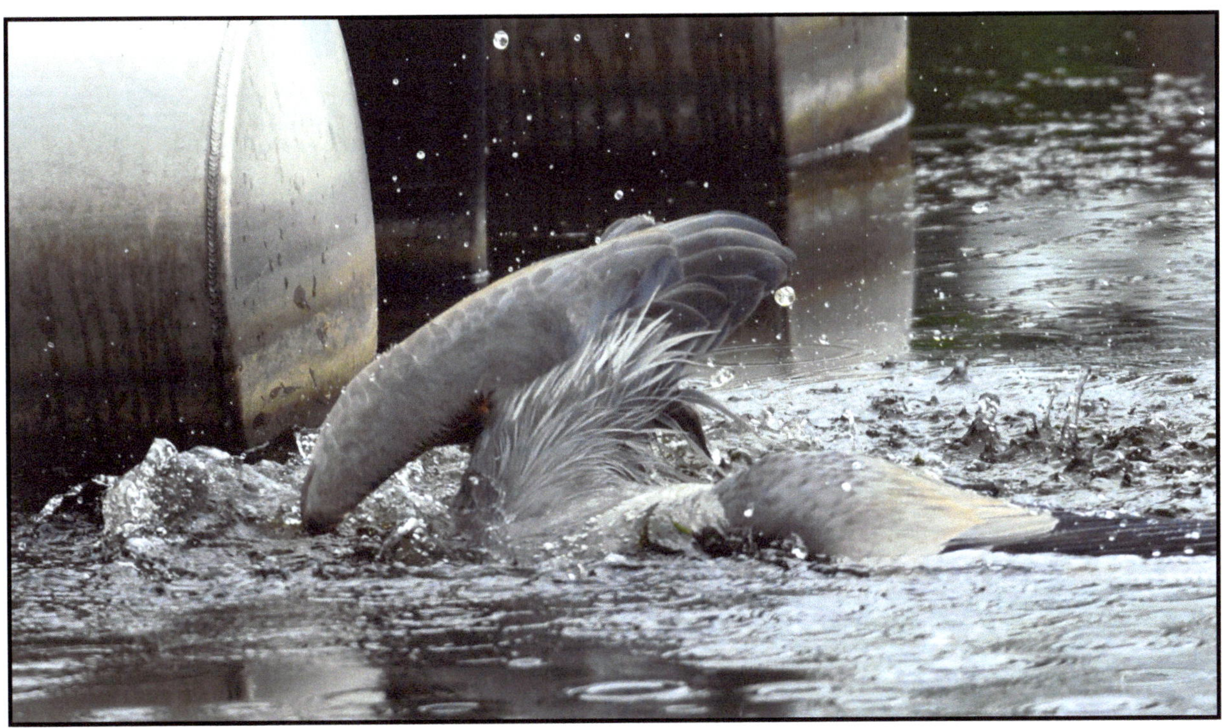

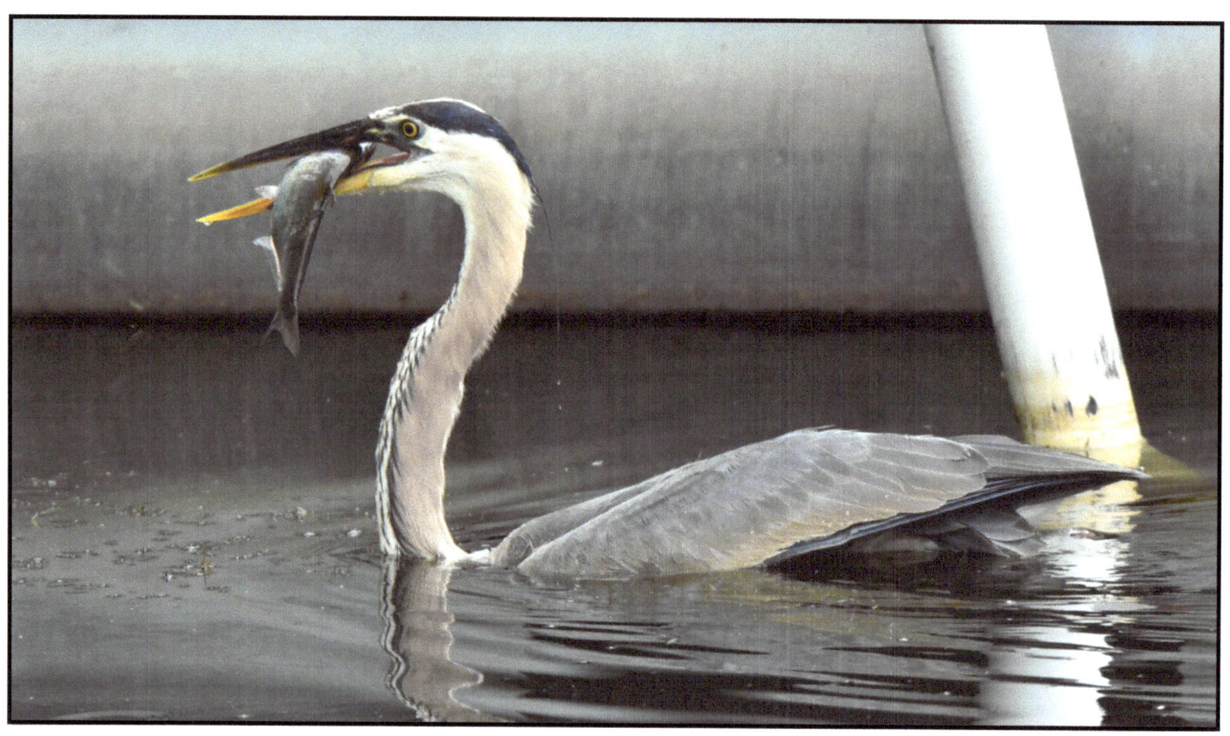

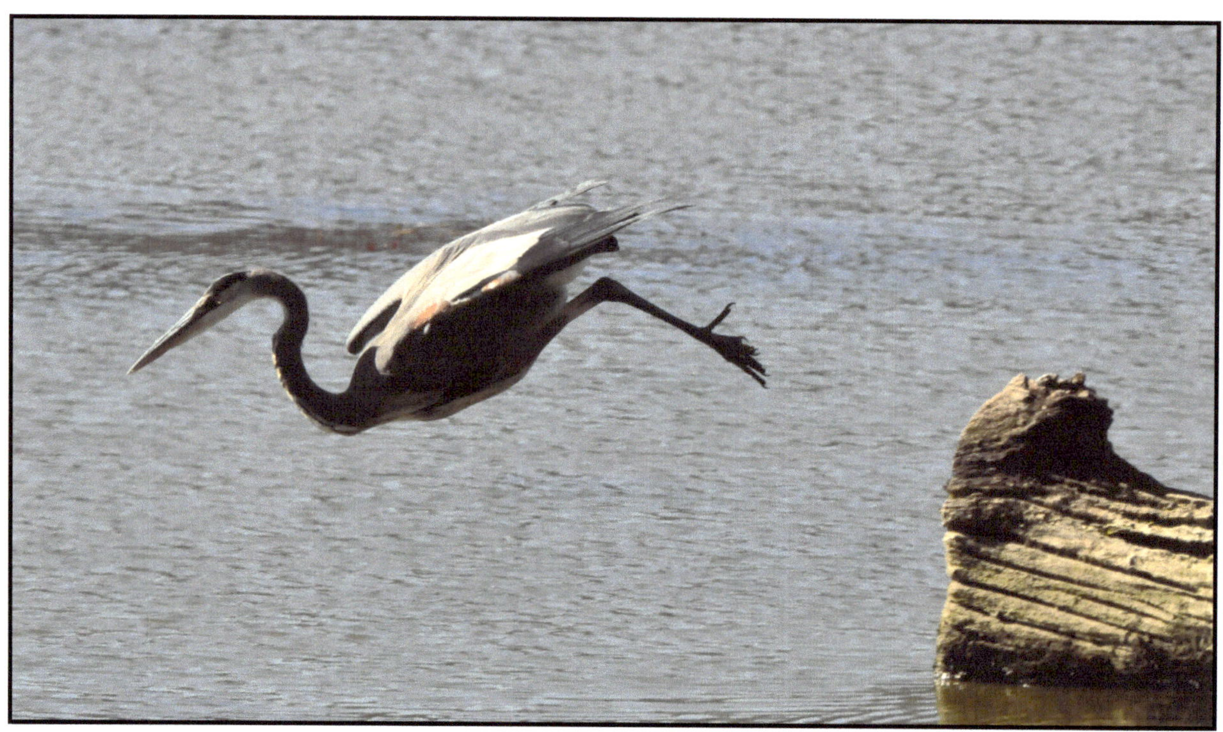

Perfect form!

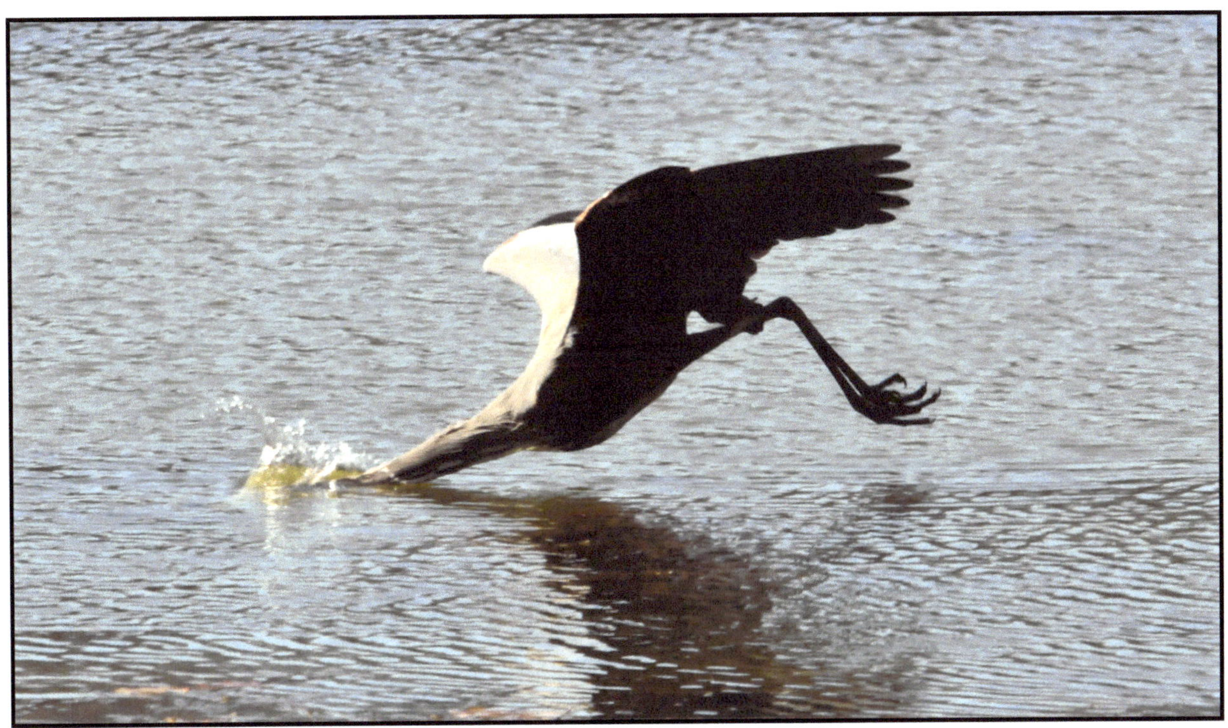

A nearly splash-free entry!

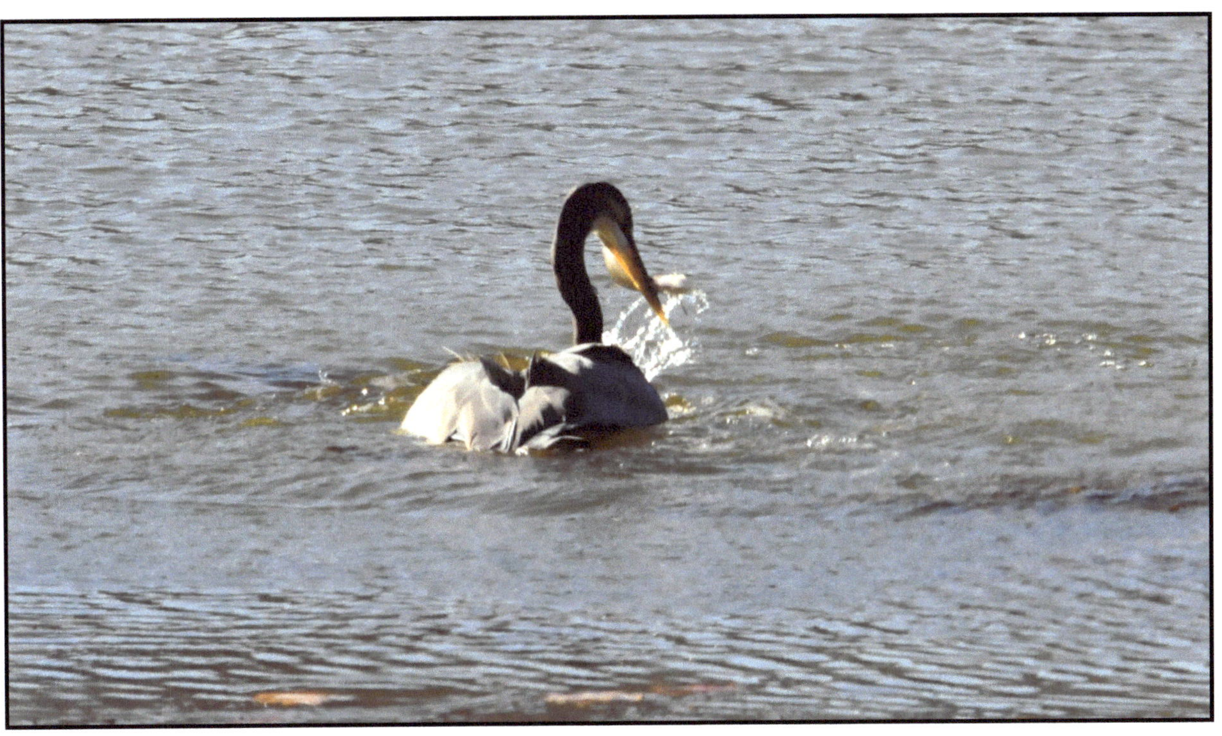

Better than a gold medal. It's edible!

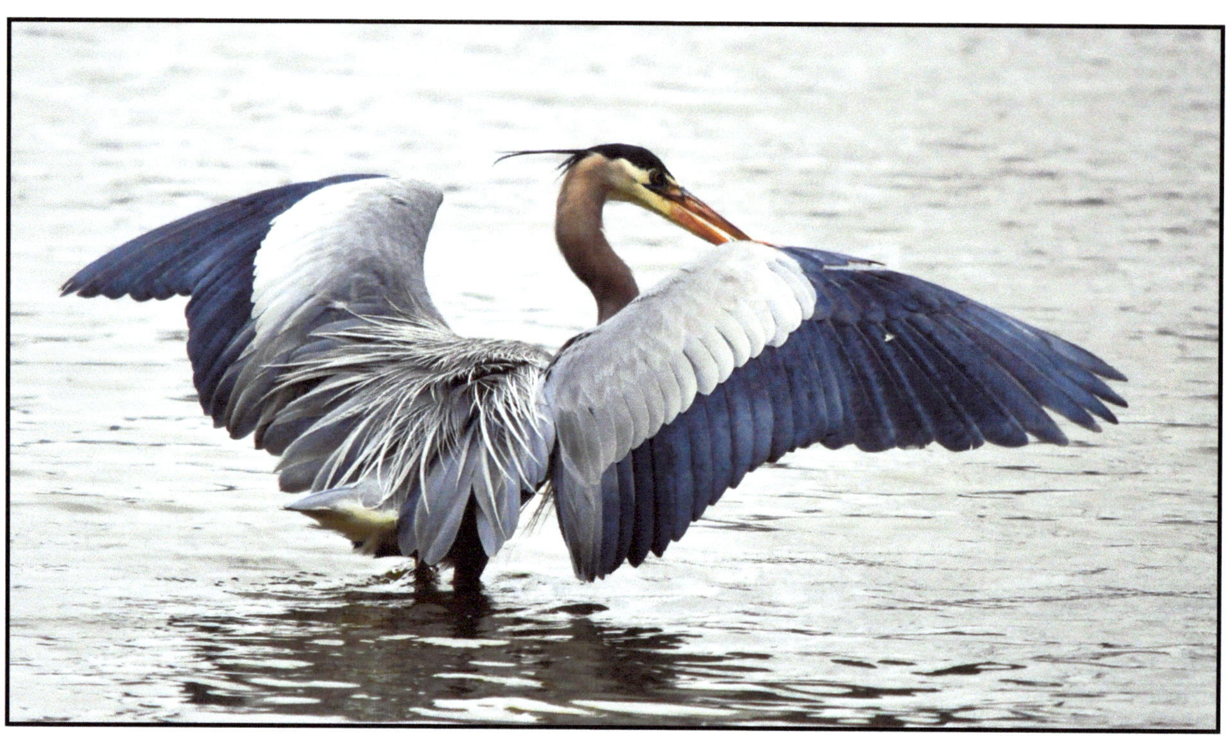

Ah, yes! Feathered wings. Those things that set the birds apart from the rest of the warm blooded creatures. Besides flying, what else could you do with a pair of feathered wings if you had them?

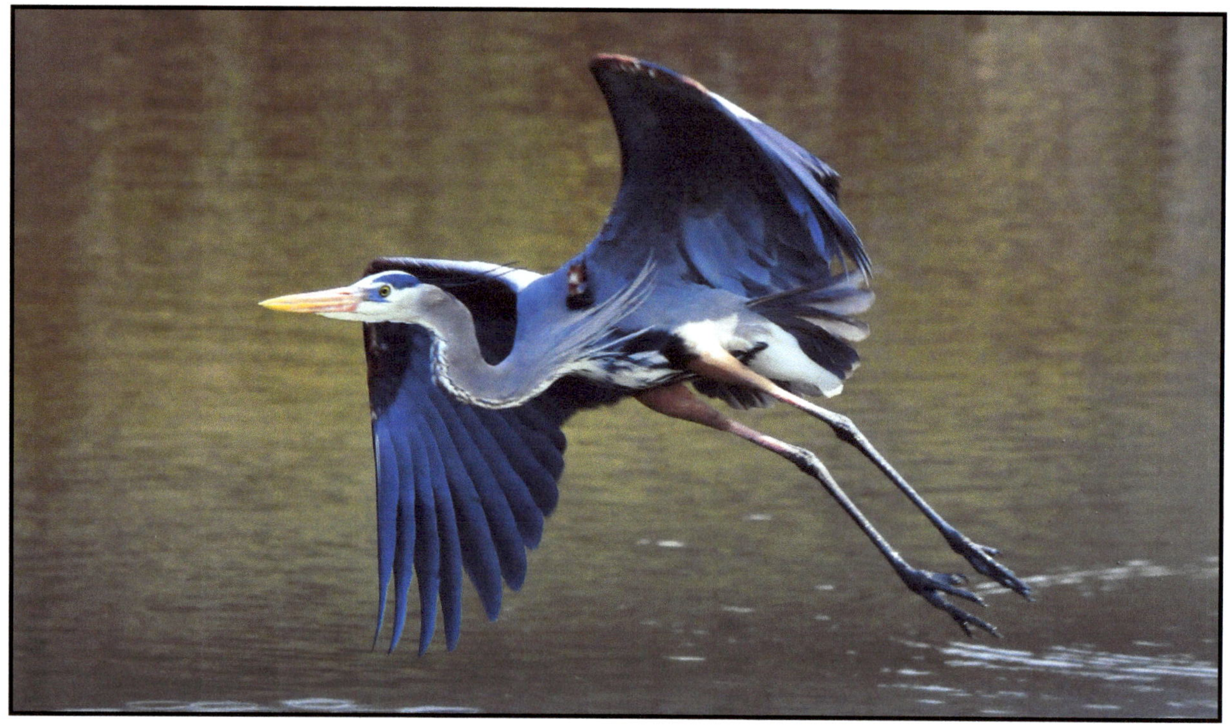

How about, taking off from the water?

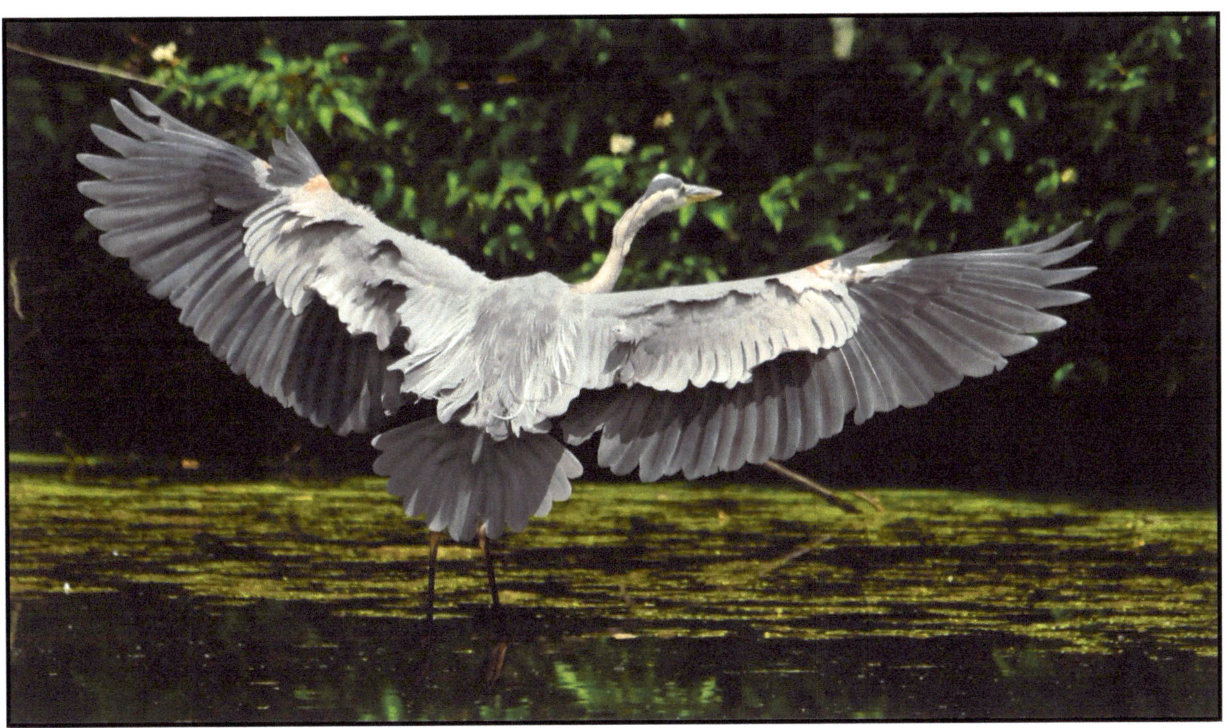

Or, how about landing in water? Shallow water is best for the Heron.

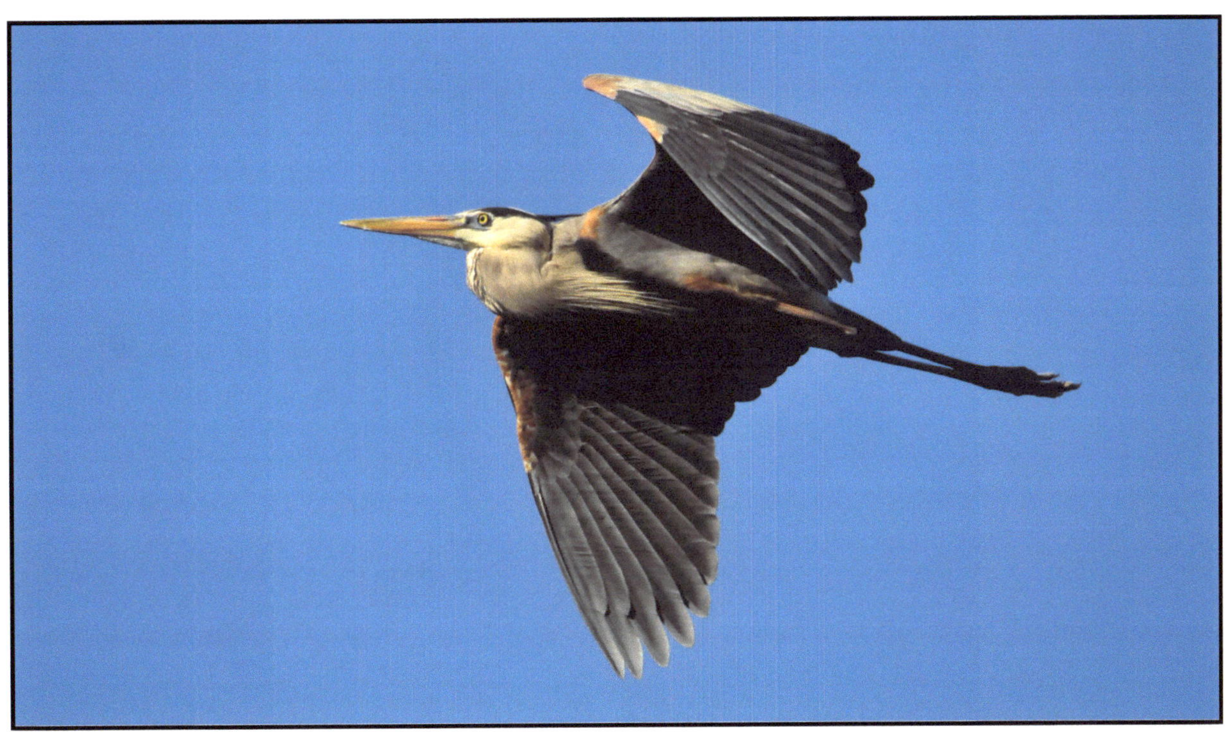

Of course, there's the obvious. Just flying around.

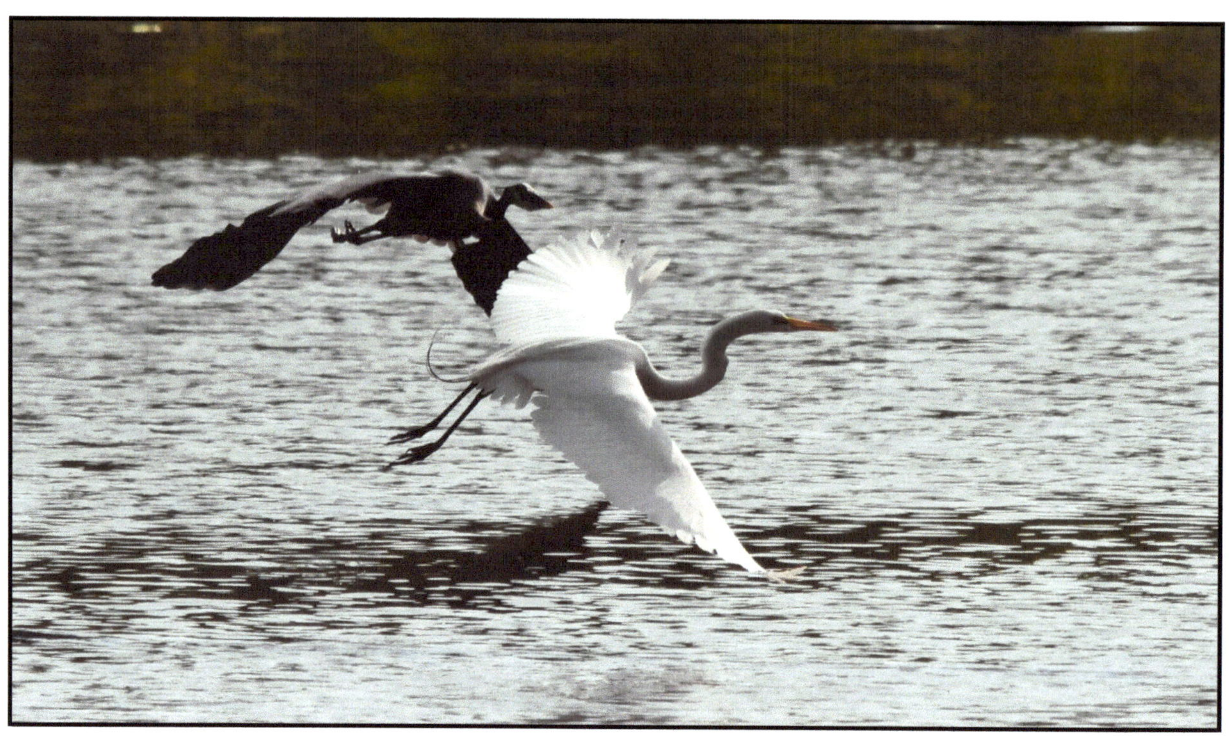

Or, using them to chase away a competitor.

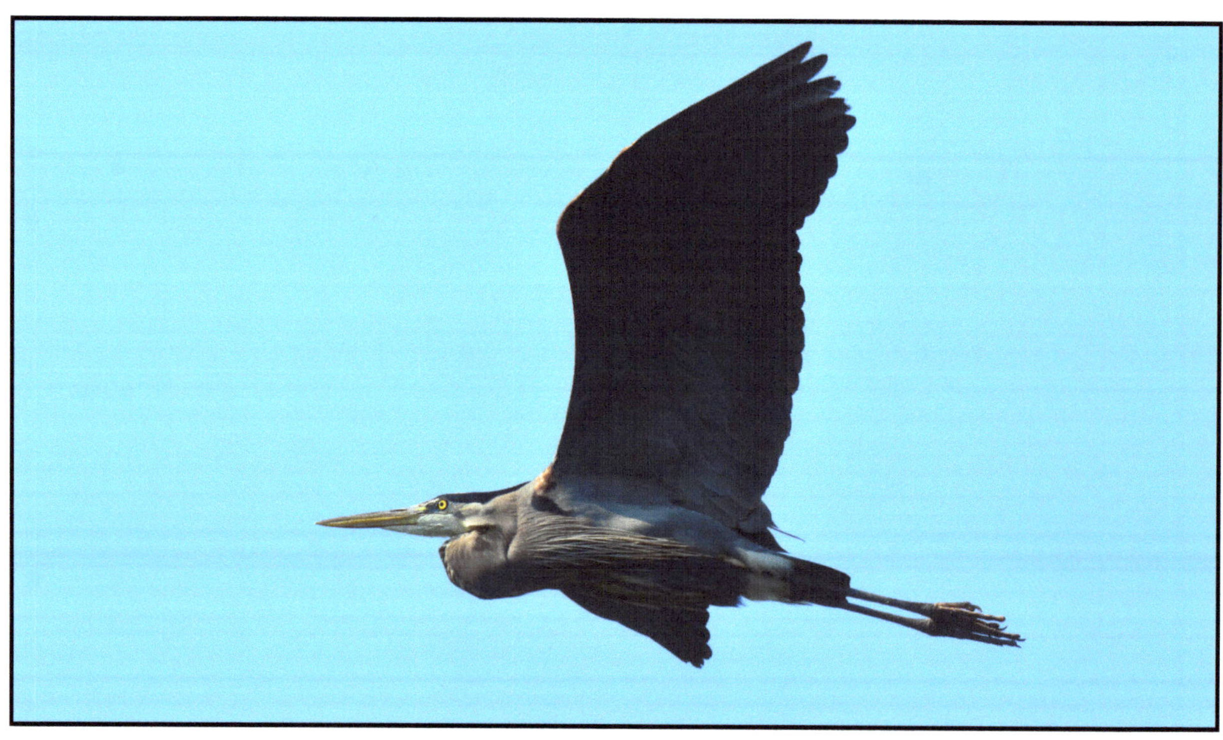

But, just flying around is a lot more enjoyable.

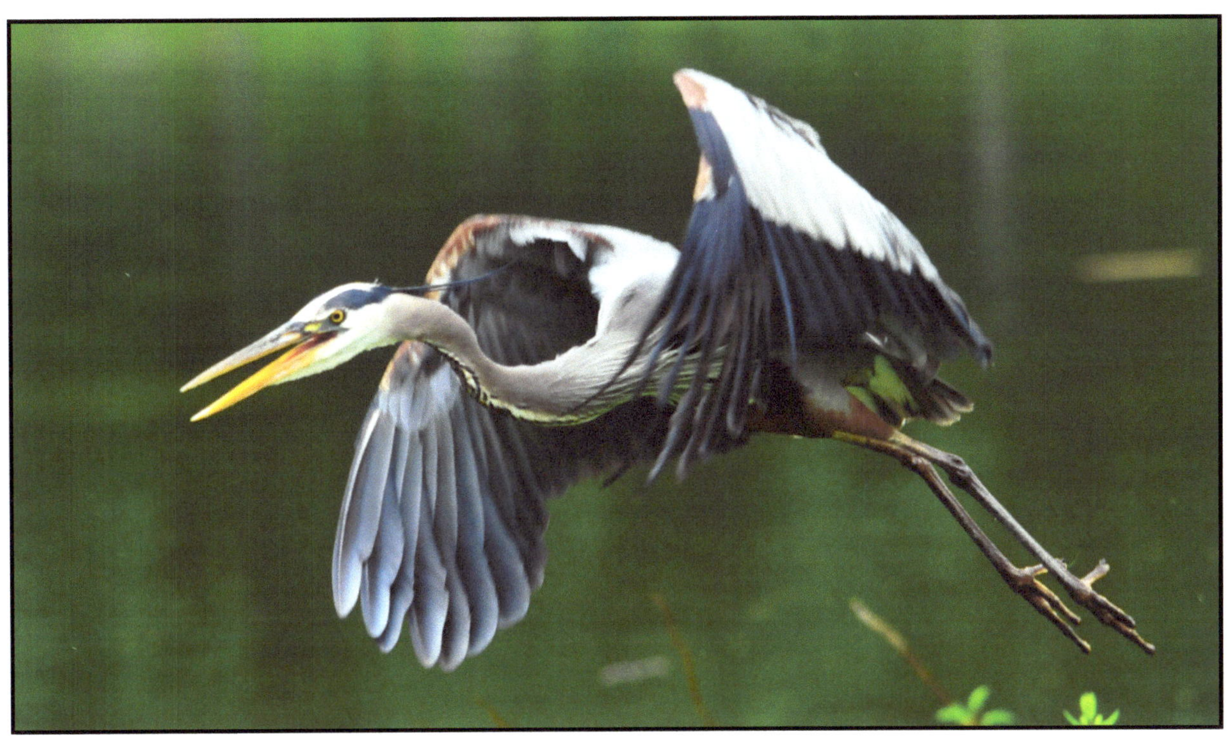

How about scaring people by uttering loud, hoarse, croaking noises as you fly away?

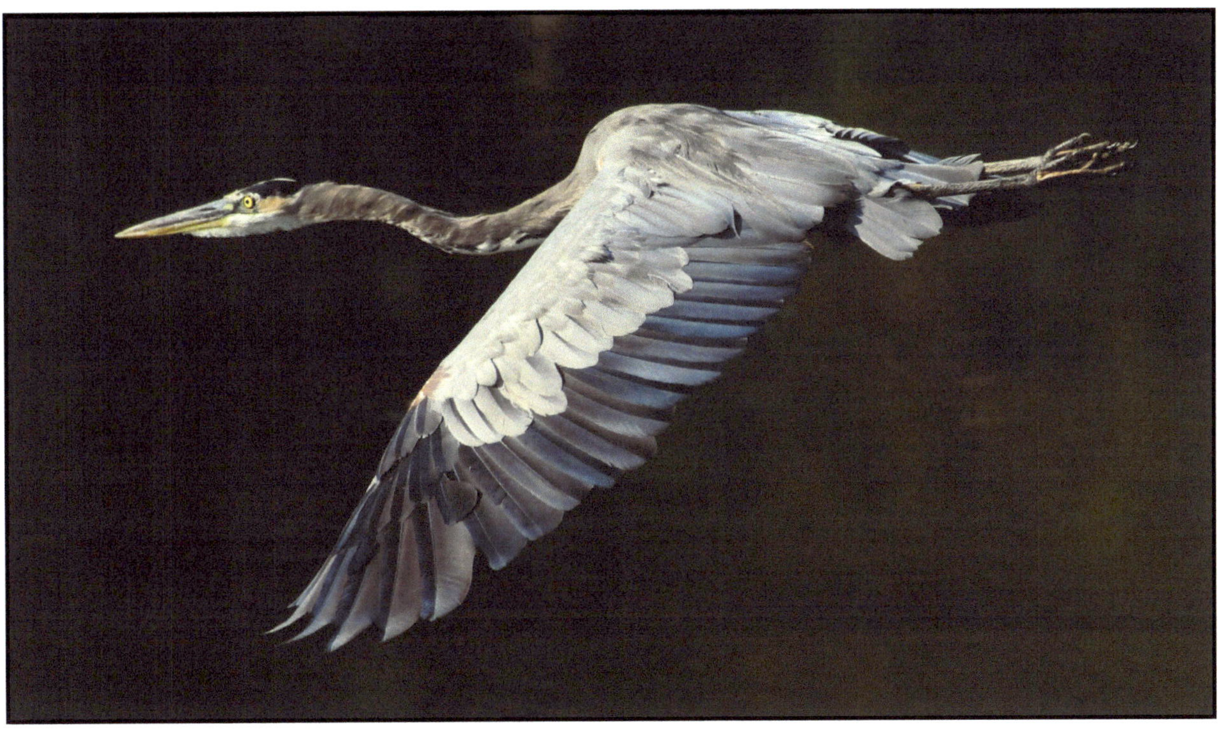

Or, just flying from point "A" to point "B"?

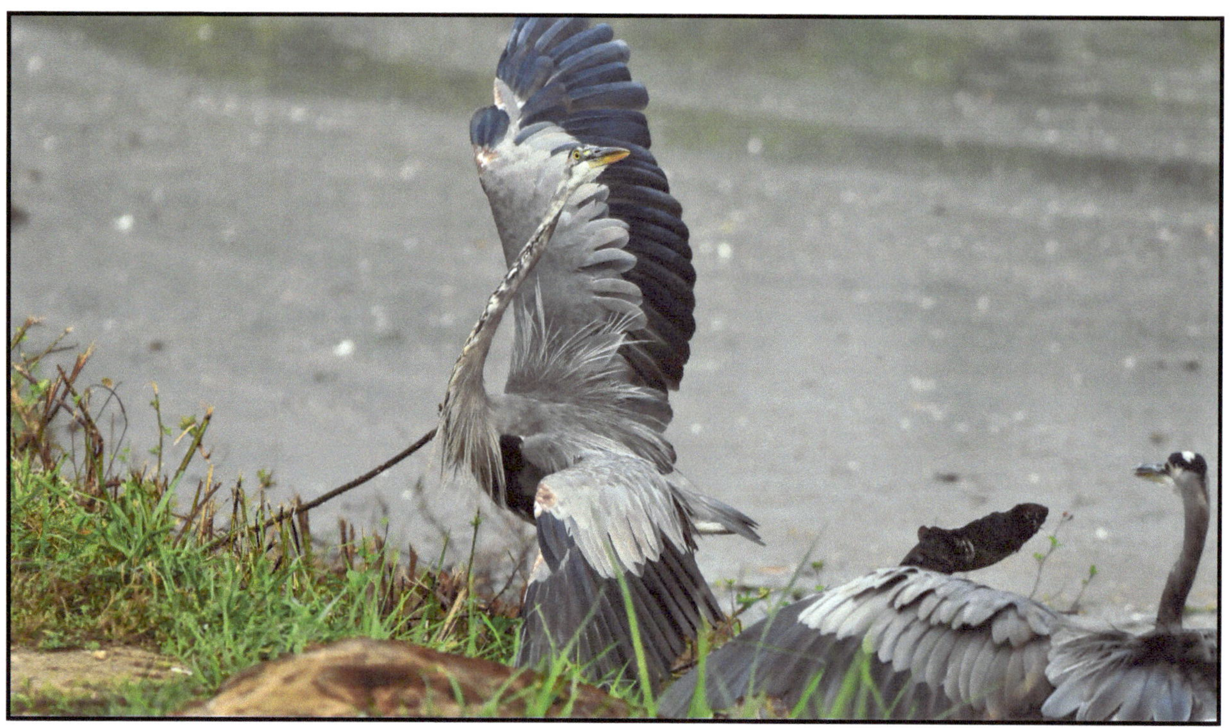

Use them to display and scare off a fellow Heron.

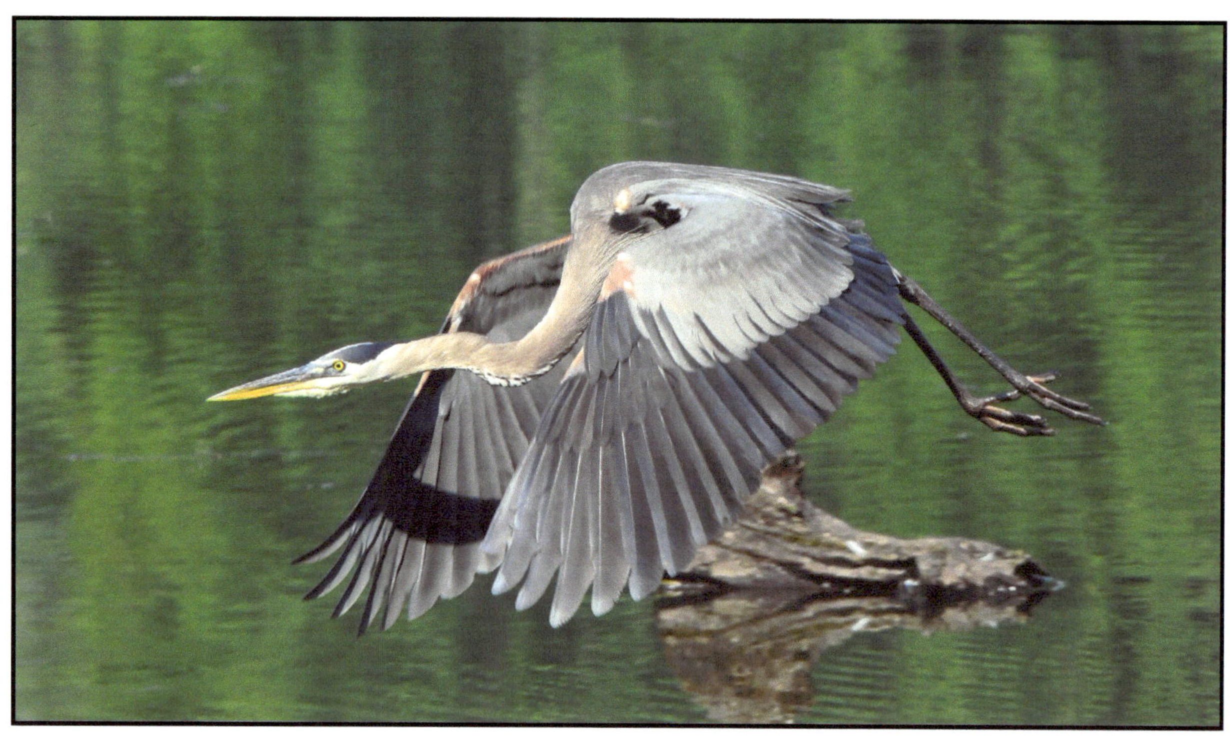

Or ... just flying some more.

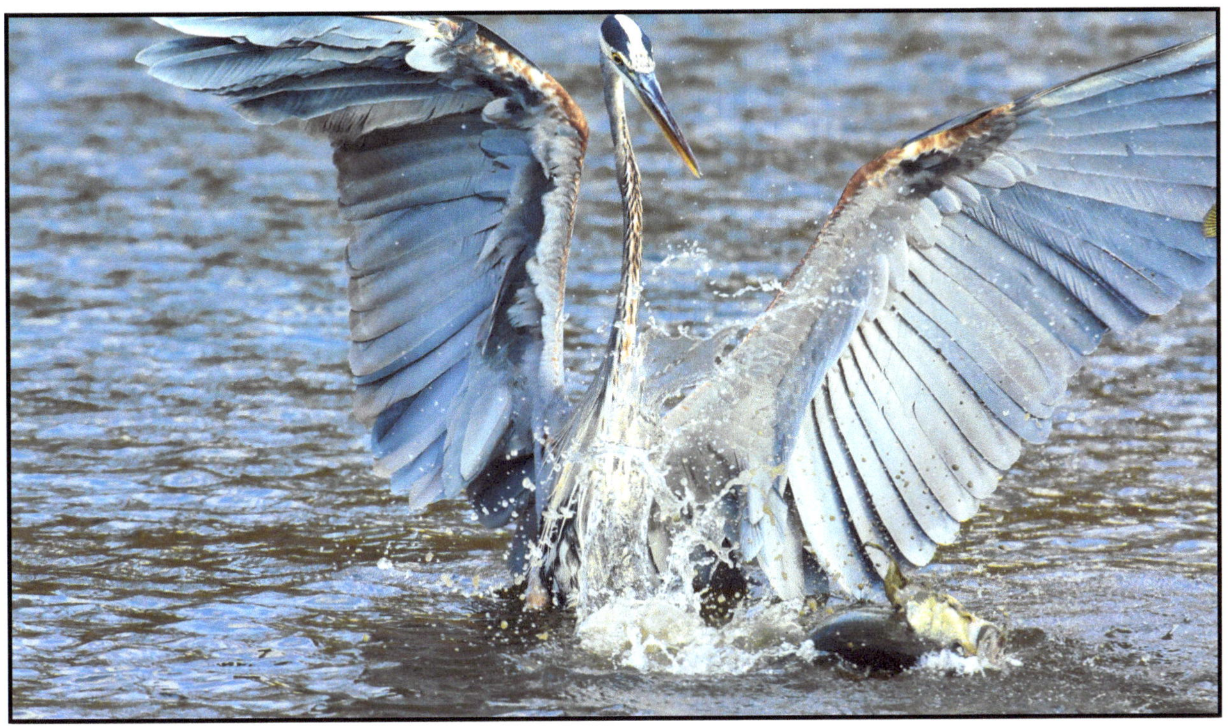

Or, use them to ward off an attacking (or escaping) Large Mouth Bass?

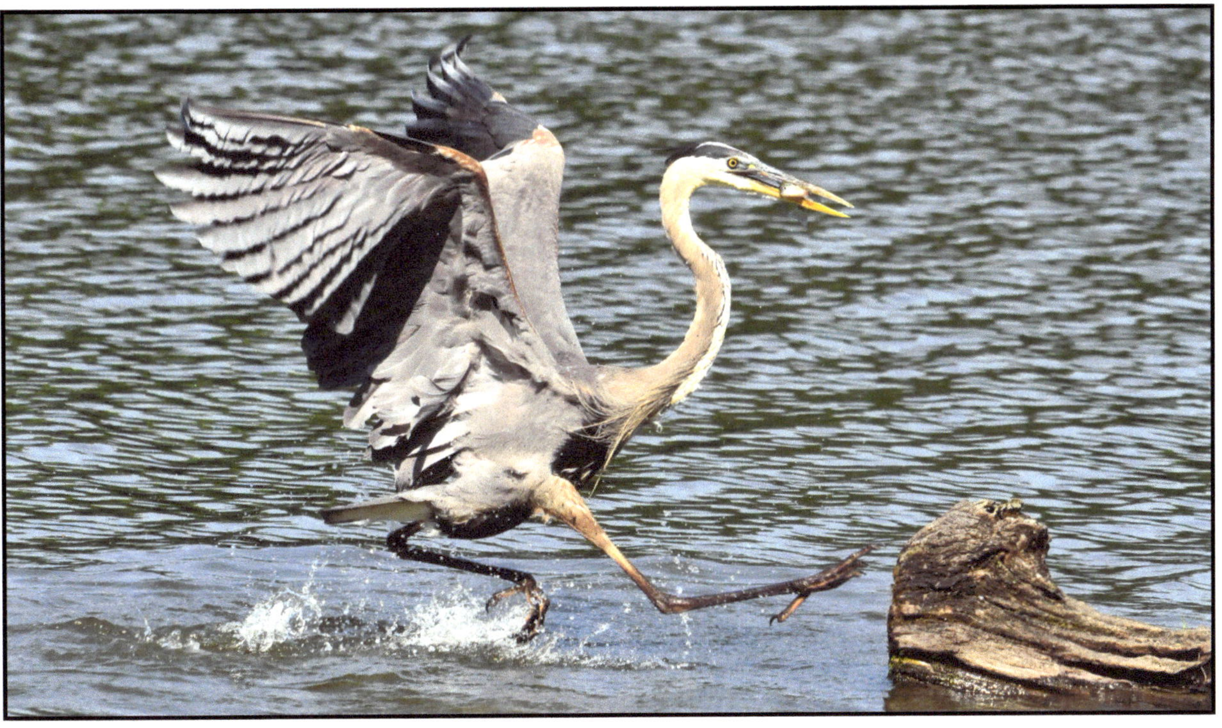

They are really nice for balance while jumping from the water onto a log

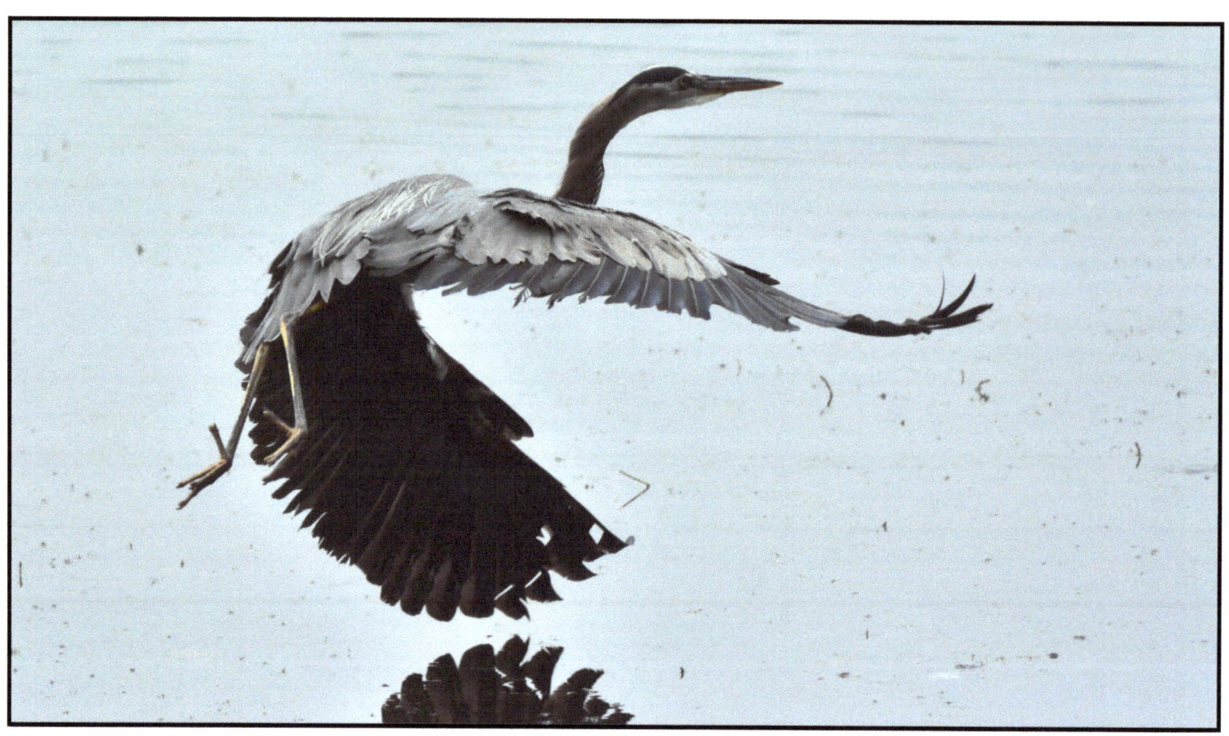

They are real handy for quick maneuvering.

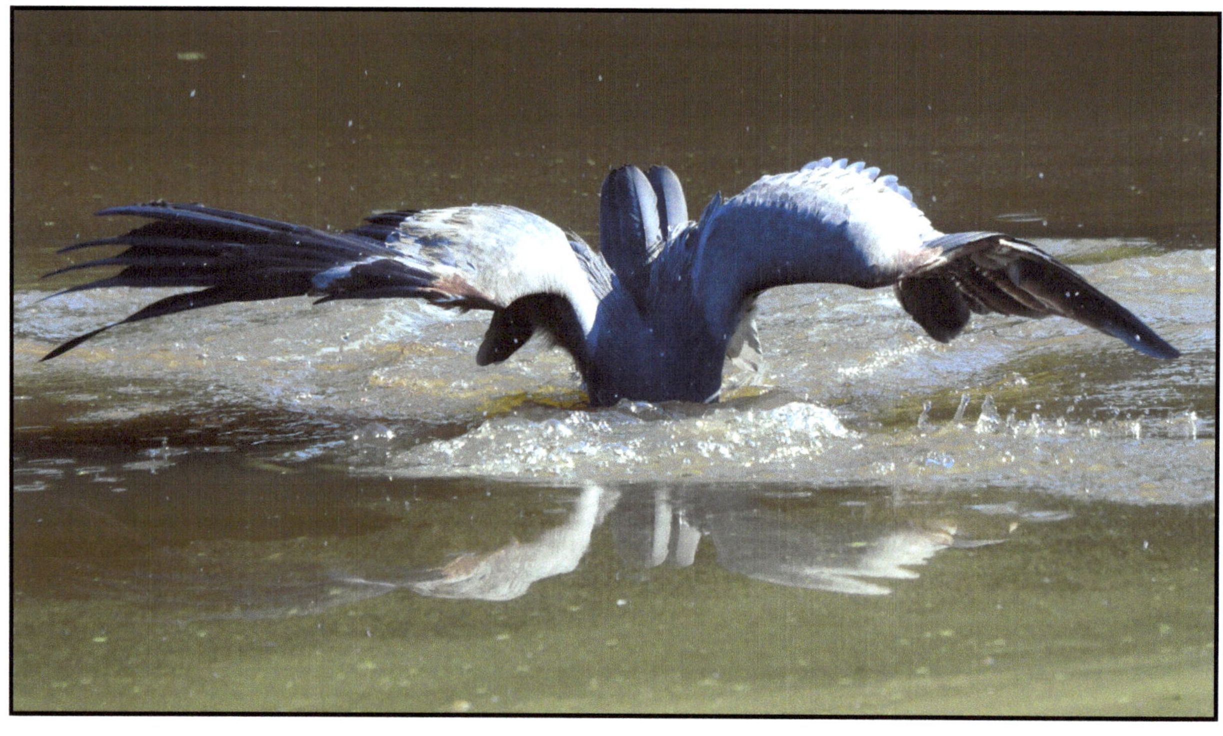

Or, for balance while capturing prey.

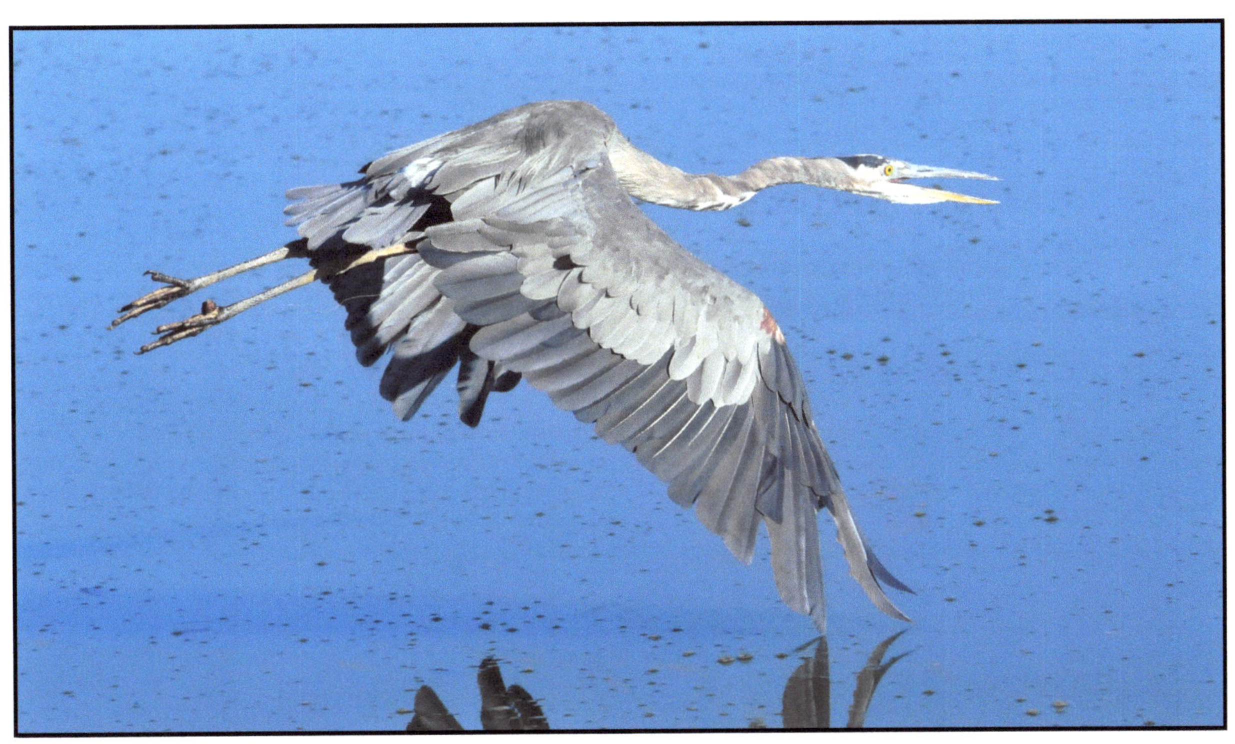

Of course, flying is always more pleasant.

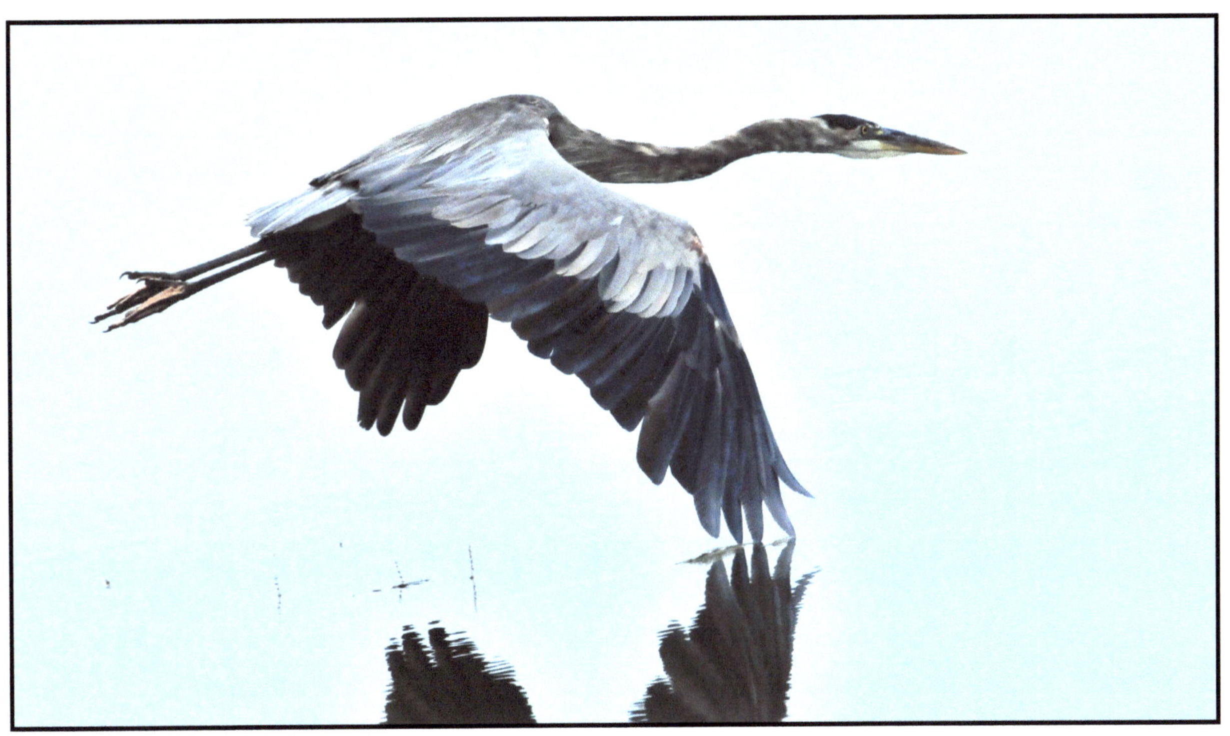

So, I'll just fly!

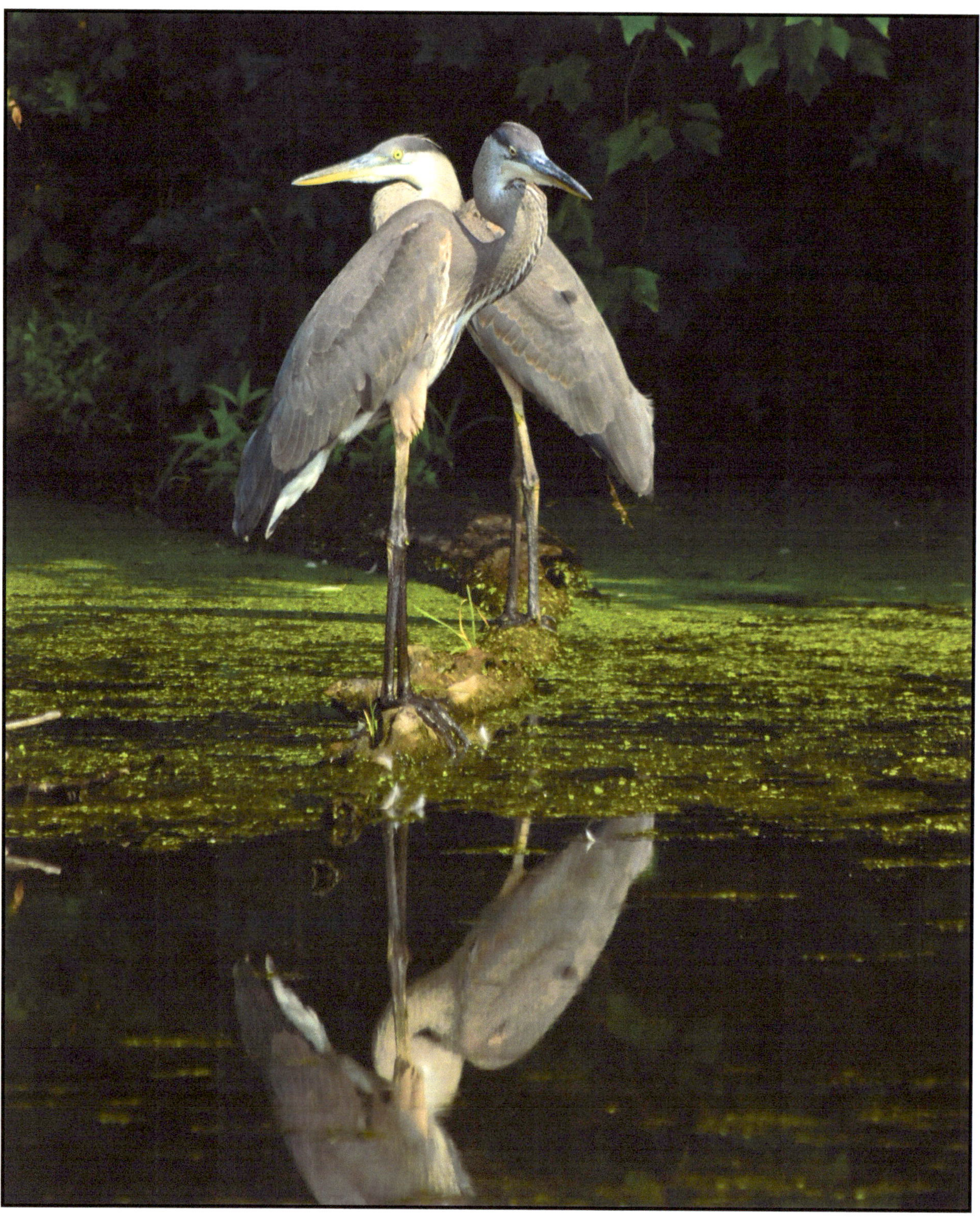

This is a pair of young Great Blue Herons. Possibly, they could be nest mates. They'll have a lot to learn in their first year. I hope they survive it.

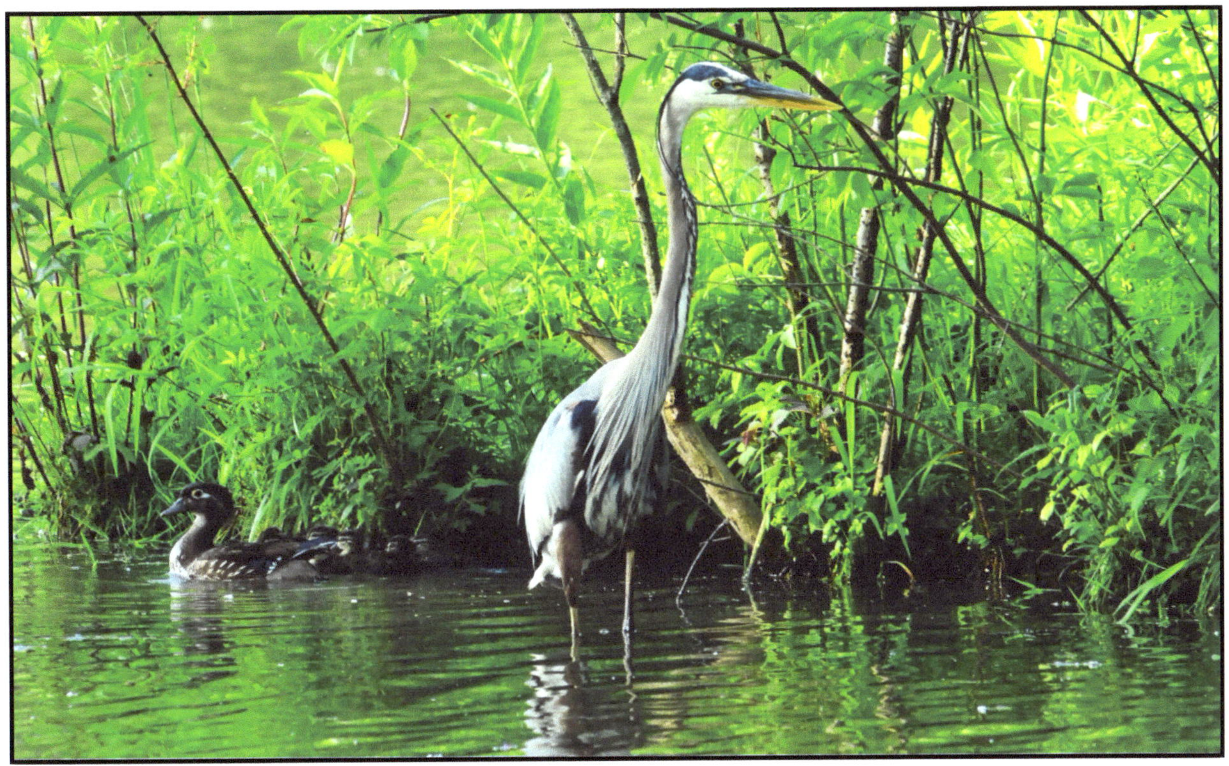

A Wood Duck family sneaks past behind this adult Heron. I have never seen a Heron take a Wood Duck duckling before, so I think they were safe. Mother Wood Duck may not think so.

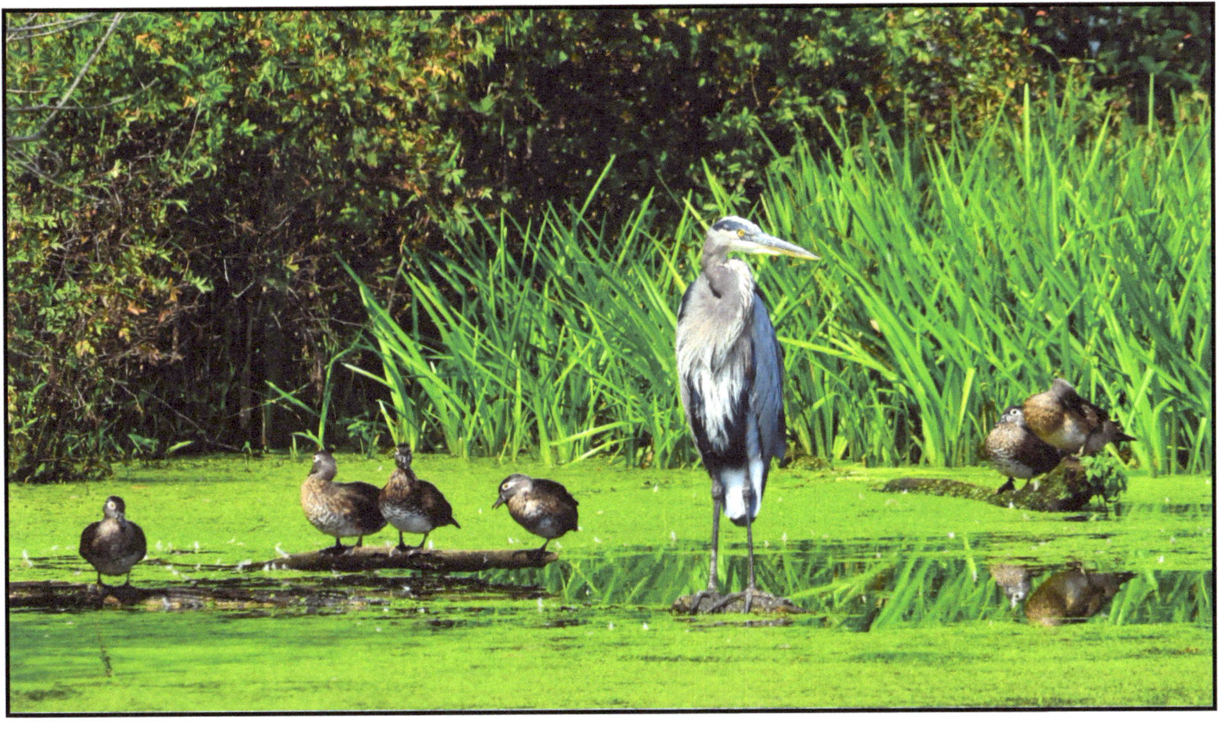

These Wood Ducks are nearly fully grown now. They have nothing to fear. Except eagles, hawks, or snapping turtles. And ... man.

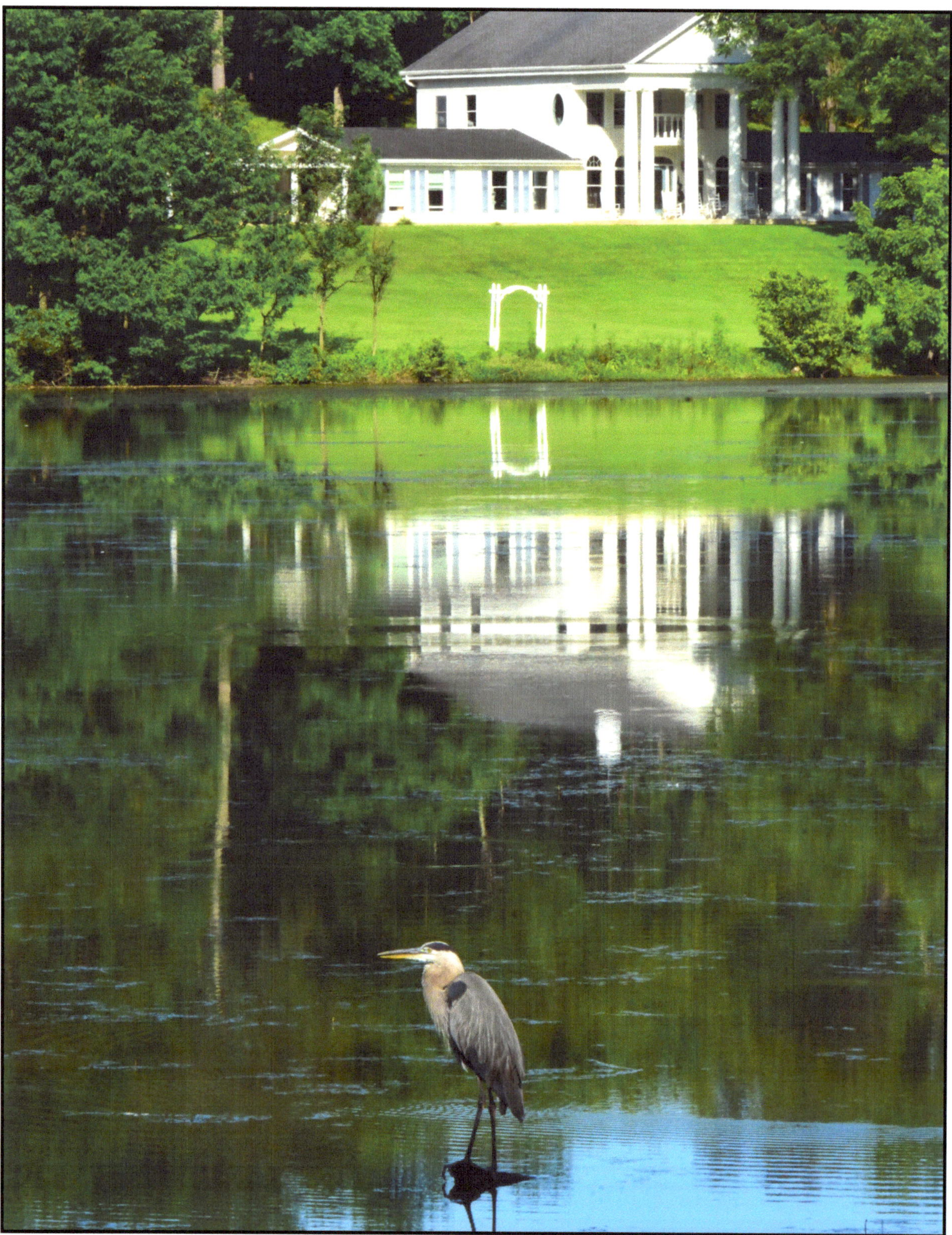

Just chillin' and thinkin'!

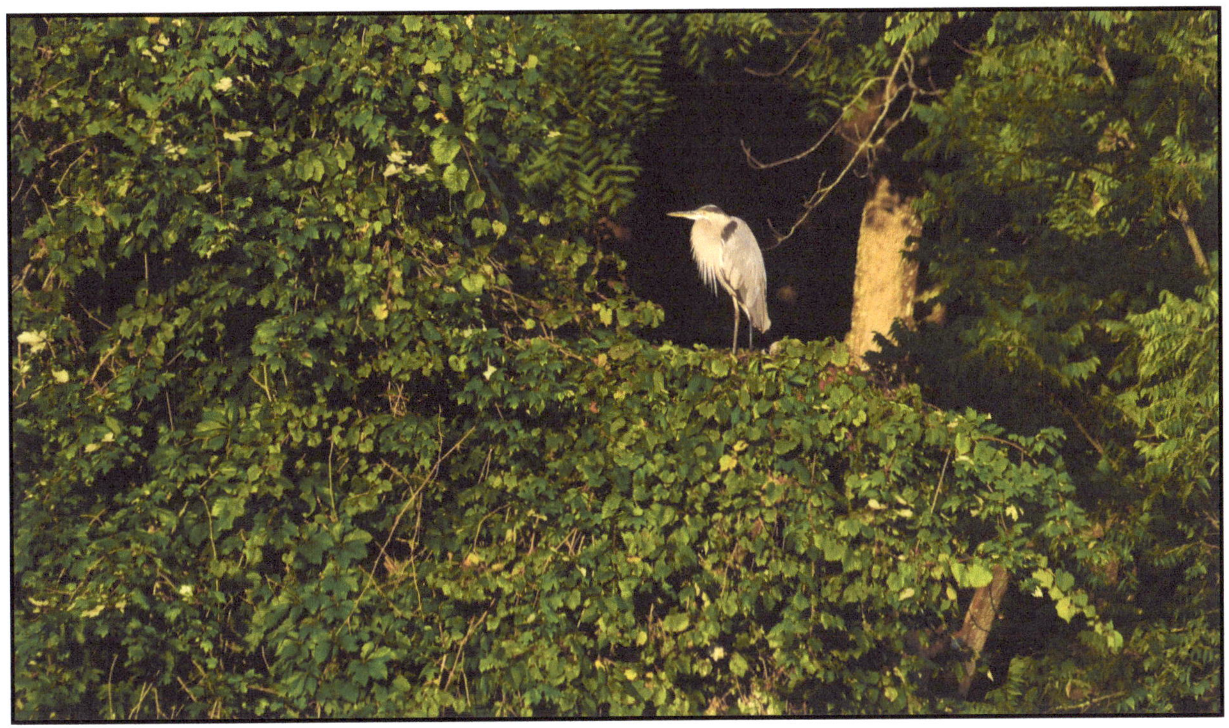

The warm, morning light greets this Heron as he greets the day.

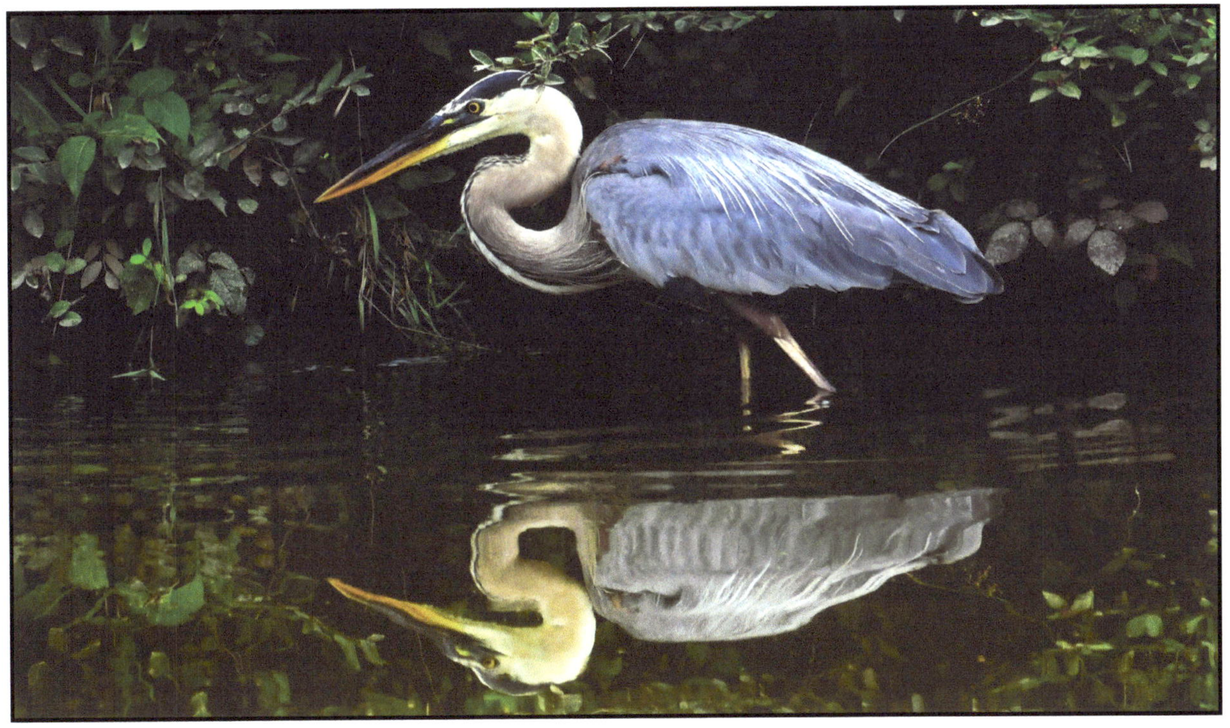

A familiar pose as this big guy hunts close to the shore.

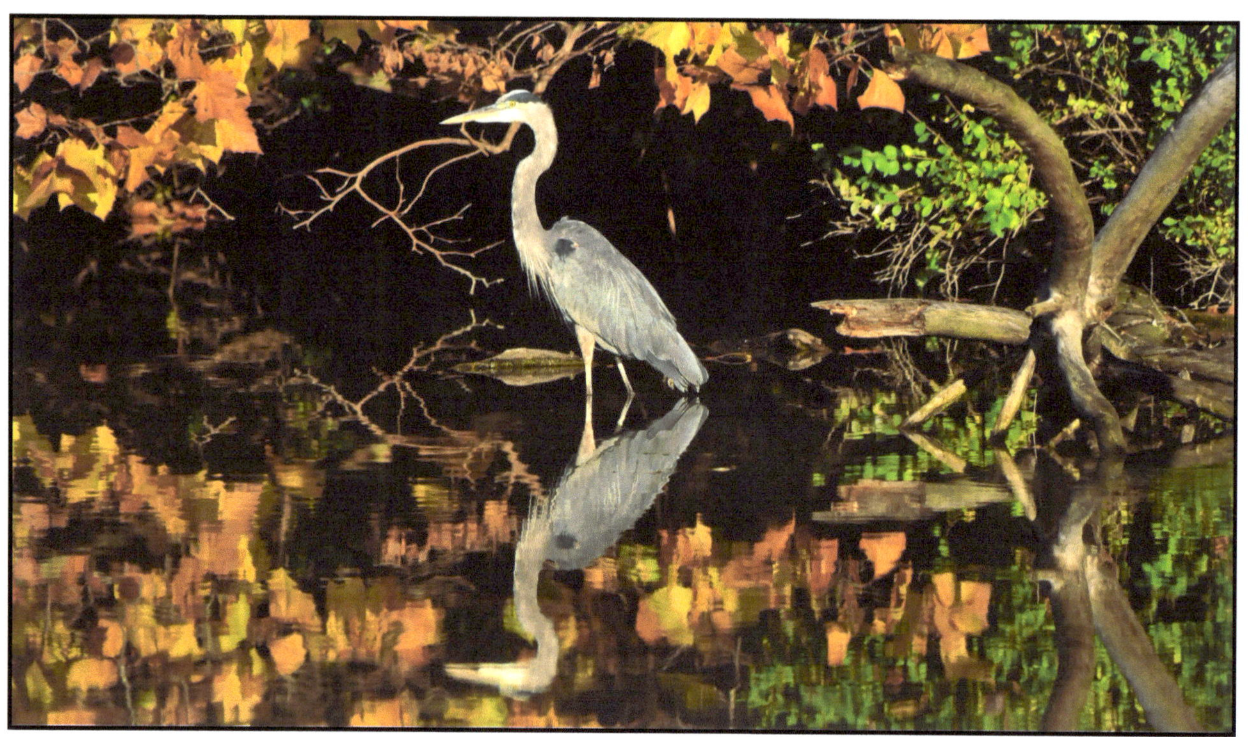

Reflections on a new day.

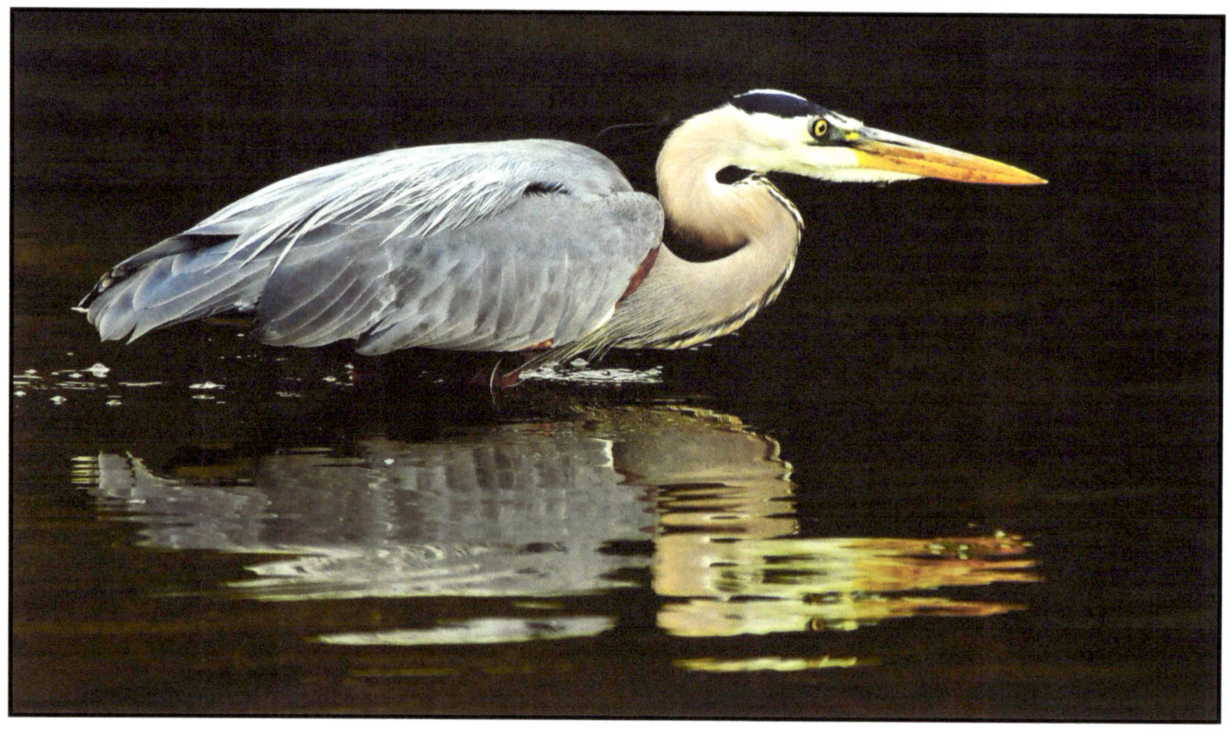

How low can you go? They can get down much lower than this.

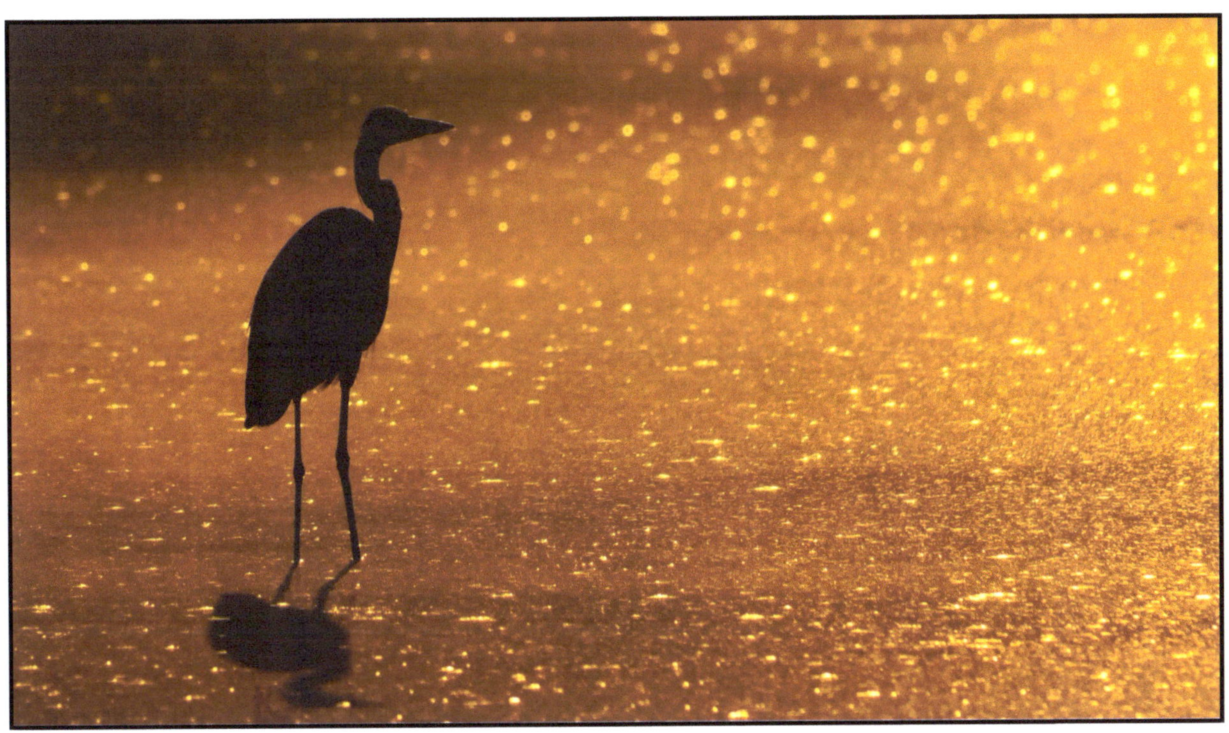

The morning sun has just risen over the hills and painted the morning gold.

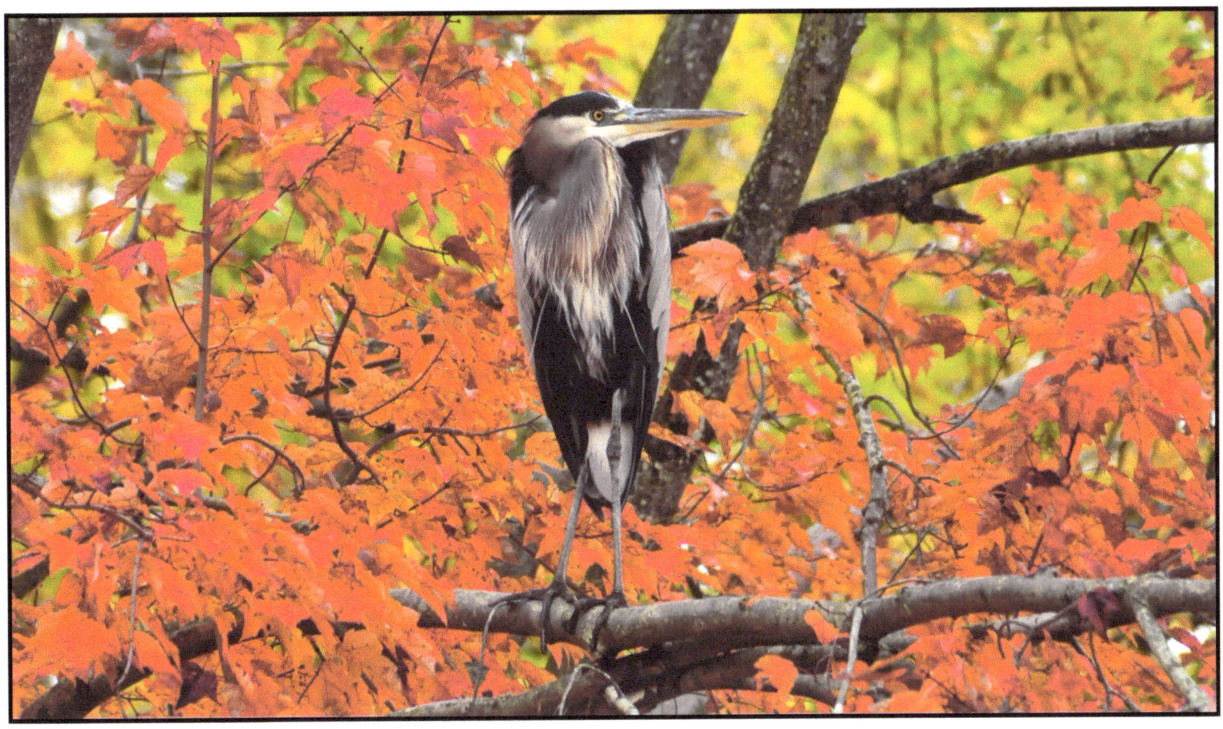

My favorite time of the year! I hope this Heron enjoys it, too!

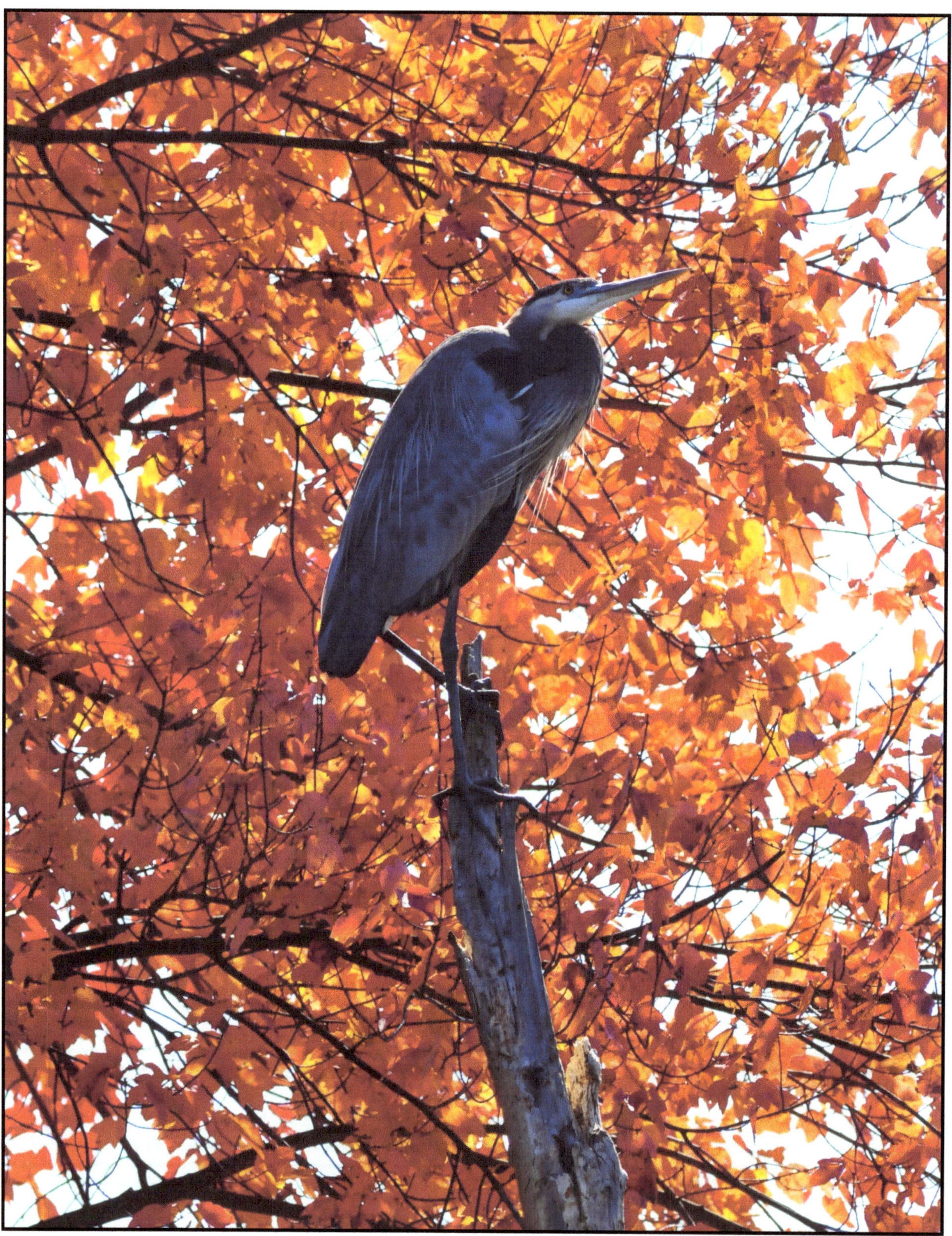

I think this is the bird who injured his wing. He has come up in his world!

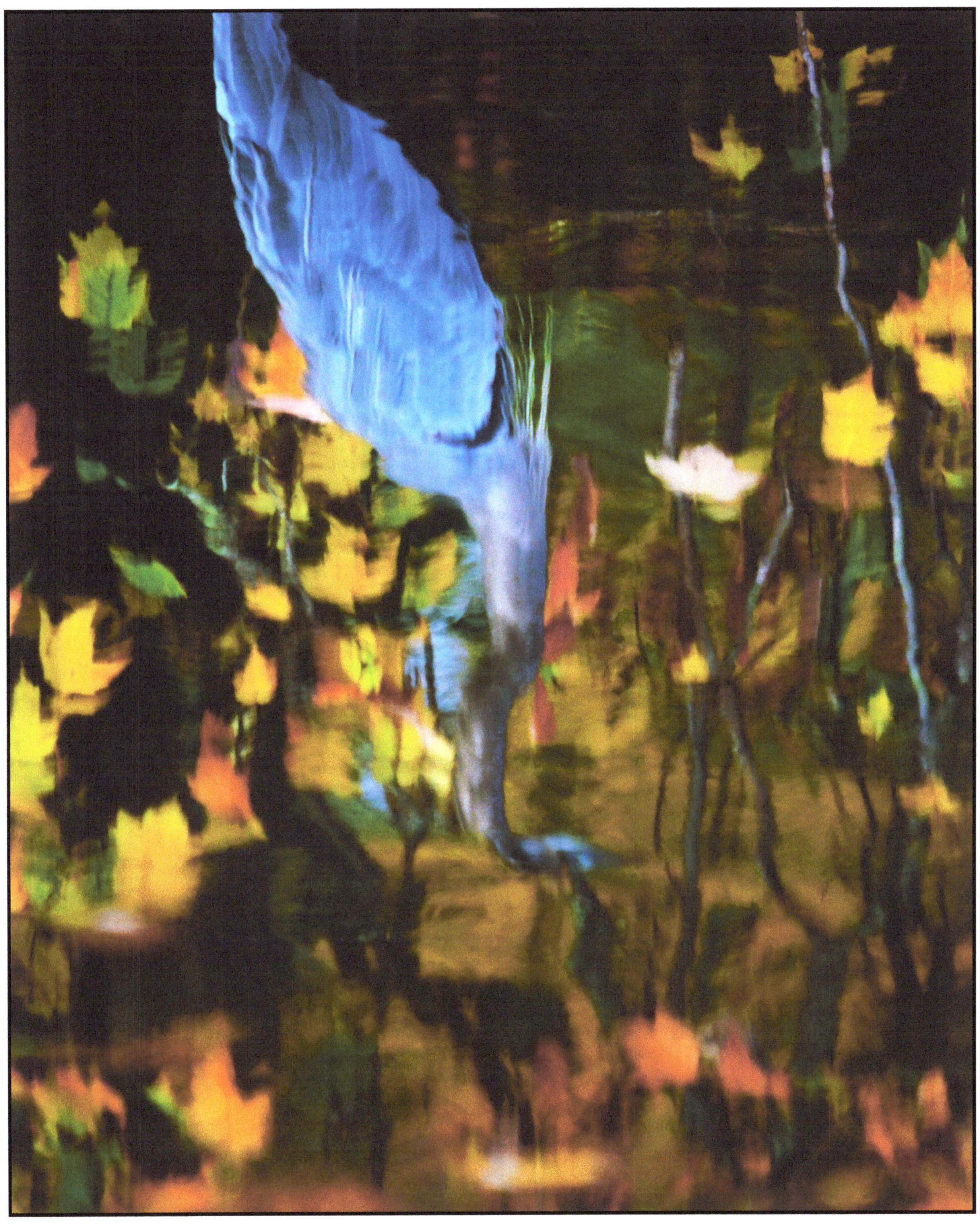

This soft, abstract photo shows the reflection of a Great Blue Heron in the waters of the lake and the fall splendor surrounding him.

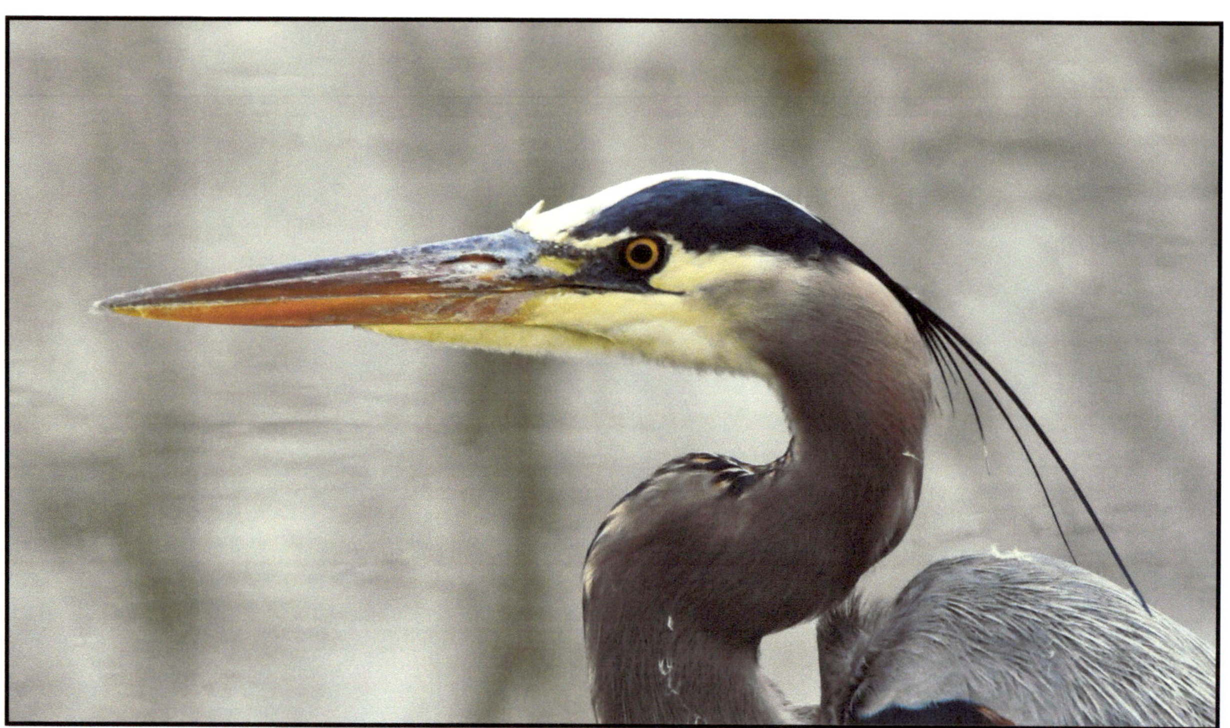

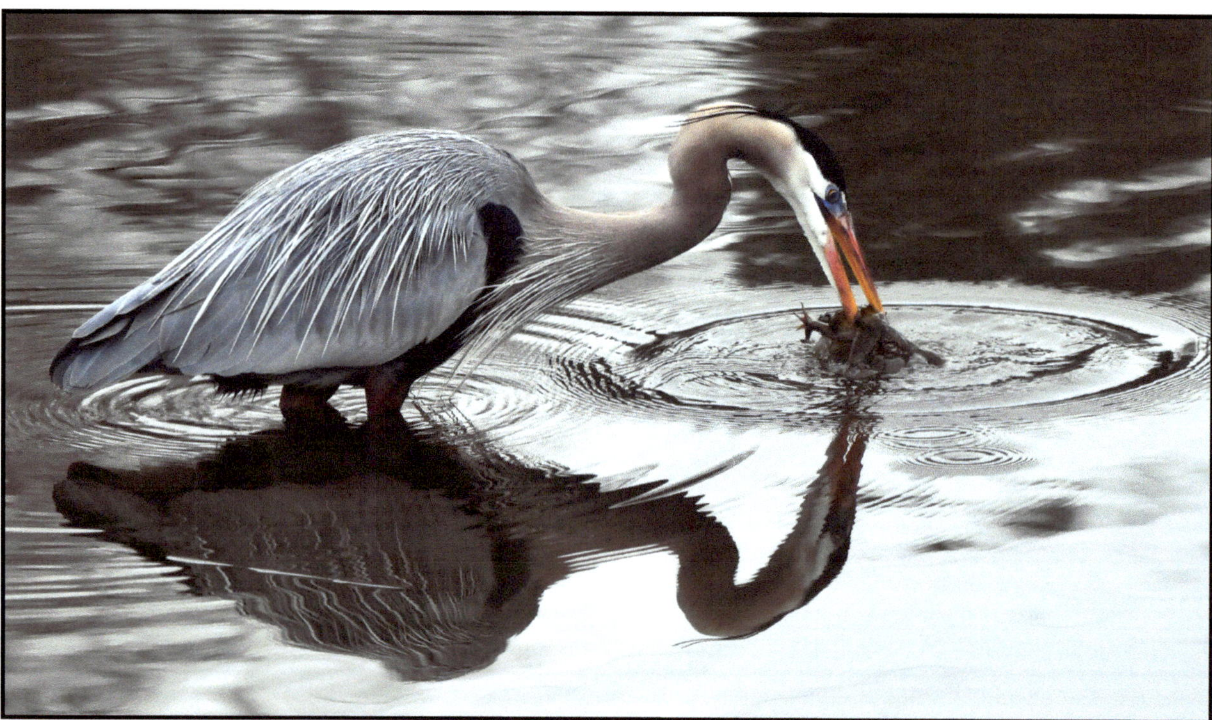

Top is a portrait of a Great Blue Heron showing close up its dagger-like bill. Bottom shows the Heron using it to capture a bull frog for its next meal. A perfect tool, always available

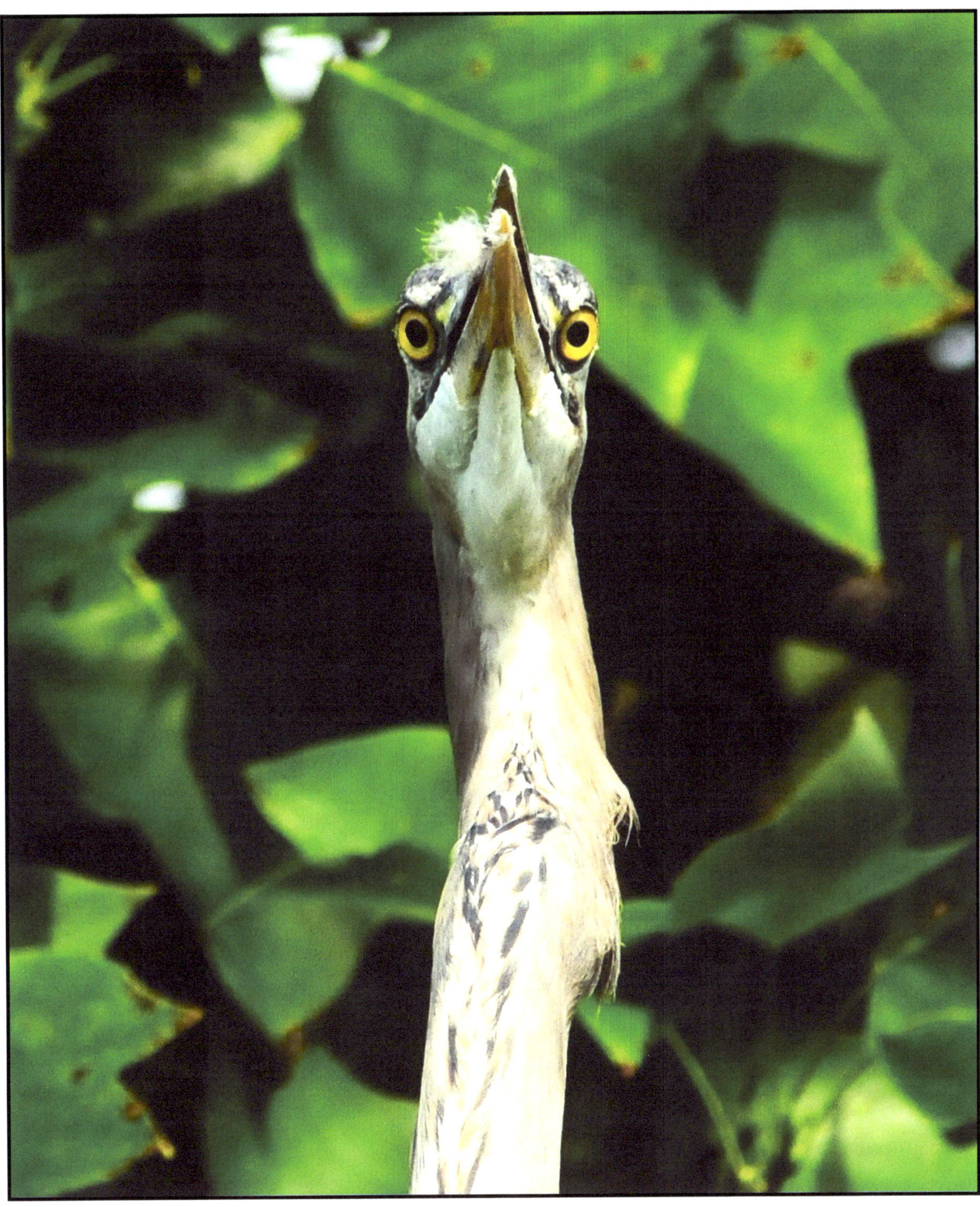

A head-on view of a Great Blue Heron showing his eyes. They give him good stereo vision enabling him to estimate hunting distances very accurately. He also has to compensate for the refraction of the water so he doesn't overshoot his underwater prey when he stabs at it.

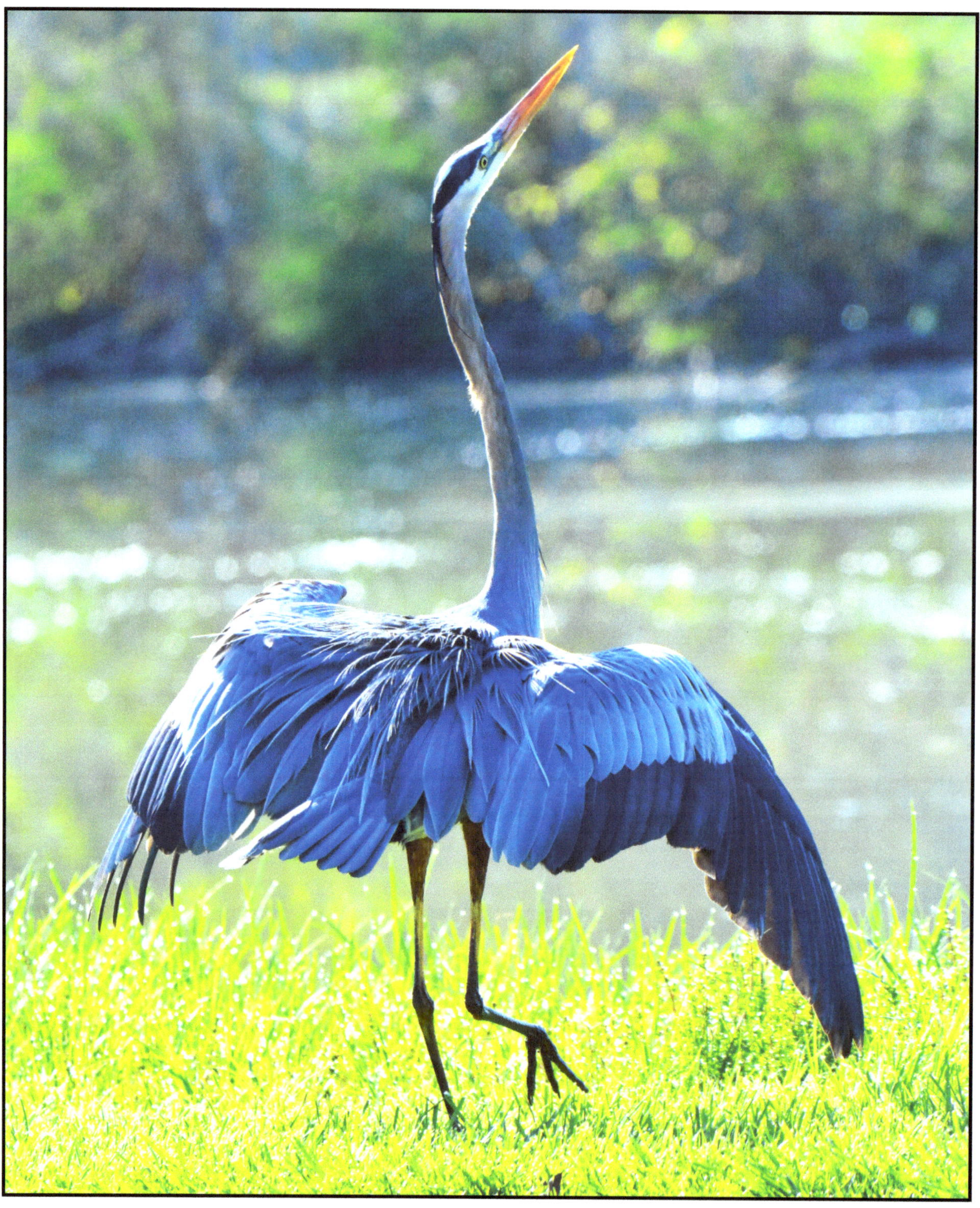

This Heron is not dancing with joy. It's displaying in a effort to let other Herons in the area know he may be top dog and is willing to prove it.

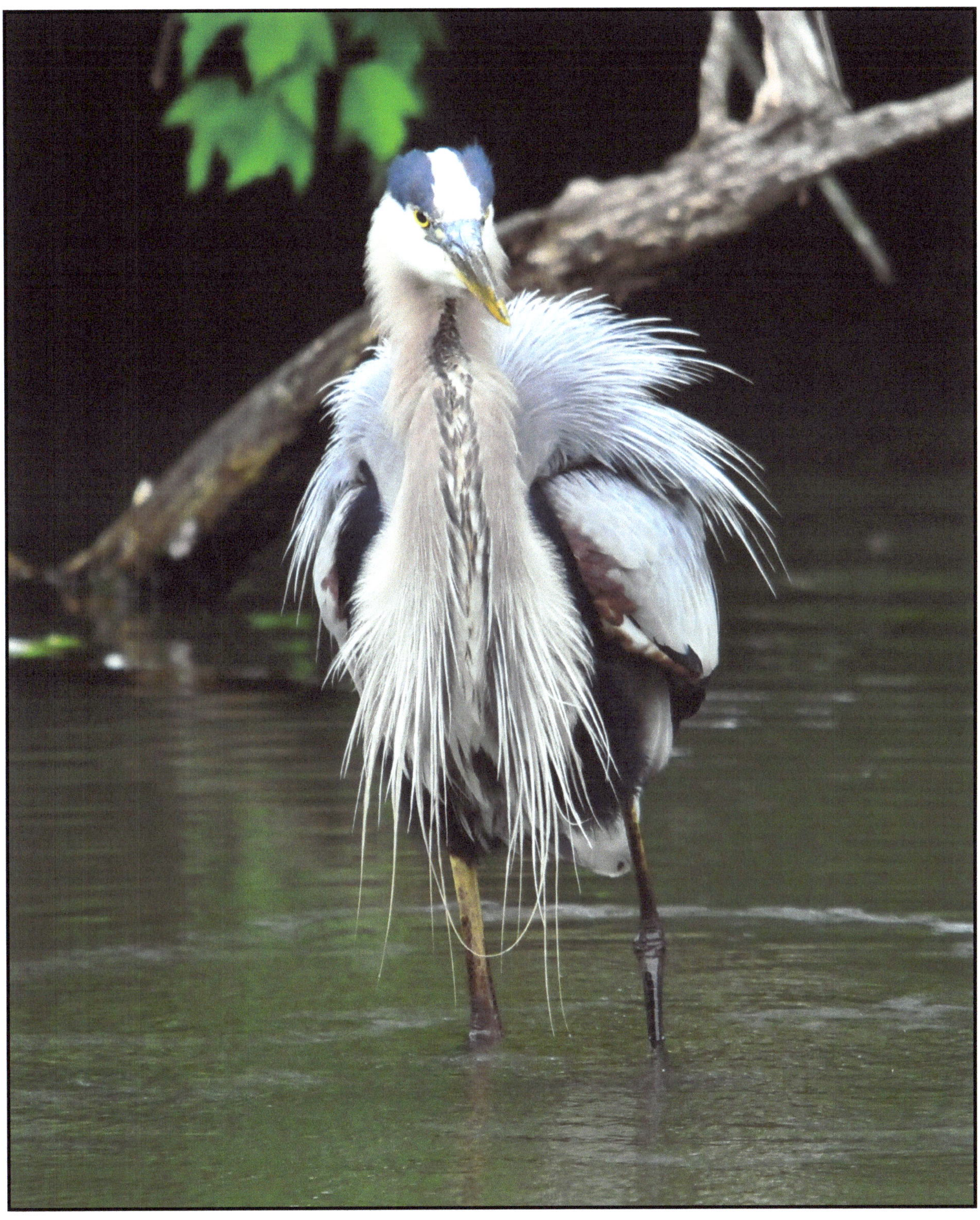

This plump looking Great Blue Heron is merely shaking his feathers and plumping up prior to relaxing his body so the feathers will fall back into their proper spots.

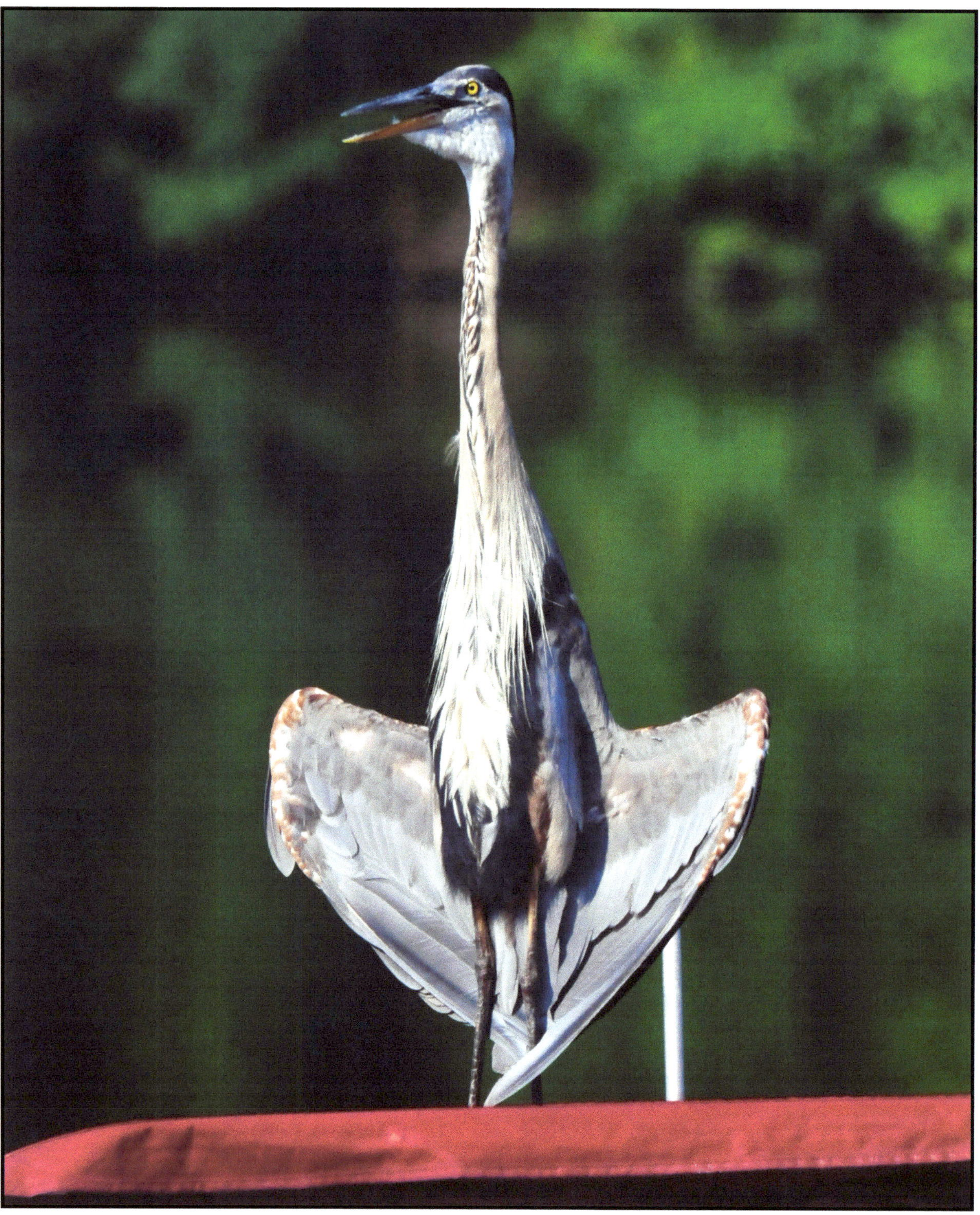

This big bird is facing the morning sun. They seem to use this strange looking pose to warm up on a sunny morning. Usually, their bill is opened slightly and they pulse their throat muscles rapidly as well. I suspect they may use this method to cool down, also.

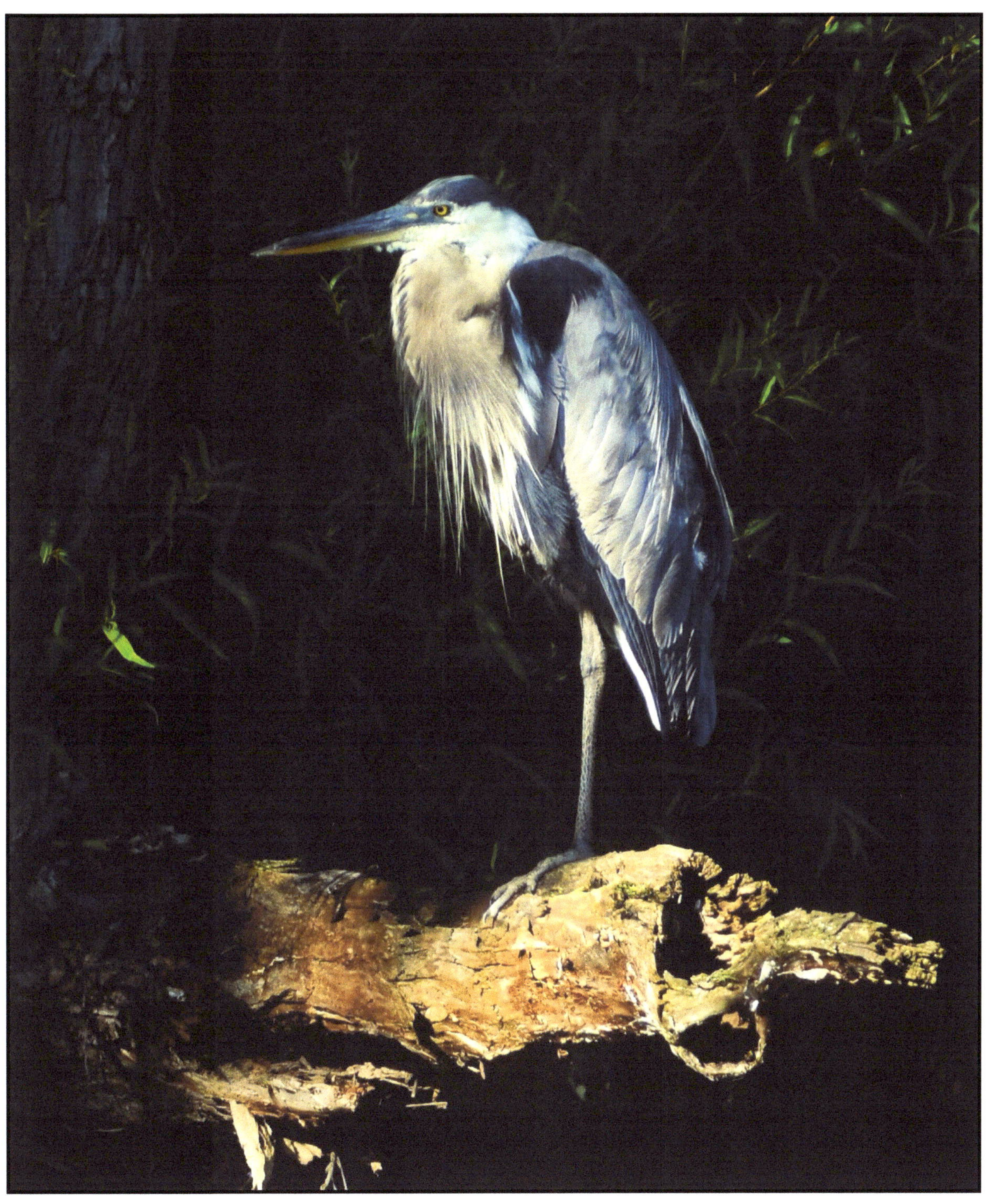

Relaxing after a hard day's work. All fishermen know how stressful fishing can be.

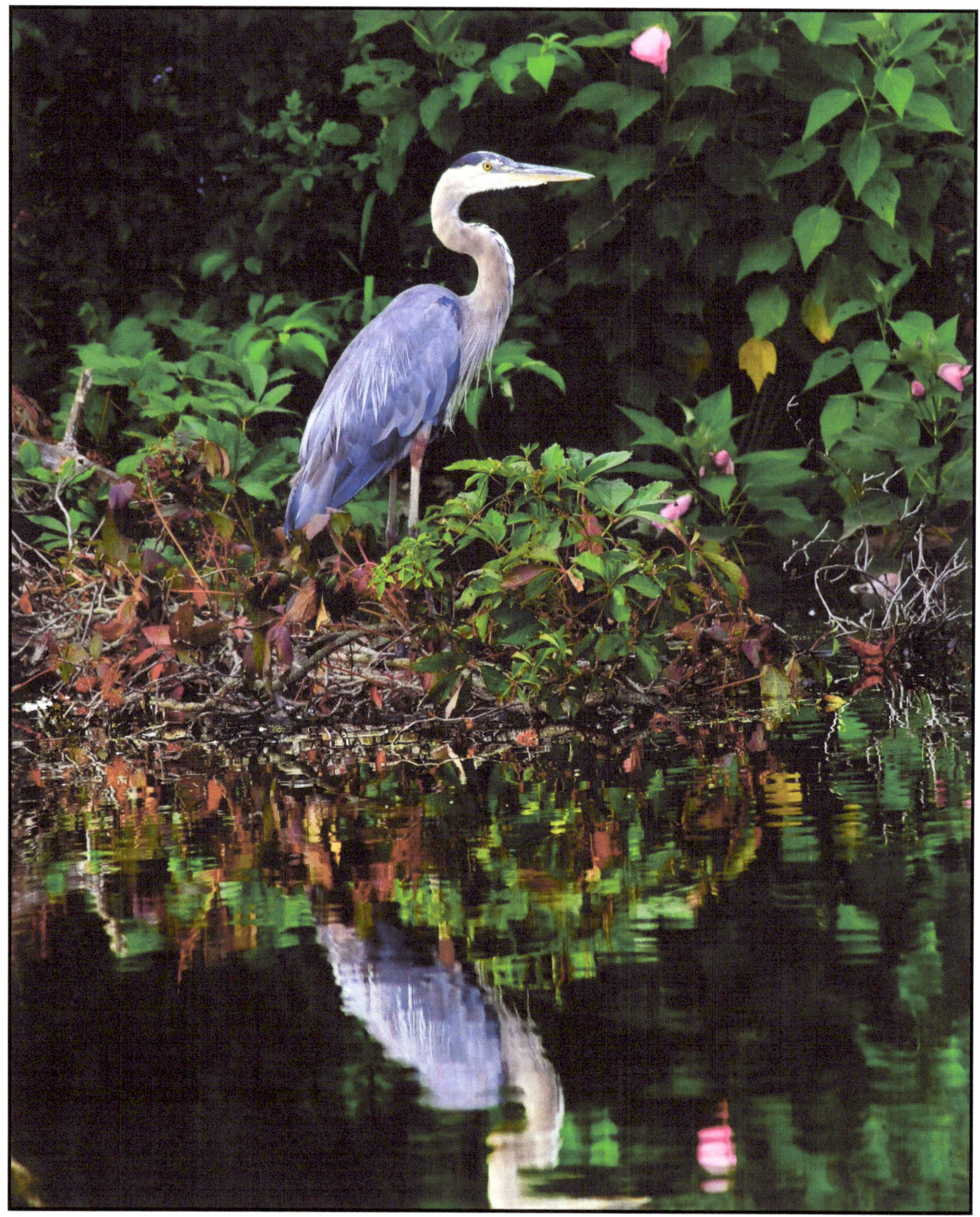

This is not a nest. Just a spot to wind down and plan for tomorrow.

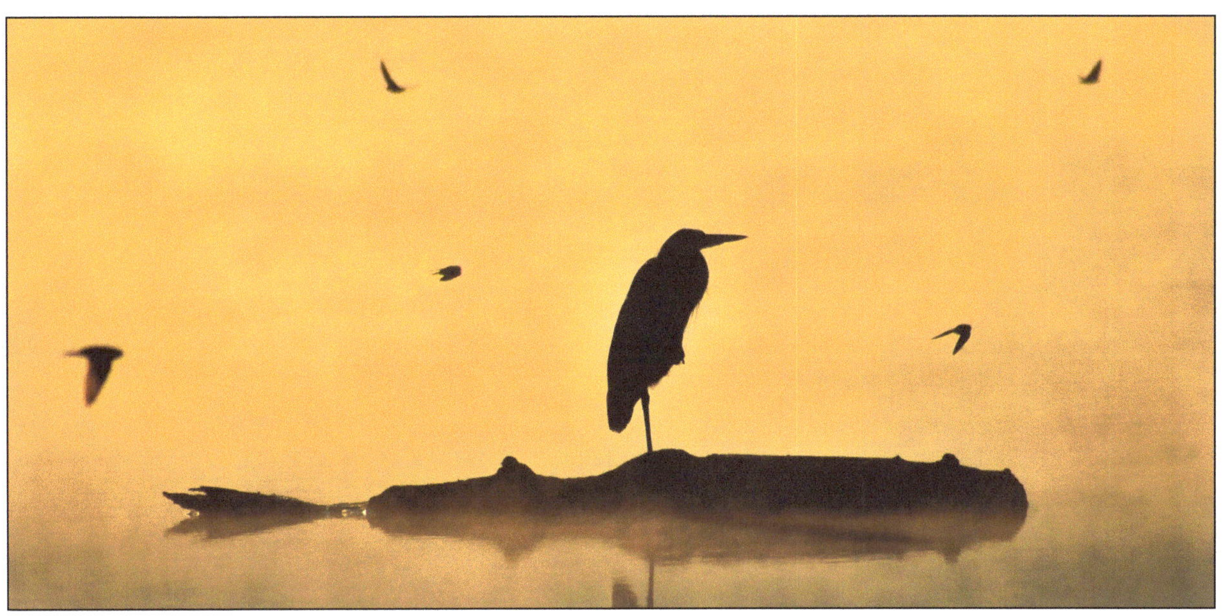

In the still, morning mists, Tree Swallows and Barn Swallows swoop around this Great Blue Heron as they feast on the abundant insect life hatching from the lake's waters.

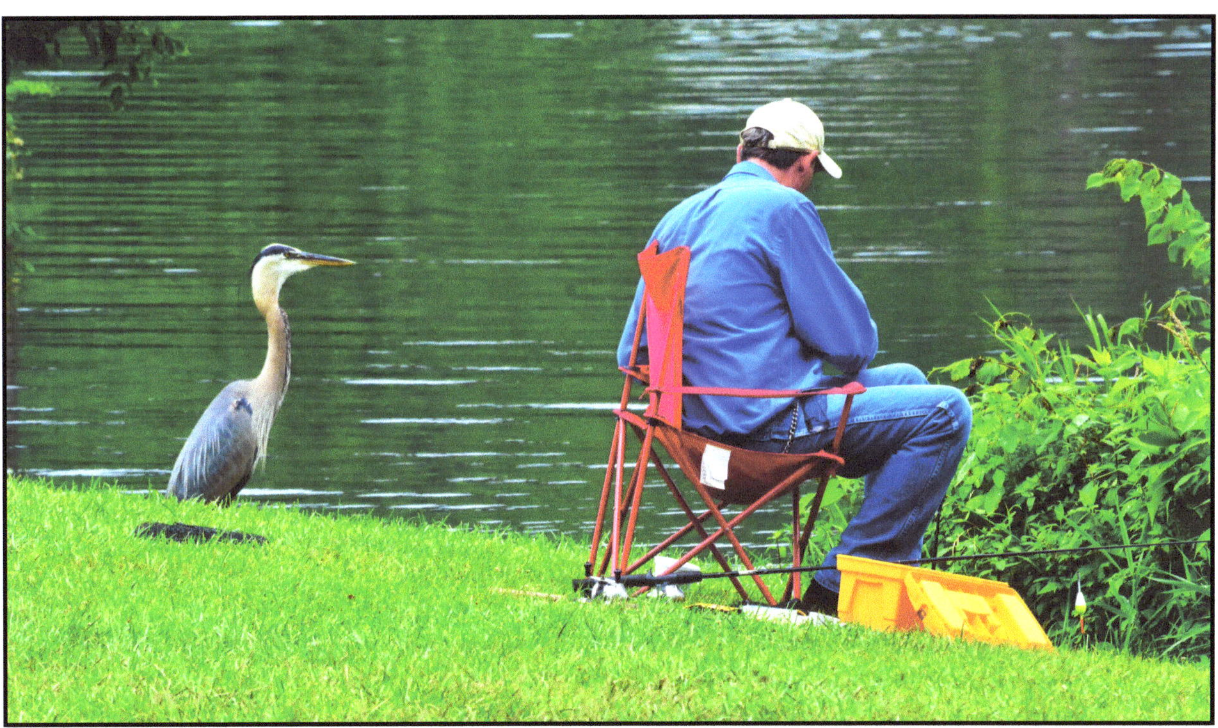

The Great Blue Heron is very familiar to many of the fishermen at Lake Logan in Ohio. They will sometimes take up a vigil near a fisherman in hopes of receiving a labor-free meal.

Bud Simpson

BUD SIMPSON was born in Brewer, Maine. He worked in the shoe industry there until joining the U.S. Navy in 1957. After being discharged from the navy in late 1960, he worked in the aerospace industry in Los Angeles, California for 14 years. Moving back to Maine, he retuned to the shoe industry until his work took him to Logan, Ohio in 1994. He retired in 2000. He and his wife, Margo, now live permanently in Logan, Ohio. The lake referred to in these pages, is Lake Logan near his home. He now writes a weekly opinion column for the *Logan (Ohio) Daily News* and, also, an occasional nature column. Nature photography is one of his loves and this book is the direct result of that. He is also an artist and has painted in several different media. He has carved and painted birds in wood and sculpted in bronze. This book is the direct result of his interest in wildlife photography and writing.

He has written several books besides this one. The first book was, *Mantawassuk: The Cove*. A book about growing up poor in the State of Maine and learning first hand about nature from daily explorations of the woods and waters near his home with his brother, Trevor. Learning about nature was his salvation from a life of poverty. He has also written four novels: *The Reluctant Guest; A Missing piece of Sky; A Dark Place;* and *Junkyard Dogs*, plus, a collection of short stories, essays, novelettes, and poetry, called; *Bud Simpson's Olio Folio.*

PAUL KNOOP, JR is a resident of Laurelville, Ohio and a graduate of Ohio State University with degrees in Dairy Technology and Biology. Early childhood days were spent exploring woods and fields in search of birds, mammals, insects, frogs, wildflowers, rocks and all other natural objects. In response to this interest Mr. Knoop acquired a job with the Dayton Museum of Natural History in 1957 and 1958 as a museum naturalist. In 1959 he accepted a position with the National Audubon Society at their Aullwood Audubon center And Farm north of Dayton, Ohio. It was here that Mr. Knoop was employed for 35 years as Interpretive Naturalist, Director and Education Coordinator before retiring in 1994. After retirement Mr. Knoop moved to Hocking County, Ohio where he became a founding member of the local land trust, Appalachia Ohio Alliance, and continued his work as a consulting naturalist.

Personal interests include bird watching, field botany, photography, canoeing, back packing, reading, traveling, environmental education programs for children and adults to preserve ecologically significant landscapes.

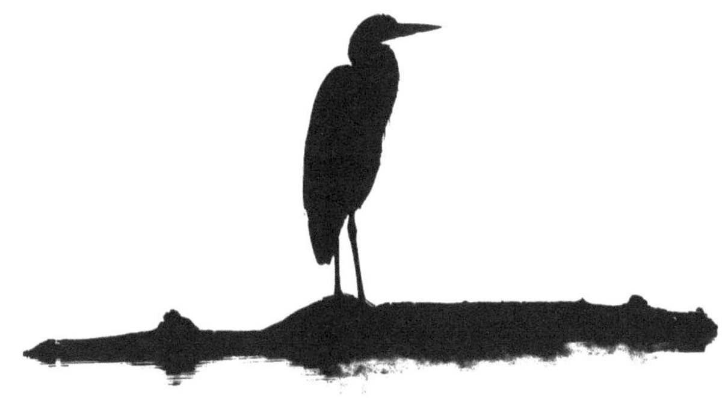

www.ingramcontent.com/pod-product-compliance
Ingram Content Group UK Ltd.
Pitfield, Milton Keynes, MK11 3LW, UK
UKHW060120300726
14090UKWH00002B/284
* 9 7 8 1 6 2 2 4 9 2 9 1 6 *